THE GENOCIDAL MIND

Sociological and Sexual Perspectives

Jack Nusan Porter

University Press of America,® Inc.
Lanham · Boulder · New York · Toronto · Oxford

Copyright © 2006 by
University Press of America,® Inc.
4501 Forbes Boulevard
Suite 200
Lanham, Maryland 20706
UPA Acquisitions Department (301) 459-3366

PO Box 317
Oxford
OX2 9RU, UK

All rights reserved
Printed in the United States of America
British Library Cataloging in Publication Information Available

Library of Congress Control Number: 2005938644
ISBN-13: 978-0-7618-3400-7 (paperback : alk. paper)
ISBN-10: 0-7618-3400-1 (paperback : alk. paper)

∞™ The paper used in this publication meets the minimum
requirements of American National Standard for Information
Sciences—Permanence of Paper for Printed Library Materials,
ANSI Z39.48—1984

Dedication

I dedicate this page to three women:

First and foremost to my 96-year-old mother Faygeh Merin Porter Arenzon, a sole survivor of the Holocaust, out of whose womb has emerged generations without end.

To Davida Navarre, my friend, who gave me the "mut", the energy, to complete this book and future books. Thank you, Davida.

To Jude Burns, an extraordinary editor who caught all the little things, and the big ones too. Any mistakes are mine. Thank you, Jude.

Contents

Foreword	vii
Preface	xi
Acknowledgments and Sources	xix

Introduction
Genocide is a New Word for an Old Crime: Toward a Social Scientific Study of the Holocaust and Other International Crimes 1

Part I. Toward a Sociology of the Holocaust

Chapter 1	The Meaning of the Holocaust for Sociologists	31
Chapter 2	The Holocaust as a Sociological Construct	47
Chapter 3	Comparative Aspects of the Holocaust and Other Genocides	53
Chapter 4	Toward a Sociology of National Socialism	59

Part II. The Holocaust and Western Civilization

Chapter 5	The Role of the Holocaust in Western Civilization	71
Chapter 6	What is Evil? Some New Post-Modern Theories to Explain the Post 9/11 Era	79
Chapter 7	The Genocidal Mind: The Contribution of Erich Goldhagen to Holocaust Studies	97

Part III. Social and Sexual Deviance

Chapter 8	Genocide of Homosexuals in the Nazi Era	115
Chapter 9	Hitler: Sixteen Theories in Search of an Explanation	131

| Chapter 10 | Sexual Aberrations Among Nazi Leaders | 141 |
| Chapter 11 | Holocaust Suicides | 147 |

Part IV. Social and Psychological Issues

Chapter 12	Toward a Sociology of Evil: Why Men Kill	167
Chapter 13	The Goldhagen Controversy: A Response and a Solution	175
Chapter 14	Is There a Survivor's Syndrome? Psychological and Socio-Political Implications	181
Chapter 15	On Therapy, Research, and Other Dangerous Phenomena	203
Chapter 16	The Affirmation of Life After the Holocaust: The Contributions of Bettelheim, Lifton, and Frankl	207

Part V. The Future

Chapter 17	Holocaust Controversies	215
Chapter 18	Impaired Memories/Distorted History	223
Chapter 19	Toward a Sociology and History of Peace	233

The Ten Commandments of the Holocaust	249
Selected Bibliography on Genocide and the Holocaust	251
Index	253
About the Author	265

Foreword

An enormous amount of work has been published in recent years illuminating how the Nazi regime came to adopt a policy of genocide towards the Jews of Europe, whose goal was to murder every Jewish man, woman and child within the Nazi sphere of influence. We now know much more about why the democratic system collapsed in Germany after 1933 and the character of the Nazi regime which replaced it. We also have a much better understanding of the role played by antisemitism in the rise to power of the Nazis and about what Kurt Schleunes has described as the "twisted road to Auschwitz," the complex path the Nazi regime took to the adoption of the policy of genocide. While the policy of mass murder was clearly adopted in the invasion of the Soviet Union in the summer of 1941 it was always at some level inherent in Hitler's *weltanschauung* and the deep-rooted antisemitism of his closest followers. Certainly the outbreak of war had largely freed the Nazi leadership from the taboos of civilization and opened the path to genocide. This war was marked by an open exultation on the part of the Nazis on the possibility for violent and brutal action to destroy their enemies.

During the first twenty months of the war, a double process took place, the barbarization of Nazi policy generally and a hardening of policy towards Jews. The barbarization of Nazi policy was seen in the vicious treatment of occupied Poland. In the first year of the war, more than 50,000 people were killed and half a million expelled from the areas incorporated into Germany. In Germany itself there was also an increase in political repression. The death penalty was now introduced for a wide range of offences, including listening to enemy radio broadcasts, economic sabotage, "disrupting the armed forces" and "crimes of violence." In the "Euthanasia" programme, which was directed against people suffering from incurable mental or physical illnesses, 70-80,000 killed in

Hartheim, Germany and elsewhere. This is well described by Michael Burleigh in his book, *Death and Deliverance*. Certainly the policies adopted by the Nazis towards congenitally ill and insane people led to the development of a technology of mass murder. It is significant that the use of the gas chamber, the characteristic instrument of the Nazi anti-Jewish genocide, with its employment of industrial technology, its practice of disinformation and deceit, and its avoidance of the need for the murderers to be personally involved in the shedding of blood was first tried in Germany in the "euthanasia" programme in 1939 and then tested on Soviet POWs in late 1941. There was also much interchange of personnel between these various programmes.

Policy towards Jews also hardened. In massacres during the September campaign in Poland 6,000 Jews were killed and there was also widespread use of Jewish forced labour in inhuman conditions in Nazi occupied Poland. By German policy, Jews in occupied Poland were to be confined to ghettos . This was not necessarily a step towards mass murder and a conflict developed between those who believed that conditions in the ghettos should be as difficult as possible to cause maximum mortality and those who hoped to make use of the productive capacity of the Jews for the war effort. These years also saw unsuccessful attempts to create a Jewish "reservation" in the area around Lublin and to much effort being devoted after the French capitulation to the question as to whether some sort of Jewish penal colony could be created on the island of Madagascar.

It was the war with the Soviet Union which began on 22 June 1941 that made genocide possible. This war was seen as an ideological conflict. According to the Order of Army High Command of June 1941:

> . . . anyone who has once looked into the face of a Red Commissar knows what Bolsheviks are. . . . It would be insulting animals if you described these mostly Jewish features as animal.

Among the legislation which preceded it was the Commissar Order *(Kommissarbefehl)* which laid down that adult male Jews and political commissars be executed. This reflected both the equation of the Bolshevik regime with the Jews and the fear that the invasion would be accompanied by sabotage and irregular warfare which would have to be ruthlessly crushed. Certainly the war was marked by extreme brutality. In its six months, half a million Soviet prisoners were left in conditions which caused their deaths.

How was the policy of killing Jewish men and commissars expanded during the first months of the war to include women and children? Was the leap to total extermination taken as a result of victory or of the setback caused by the failure to take Moscow? It does seem that Nazi policy in this area was radicalized in "quantum leaps" in the first months of Operation Barbarossa. The most convincing account of this problem is that provided by Christopher Browning. He argues that between 16 September, when the Germans completed the encirclement of Kiev, and 18 October, when the last resistance ended in Bryansk, Hitler approved the deportation of Jews to the east, the first practical steps for the construction of the death camps of Belzec and Chelmno were taken, the first Jewish transports departed for Lodz and Jewish emigration from Europe was banned. These were clear signs that a policy of mass murder had been embarked on.

Was there a direct order from Hitler? The closest we have got to an actual order is the letter sent by Hermann Goering, Commander of the Luftwaffe, President of the Reichstag and Prime Minister of Prussia, the number two man in the Nazi hierarchy, to Heydrich on 31 July 1941. This letter gave Heydrich the plenipotentiary powers he had sought for "the overall solution of the Jewish question in the German sphere of influence in Europe." One has to take into account the way Hitler acted. He did not need to communicate the details of what he wanted. The most zealous National Socialists were those sent to the front. To quote Browning again, "Hitler ordered, or to be more precise, incited or solicited the preparation of an extermination."

The path was now open to genocide. It was carried out in three stages. In the first, as we have seen, mobile killing squads, the *Einsatzgruppen,* advanced behind the *Wehrmacht,* killing Soviet officials and first Jewish adult men and then, after a period, also Jewish women and children. At least one million Jews were killed in this way between July and December 1941. This method of murder was abandoned because of its deleterious effect on the morale of those required to carry it out. It was replaced, in the second stage, by the creation of death camps, where assembly line techniques of mass murder were developed using first carbon monoxide and then an insecticide, Zyklon B. During this period of the genocide, which came to an end in late 1942, the Germans were operating in areas where there was no limitation on their absolute freedom of action, when their power was at its height and the ability of the Allies or the subject populations under the control of the Third Reich to exercise influence on their behaviour was minimal. Most of the actual genocide was also at this stage carried out by Germans. It was during this period that at least another 2.7 million Jews were murdered. In the third stage of the genocide, which lasted until the end of the war, the Nazis found themselves obliged to persuade or coerce their allies, satellites and puppets in the New Europe to hand over their Jews. By this time, both these governments, the Western Allies and virtually everybody else in Nazi occupied Europe knew that Nazi policy towards the Jews involved genocide and were obliged to articulate some sort of response. The total number of those murdered in this way is now accepted to be around six million.

The investigation of these topics in recent years has been largely the work of historians, who have sought to investigate a large corpus of archival material and to elicit from it answers to specific questions which would enable Nazi policy to be described and analysed. What is striking is how few sociologists have attempted to investigate these important topics and to apply the specific tools of their profession to these problems. Sociologists have rather sought to examine the holocaust in the general framework of genocide and have stressed its general rather than its specific features. Apart from the work of Zygmunt Bauman and Helen Fein, one is hard put to identify any specific sociological approach to the problems of examining the holocaust. It is the great virtue of this collection that it is written by a leading sociologist and attempts to use sociological techniques to explicate a number of key problems, including an analysis of the general problems of the sociology of the holocaust, its relationship to western civilization, the issue of social and sexual deviance in the Nazi state, some of the key psychological and social issues it raises, and the question of resistance to Nazi genocide. There is a great deal to be learned from these essays and I very much hope they reach the wide audience they deserve.

Antony Polonsky
Department of Near Eastern and Judaic Studies
Brandeis University

Preface

These essays represent the culmination of over 25 years of hard work and deep thought on two of the most important issues of our age: the Holocaust of World War II and the phenomenon of 20th century genocide.

They are not simply a retrospective of my work over the past three decades, but something more: Holocaust studies in particular has stagnated in recent years and the field has suffered too many controversies, too much special pleading, too much emphasis on Holocaust uniqueness, too much emphasis on historicism and historical analysis and too little on the sociological and political, too little comparative analysis, and simply too little creative research. It has become dominated by historians and by the top-down institutional needs of the US Holocaust Memorial Museum in Washington, DC, the Spielberg Foundation, Facing History and Ourselves, and other similar institutions.

Younger scholars have been crucified by senior for simply trying out new ideas. The Daniel Goldhagen case at Harvard University in the late 1990s is a perfect case in point, but every month brings more and more scandal and controversy. (Thankfully, it has, I will admit, settled down a bit.) This fear of approbation and condemnation has led to a subsequent loss of nerve and an end to creative scholarship.

I have attempted in these essays to try out new and fresh approaches to Holocaust research. My goal is to entice a new generation of graduate students and younger scholars back into the field. I have done this through the use of a fresh new "post-modern" approach, a sociological and psychological approach (in a field dominated by historians), and a comparative, analytical approach. If I have failed, it is not for lack of trying. As in any scientific endeavor, there will always be some approaches that will fizzle out and fail, but what magnificent failures they be if they enthrall a student or a benefactor to take up the grail and push on by supporting these new approaches.

So, that has been my desire in these essays: to educate, to entertain, perhaps even to titillate, if one can use such a word in scientific circles . . . to excite, to enervate, and to revise two fields that have been mired too long in stagnation and scandal: Holocaust and genocide studies.

If I have succeeded in energizing a new generation of scholars, that will be my greatest pleasure.

> Jack Nusan Porter, Ph.D.
> Newtonville, MA
> jacknusan@earthlink.net
> July 15, 2005

Nota Bene: My writings on resistance to genocide will be gathered in a separate volume as will my research on chaos theory as it applies to terrorism and genocide. This book is volume 1 of my collected essays in a projected six volumes of such essays. They will include sociological theory and social praxis, the sociology of Jewry, Jewish radicalism and radical Judaism, Black-Jewish relations, and Holocaust controversies. Watch for them.

From the Author

For too long historians have dominated Holocaust studies. We need fresh new voices and ideas. Genocide studies, on the other hand, was founded and is dominated, not by historians but by sociologists: Helen Fein, Vahakn Dadrian, Kurt Jonassohn, Irving Louis Horowitz, and the present author. One could add others such as William Helmreich and Nechama Tec who are also sociologists but have written more on Holocaust history (Jewish partisans, Christian-Jewish relations on the part of Tec) or post-Holocaust history (the lives of Jewish survivors in America, on the part of Bill Helmreich).

I would not put the latter two in the same category as "genocide" scholars as I would with Helen Fein, et al. They are more Holocaust scholars. But the point is, that most sociologists have not only disregarded but marginalized the Holocaust in their literature, and the voices of sociologists who have done work have often been overlooked by mainstream Holocaust scholars, who tend to be historians or Jewish studies professors.

Preface

The title for this book was derived from a course I took at Harvard University in the fall of 1994. It was called "The Holocaust and the Phenomenon of Genocide" and was taught by Erich Goldhagen, the father of the more famous Daniel Jonah Goldhagen. Goldhagen, the father, taught me more about the Holocaust than almost any other teacher, and his perspective was sociological and social-psychological, a position that differed from his son in some ways. The elder Goldhagen had always wanted to write a book entitled "The Genocidal Mind" but writer's block stopped him from doing so. I have been influenced over the name by him even though this is a very different book than he might have written. However, Goldhagen and I both share the "sociological imagination." I suppose I should have called it "The Genocidal Experience" since it deals as much with the Jewish experience as the Nazi temperament and Hitler's state of mind, but "The Genocidal Mind" is a more accurate title.

This book is both psychological and sociological. I have tried to deal with the mind of the genocidal killer as well as the structure of the genocidal society, mind and body. I have also examined the mind of the victims and the survivors as well as the social structure of the "victims", in most cases, Jewish victims. In this postmodern world, we must flow easily between the sociology and psychology of evil and between the anthropology and history of evil. Many approaches, many venues, will lead to many creative results.

* * * * *

This book is also a direct response to two colleagues with whom I have had a friendly yet profound disagreement—Daniel Goldhagen and Steven Katz.

A recent conference in March 26-29, 2000 held at Brandeis University sponsored by Yad Vashem, the Holocaust Memorial Museum and Archives in Jerusalem, Israel, brought together for the very first time Israeli, European, and American scholars from both camps—Holocaust-centered and genocide-centered—with what I believe will have healthy long-term effects of cross pollination and cooperation for years to come.

In fact, if for no other reason than having these scholars meet and dispel myths and rumors about each other, the conference should see itself as a success. The key figure in this dialogue will probably be Professor Yehuda Bauer of the Hebrew University and Yad Vashem, a scholar of international repute, who has managed to bridge the gap so to speak as a "universalist" rather than as a "Jewish exclusivist." Bauer understands the "uniqueness" of the Holocaust though he calls it "unprecedented", a much better term, while at the same time recognizing the Armenian, Gypsy, Cambodian, Rwandan, and even the Bosnian genocides.

While he has serious reservations about calling every mass killing a "genocide", he is by and large in the "universalist" camp, and has good relations with such genocide-oriented scholars as Helen Fein, Vahakn Dadrian, and myself.

I should be considered a member of *both* camps—Holocaust and genocide-centered—since I have written on both topics, and of course I am a "universalist" though I too recognize the "unique" nature of the Holocaust.

On the other hand, Bauer's colleague from the Judaic department of Boston University, and a friend of mine as well—Steven Katz—stands as an example of the "Jewish exclusivist" camp, even though he takes great pains to deny it. Katz feels there is *only one* true, phenomenologically defined genocide in history—the Jewish one of the Holocaust. All others belong to another category or definition, or what he calls "genocide-plus" or better yet, "Holocaust-plus". . . "plus" meaning some other type of persecution besides genocide. While he is well-meaning and sensitive to other genocides (i., the Armenian, Gypsy, Rwandan), he will not call them genocides.

The "uniqueness" debate is important but ultimately sterile and dysfunctional. I could argue that the Jews are a "chosen people", and they are but who cares and to what end is this argument leading? What indeed is the purpose of the debate? I would rather emphasize not the uniqueness nor "chosenness" of the Jewish people (and I am a Jew despite my name) but rather that Jews should be seen as a "role model" to the world and bring their sense of justice and humanity to all people. In other words, the phrase "never again" does not mean "never again to Jews" but "never again" to anyone, to any people, anywhere on earth. (For more on the uniqueness issue, See Alan S. Rosenbaum, *Is the Holocaust Unique? Perspectives on Comparative Genocide*, Boulder, Colorado: Westview Press, USA, 1998)

But this is politics, and the Brandeis conference could not avoid politics, and neither can many of us. As Elie Wiesel recently told me, controversy will always be a part of the Holocaust and genocide. The real point for us as scholars is to try to put aside our "politics" and passions for a moment and explore new areas of research, in order to build a new generation of graduate students and younger scholars, and that is what this book hopes to do.

The essays in this book give a clue to what I have been doing over the past two and a half decades since my earlier books *Genocide and Human Rights* and *Confronting History and Holocaust* came out more than twenty years ago.

* * * * *

Let us now examine the breakdown of chapters and sections:

First, as Section I "Toward a Sociology of the Holocaust" shows, I have tried to hone and clarify the role of sociology in Holocaust studies, explaining why sociology came late to the field and why it was more comfortable in genocide studies than Holocaust studies. The reason is simple: sociology as a discipline, unlike history, is uncomfortable with unique events like the Holocaust or Hiroshima or My Lai. Sociology is a comparative, generalizing, muckraking discipline, always probing the commonalities of phenomena and exploring the radical and sensitive corners of society. It was, until recently, uncomfortable with the mystical singularity of the Holocaust; it didn't know how to deal with it, and the way it "handles" it today is through an objective comparative approach. And that is the second purpose of this book—to prod students into a more comparative methodological and theoretical analysis without ignoring the unique aspects and humanity of each individual genocide. A delicate balance is indeed needed.

In Section II, I embed the Holocaust into the history of Western Civilization and show how the Holocaust exposed the logical conclusion of certain tendencies in Western Civilization—scientism, bureaucracy, technology, and ideology. In essence the Holocaust represents the breakdown of Western Civilization, the false promise of progress as being inevitably humanistic and progressive. It represents the dark side of civilization. I also explore what postmodern theory has to offer Holocaust studies. Postmodernism is very popular in sociological circles; in fact, one could make claim that it was sociology and literary criticism that brought postmodernism, warts and all, into academia.

Conservative scholars in Jewish and Holocaust studies are very wary of postmodern theory, wary of its political agenda, wary of its political "correctness", wary of its balkanization and dissolution of the field into special interest groups, wary of its emphasis on textual analysis, and wary of its general "wonkiness" and even fascist tendencies.

I however point out that postmodern theory has much to offer Holocaust scholars if only they will put down their blinders and put away their prejudices. For example, many scholars think that postmodern thinkers such as Foucault and Derrida are "fascists" and glorify dominance and sexual deviance. Not so. They emphasize power relations, including the sexual, and they are not "fascists"; but often progressive antifascists.

Section III explores social and sexual issues. I am quite aware of the danger as George Wills puts it, to turn the Holocaust into one huge case of "sexual harassment." I feel that women and homosexuals have had a different experience during the Holocaust. Their "definition of the situation" as Erving Goffman would say, was different than heterosexual men. The issue of rape comes to mind, for example, rape as a genocidal act.

We should not, however, divide the Holocaust into a male and a female Holocaust—or a gay or straight Holocaust—there is only *one* Holocaust—but there is a mine-full of data that should be explored on these issues. I, however, warn scholars, especially female or gay scholars, not to turn the Holocaust into a sub-field of feminist or gay studies. I would caution them that before you can run, you must first walk. Read the vast history of the Holocaust first and know it well before plunging into these sub-fields.

Section III discusses my longtime work on sexual politics in Nazi Germany—the victimization of homosexuals and lesbians. I place them in this chapter because of my early training with Howard S. Becker and John Kitsuse at Northwestern University in the late 60s where the theories of "social deviance", not "deviates", but "deviation," from the norm, was in its heyday. I will admit that sociologists do not use the term as often as they did because of backlash from gay rights activists. Sociologists now use the terms "gay subculture" or "gay lifestyle" or "gay minority rights" or "sex and gender issues." But I was trained to use the term "social deviance" and I will use it because the other essays in this section deal with "deviance"—sexual aberrations among Nazi leaders and the perverted mind of Hitler. People who commit terrible deeds need a means to cope with the stress, and sex is often a excellent way to relieve such stress.

Orgiastic sexual activities were common among Nazi officials, whether in Berlin or Paris or even within the death camps. As medical pioneer

Dr. Axel Muenther wrote in his book *San Michele* (p. 129) as quoted in Comer Clarke, *Eichmann: The Man and His Crimes* (1960, p. 97): "Death is the great aphrodisiac." The connection between death and sex is of course provocative and rarely discussed in Holocaust literature.

I conclude the section with a controversial essay on Holocaust survivors and suicide, sexuality coming into play in a few cases. Here I discuss the suicides of Primo Levi, Jerzy Kosinski, Bruno Bettelheim, Robert Maxwell, and Terrence Des Pres. I tried to find a sociological pattern in their suicides following the theoretical formulations of Emile Durkheim and his classic book *Le Suicide,* written 100 years ago.

Section IV continues in the same vein as Section III, with social and psychological issues, but here the emphasis is more on traditional psychological and psychiatric issues rather than sexual ones. I begin with an overview of theories of evil, traditional, social-psychological and group dynamic theories of why men commit unspeakable evil, and end with the famous Milgram experiments.

Naturally, the famous Daniel Jonah Goldhagen book *Hitler's Willing Executioners* (New York: Knopf, 1996) threw a monkey wrench into this debate by rejecting all social-psychological group pressure theories and positing only one: the "eliminationist anti-semitism" of the German people and not just German Nazis but the German people as a whole. Evil, I will show, is much more complex than even anti-semitism can explain.

I also return in this section to an earlier interest of mine: "survivors' syndrome" and its actuality. Then, I explore the thorny question of therapy for survivors and why the psychiatric "medical model" is outdated today. It was, however, pointed out to me that this approach, utilized mostly by post-World War II psychiatrists, was necessary in order to get *Weidergutmachung*, German reparations. But today, a more sophisticated approach is necessary. I conclude with a discussion of life affirmations in the wake of the Holocaust.

And the final section, Section V, looks toward the future with three essays: Holocaust controversies that never seem to end; distorted memoirs leading to fraudulent history, another controversy without end; and a wish for the future, a positive note to end on—toward a sociology of peace.

I have used a variety of styles and content in these pieces; some may be controversial for a scholarly book, there may also be some minor repetition, but in any case, I hope it provokes a new generation of graduate students, scholars, and writers to tackle the Holocaust and comparative genocide in fresh, new and innovative ways. We've gotten stale this past decade and it's often the same old thing over and over again. I've tried to shake things up.

Acknowledgments and Sources

I wish to acknowledge the Creator for having given me the strength to carry out this work and for all future works; to Israel Charny, Sam Totten, and Steve Jacobs, all superb colleagues, for their spiritual and intellectual support over the years; they have helped me weather the storms; to Gershon (Jerry) Weissenberg for his friendship, his great mind and his deep insights; to Steve Katz who I hope will still be friends with me even as we disagree without becoming disagreeable; to Helen Fein, Vahakn Dadrian, Yehuda Bauer, I. L. Horowitz, Roger Smith, Robert Melson, Peter Balakian, Levon Chorbajian, and to all my colleagues, friends, and family for their support and even nonsupport over the past quarter century. Even when you criticized and condemned me, and while it hurt, it spurred me on to greater heights. To Peggy Sunshine for her inspiration, and to Jude Burns for her excellent editorial skills. She made this a much better book.

As for particular sources: my introduction "Genocide is a New Word for an Old Crime," it is an updated version of my introduction to my first book on the subject *Genocide and Human Rights: A Global Anthology*, Lanham, MD and London: University Press of America, 1982.

The essays in Section I on the sociology of the Holocaust first appeared in my book *The Sociology of the Holocaust and Genocide*, compiled with Steve Hoffman, American Sociological Association, 1307 New York Avenue, Washington, DC 20005, 1999. My essay "Toward a Sociology of National Socialism" first appeared in *Sociological Forum*, Vol. 9, No. 3, 1994, pp. 505-511.

All the essays in Section II are original and have never been published anywhere though they have been read as lectures in several venues and conferences around the country these past few years.

In Section III, portions of "Genocide of Homosexuals in the Nazi Era" appeared in Jack Nusan Porter's *Sexual Politics in the Third Reich:*

The Persecution of the Homosexuals During the Holocaust, Newton, MA: The Spencer Press, 1991, 1995 and appears by permission of the author. The bibliography, the photos, and charts also appear from that book. "Holocaust Suicides" by Jack Nusan Porter originally appeared in Harry James Cargas (ed), *Problems Unique to the Holocaust*, Lexington, KY: The University Press of Kentucky, 1999, pp. 51-66. It was first read at the Society for Applied Sociology meetings in Atlanta, GA. October 18, 1996 and at the "Working with Holocaust Survivors" Conference in New York City, October 11, 1996 sponsored by the New York Self-Help Community Services, Inc. organization. I would like to thank Dr. Yael Danieli and others at the conference for their comments as well as to Prof. Larry Langer. The photos are from the National Archives (USA).

In Section IV, "Is there a Survivor's Syndrome?" first appeared in Byron L. Sherwin and Susan G. Ament (eds.), *Encountering the Holocaust: An Interdisciplinary Survey*, Chicago, IL: Impact Press, 1979, pp. 189-222 under the title "Social-Psychological Aspects of the Holocaust" and also appeared under the same title in the *Journal of Psychology and Judaism*, Vol. 6, No. 1, Fall/Winter 1981. Funding for this research came from the Wein Foundation of Chicago under the direction of Prof. Byron Sherwin of Spertus College of Chicago. I would like to thank him, the late Dr. Robert Ravven, and the staff of the Countway Medical Library of Harvard University for their support and assistance. It was reprinted in my collection of essays *Confronting History and Holocaust: Collected Essays: 1972-1982*, Lanham, MD and London: University Press of America, 1983, pp. 83-105.

"On Therapy, Research, and Other dangerous Phenomena" first appeared in *Shoah*, Vol. 1, No. 3, 1979 and was reprinted in Jack Nusan Porter, *Confronting History and Holocaust*, op. cit., pp. 79-82. I would like to thank Prof. Leo Eitinger of Oslo and Haifa for his post-publishing comments.

"The Affirmation of Life after the Holocaust" first appeared in the *Association for Humanistic Psychology Newsletter*, August-September 1980, pp. 9-11 and was reprinted in Jack Nusan Porter, *Confronting History and Holocaust*, op. cit, pp. 122-129. I would like to thank Robert J. Lifton for his post-publishing comments.

In Section V a shorter, edited version of "Holocaust Controversies" appeared in Israel Charny (ed), *Encyclopedia of Genocide*, Volume 1, Santa Barbara, California: ABC-Clio, 1999, pp. 307-311.

"Impaired Memories/Distorted History" first appeared in *International Network on Holocaust and Genocide Newsletter* of Macquarie University, Centre for Comparative Genocide Studies, in Australia, Fall 1998. The charts in "Toward a Sociology and History of Peace" appeared in Matthew Melko, *52 Peaceful Societies*, Ontario, Canada: Canadian Peace Research Institute, 1973 and "The Remission of Violence in the West," *International Journal on World Peace*, Vol. II, No. 2, April-June 1985, page 53.

This paper was requested to be read at the annual International Association of Genocide Scholars held June 7-10, 2003 in Galway, Ireland at the Irish National University, Irish Centre for Human Rights.

Introduction

Genocide Is a New Word for an Old Crime: Toward a Social Scientific Study of the Holocaust and Other International Crimes

Genocide is a new word for an old crime. The originator of the term was Raphael Lemkin, a Polish legal scholar. The word first appeared in 1944 in his *Axis Rule in Occupied Europe* (1973 reprint). Lemkin coined a hybrid word consisting of the Greek prefix *genos* (nation, tribe) and the Latin suffix *-cide* (killing). He felt that the destruction of the Armenians during World War I and the Jews during World War II called for the formulation of a legal concept that would accurately describe the deliberate killing of entire human groups. Lemkin was more than a scholar. He inspired and promoted action on the international level to outlaw genocide. It was largely due to his efforts that the United Nations decided to debate the issue of genocide, to organize a convention to discuss it, and to eventually include it as a part of international law in 1948.

Before 1944 no dictionary, encyclopedia, or textbook used the term genocide, and even after 1944 there have been some glaring omissions. For example, there is no mention of the term in *Webster's International Dictionary* until 1961. All three major sociology dictionaries have also ignored the term (Gould and Kolb, 1964; Theodorson and Theodorson, 1969; and Hoult, 1969). Both the earlier *Encyclopedia of the Social Sciences* (Seligman and Johnson, 1933) and the *International Encyclopedia of the Social Sciences* (Sills, 1968) have no separate descriptive and analytical listing for "genocide." The Sills' encyclopedia does mention genocide but only under the heading of "international crimes" where genocide is defined in the context for international law, not sociologically or historically (Sills, 1968: Vol. 7:515-519).

On the other hand, the encyclopedias written by minority groups affected by genocide (Armenians and Jews are two examples) have excellent coverage of the topic. For example the new *Encyclopedia Judaica* has a long and comprehensive account of the Holocaust in Europe by Jacob Robinson, yet, ironically, even in this Jewish publication the actual term "genocide" cannot be found as a major listing. Only "genocide convention" is mentioned.

The United Nations General Assembly, during its first session in 1946, carried out the mandate proposed by Raphael Lemkin and adopted two resolutions: the first affirmed the principles of the charter of the International Military Tribunal in Nuremberg, Germany (the so-called Nuremberg Trials of Nazi leaders) and the second affirmed that genocide was a crime under international law and, if committed, would be punished. The U.N. asked for international cooperation in preventing and punishing genocide and invited member states to enact necessary national legislation.

In a final provision, the Assembly called for studies aimed at creating international legal instruments to deal with the crime. That was the origin of the Convention on the Prevention and Punishment of the Crime of Genocide which was unanimously adopted by the Assembly on December 9, 1948. The Convention, which in international law means an agreement among sovereign nations pledging them to specified obligations, went into effect on January 12, 1951. By January 1973, seventy-six governments had ratified the Convention. The United States, however, hadn't, claiming that it had existing legislation that covers genocide; that the wording of the Convention is vague in certain areas; that the Convention violates national sovereignty in its provision for an international tribunal; and that an entire nation cannot be charged with the crime of genocide because of the acts of a few individual citizens.

Several sections of the Article II of the Genocide Convention in particular, make the United States hesitant. Article II reads as follows:

> In the present Convention, genocide means any of the following acts committed with intent to destroy, in whole or in part, a national, ethnical (sic), racial or religious groups (sic), as such:

(a) Killing members of the group;
(b) Causing serious bodily harm to members of the group;
(c) Deliberately inflicting on the group conditions of life calculated to bring about its physical destruction in whole or in part;
(d) Imposing measures intended to prevent births within the group;
(e) Forcibly transferring children of the group to another group.

Sections (b) and (d) caused the most controversy in the United States Senate. The senators who voted against the United States' ratifying the Convention were mindful that American blacks had charged the United States with genocide, basing their accusations on sections (a), (b), (c), and (d) of the United Nations Convention. Furthermore, America was charged with genocide in Vietnam in the late 1960s and early 1970s; this was another reason why some senators were extremely reluctant to ratify and support the Convention.

While the U.N. does provide for enforcement of the Genocide Convention by the use of international courts, the actual implementation has been limited. In essence, the U.N. Convention is more of a symbolic than a legislative contract, and those U.S. senators who voted against it have little to fear; the United States will not be brought before a tribunal. Claims of genocide have been made, inter alia, to the United Nations with regard to blacks in Southern Sudan, Kurds, in Iraq, Nagas in India, Communists and Chinese in Indonesia, Ibos in Nigeria, and Beharis in Pakistan, but no formal decision in these cases has been reached by the United Nations. Because of political pressures and lack of real opportunity for enforcement, the United Nations has never formally applied the Convention to any genocide in the post World War II period, though numerous private citizens and groups have.

Furthermore the U. N. Convention is not retroactive. Therefore the United States could not be charged with genocide against the American Indians, the blacks, or the Vietnamese. The legal scholar Cherif Bassiouni maintains that the US. cannot be charged with genocide regarding the Indian massacres or the Vietnam war because it has never ratified the U.N. Genocide Convention. He also argues that because the Convention states that only individuals can be charged with genocide, it would require an extremely loose interpretation of the Convention text to charge a government with a crime. And, finally, Bassiouni contends that in both the Vietnam and Indian frontier situations, the requisite and specific intent of the United States government to commit genocide has never been established. (Please note that despite these concerns, the U.S. eventually ratified the genocide convention in November, 1988.

The problems of intent and application of the term genocide to specific cases will be discussed in the next section, but, in summary, the following points should be emphasized. First, the U.N. Convention on Genocide has been charged with controversy from its very inception, and it has never been used to enforce specific punishment for cases of genocide. Secondly, there is a difference between the legal and the sociological definitions of genocide. Genocide has taken place in the past (e.g., the persecution of American Indians), but legally the United States cannot be charged with genocide. There can thus be a number of responses to genocide: the act is committed but the victimizer is never found; the act is committed but the victimizer is never charged; the act is defined as genocide by the victims, but the victimizer does not concur that it is in fact genocide, and therefore will not be charged with the crime. From both a theoretical and a practical point of view, the problem of genocide is confusing and frustrating in definition, application, and enforcement.

My definition of genocide is slightly broader than that of the United Nations. I include the deliberate extermination of political and sexual groups as well as racial, religious, tribal, or ethnic groups. Thus the attempt to exterminate homosexuals in Nazi German could be labeled genocidal. In the early 1950s, under pressure from Soviet Russia, extermination of groups for political persuasion or beliefs did not fall under the rubric of genocide in the U.N. definition. Thus the elimination of anti-Communist Poles or Ukrainians in the USSR in the 1930s and 1940s and, in recent times, the massacre of anti-Communist Cambodians could not be labeled genocide. Annihilation based on political beliefs is not considered genocide according to the legal definition of the United Nations Convention.

The U.N.'s exclusion of political and sexual groups from its Convention proves that we do not have the conceptual categories to describe all forms of mass violence and murder we have seen in this century. Our sociological concepts are inadequate to cope with the phenomena. The term "massacre" describes mass killings without the intent to kill all members of the groups in question. Since the popular and classical definition of genocide implies the murder or attempted murder of an entire group (be it racial, tribal, sexual, or ethnic), then the killing of anti-Communist Cambodians or Ukrainians would not technically be genocide, because the aim of the victimizers was not to kill all Cambodians or Ukrainians, just those with a particular set of political beliefs. I disagree with this narrow definition and believe genocide can include the extermination of groups for strictly political beliefs. (See Chart IV.)

The Problem of Application and Intention

Recently there has been heated debate about the use and abuse of the terms "racism" and "racist." The term "genocide" has been similarly abused. Since "genocide" has become such a powerful catch-word, it is often used in political and cultural rhetoric. It is at least understandable that the term has been abused by political activists. However, even professional scholars have misused the concept. Because of the vague wording in some sections of the U.N. Genocide Convention, some scholars have applied the term genocide to the wrong phenomena.

For example, genocide has been applied to all of the following: "race-mixing" (integration of blacks and non-blacks); drug distribution; methadone programs; the practice of birth control and abortions among Third World people; sterilization and "Mississippi appendectomies" (tubal ligations and hysterectomies); medical treatment of Catholics; and the closing of synagogues in the Soviet Union. In other words when one needs a catch-all term to describe "oppression" of one form or another, one often resorts to the extreme of labeling it "genocide." The net result is a debasement of the concept.

Often the concept is applied to phenomena that are total opposites: integration and lack of integration; drug abuse and programs to curb such abuse. Consider the following linguistic abuse:

- The Nazi Party of America, demonstrating in Milwaukee in February 1976, argued at a school board meeting that "integration is genocide for the white race." Before the meeting the Nazis distributed literature that charged the Jews with genocide against whites in America. One handbill read: "Deport Blacks to Africa and Jews to Israel or some other island (sic) except . . . those Jews who are suspected of treasonable activities such as genocide against whites." Treasonable activities were defined as "race-mixing" and the distribution of obscene movies and magazines by "pornographic Jews." The

handbills also condemned those "sick, depraved Jews who monopolize the motion picture industry (and who) can hardly wait to turn America into a mongrel cesspool" because these Jews promote racial integration and harmony.
- Regarding government-sponsored methadone programs, Black Panther Party leader Ericka Huggins said: "We don't need methadone. We don't need the government making any more good citizens. Methadone is just genocide, mostly against Black people. What we need is political education."
- At an anti-abortion rally in Washington, D.C. in 1978, Senator Orrin G. Hatch (R-Utah) states: "I call (abortion) an epidemic and it has to be stamped out now." He noted that federal payments for abortion make it "possible for genocidal programs as were practiced in Nazi German." (From literature distributed by the National Abortion Rights Action League, 1979)
- Weisbord (1975) cites numerous instances of blacks viewing birth control as a "diabolical plot." His examples include reaction to the sterilization of the Reif sisters in South Carolina in June 1973, which Black Muslims and other black organizations called "a deliberate act of genocidal sterilization."
- Sociologist Rona Fields (1976), in a study of medical treatment of Catholics in Northern Ireland, charged the Protestants with "psychological genocide." She identified social control mechanisms which produce a mixture of chaos and docility and argued that such mechanisms were established in order to destroy the cultural identity of Catholics.

These examples point out the many ways the term has been misused. Which applications of the term can be considered legitimate and which not? To some extent that depends on which definition one follows. Naturally some applications, such as those used by the American Nazis, are blatant distortions of reality. Other applications, however, that may sound exaggerated rest on the definition of genocide used in the United Nations Convention. Rona Fields' application of the term, for example, is based on the clause ". . . causing serious bodily or mental harm" [Article II, section (b)]. This vague and controversial clause has led to several uses or abuses of the term "genocide." To Fields (1976) "psychological genocide" can occur if such "mental harm" is present. The question is what constitutes mental harm? How much mental harm is necessary in order to label it genocidal?

Some sociologists have expressed an abhorrence of the abuse that some terms and concepts take within sociology and in the general society. Dennis Wrong (1976) has called the abuse of the term genocide an example of the "banalization and trivialization of a subject and its exploitation for partisan purposes." He is especially vehement about using the concept of genocide to describe the treatment of blacks in the United States: "Slavery and color castes were evil institutions to be sure, but by no stretch of the imagination can they be compared to the extermination of 10,000 Jews a day in the death camps of Auschwitz." (Wrong, 1976, personal communication to author)

In the area of intent and in the area of "causing serious . . . mental harm," the United Nations definition seems too broad or too vague. The problems confronting scholars in the field will be whether to use *a* narrow or a broad definition at this stage of research. Will the concept be used so broadly that its meaning and application will become useless? Or will it be used in such a narrow manner that certain genocides will be overlooked because they do not fall within the parameters of the definition? Furthermore should sociologists use only a legal definition of genocide such as that of the United Nations, or should they formulate their own definition? In short do we want definitional precision or phenomenological inclusion at this juncture? I would like to find a golden mean between these extremes if in fact that is possible—that is, to reject overly broad applications while remaining flexible.

What is Genocide?

Genocide is the deliberate destruction, in whole or in part, by a government or its agents, of a racial, sexual, religious, tribal, ethnic, or political minority. It can involve not only mass murder, but also starvation, forced deportation, and political, economic, and biological subjugation. Genocide involves three major components: ideology, technology, and bureaucracy/organization. (See Charts I and II.)

Ideology

A key element in the act of genocide is an ideology that the victimizer utilizes in order to exterminate the victim. This ideology, usually based on racial or religious grounds, serves to legitimize any acts, no matter how horrendous. Racist or religious propaganda is used to spread the ideology. Such propaganda defines the victim as outside the pale of human existence and therefore vulnerable to attack. Words such as "sheep," "savages," "vermin," "subhumans," "gooks," and "lice" are commonly used, especially during war or colonialization, to reduce the victims to the level of non humans, thus making it easier to annihilate them.

Helen Fein has added immensely to theory building in genocide studies by emphasizing this key element of ideology. She describes the role of myth, or what Gaetano Mosca would call a "political formula," which legitimizes the existence of a state of *volk* as a vehicle for the destiny of the dominant group and, by definition, excludes the victim-group as being outside the realm of the "sanctified universe."

Fein presents a theory to explain the genocide of Jews, Armenians, and Gypsies. Historically these groups have been the victims of repeated collective violence—Jews for nearly 2,000 years; Armenians for 500 years of Turkish Ottoman domination; and Gypsies for nearly a thousand years. For Fein, genocide is a rational, premeditated action with particular goals. She notes that the liberal ideal of 19th-century nationalism justified removing authorities who were deemed illegitimate because they did not represent the people the 20th-century "formula" justified eradicating people to assure the legitimization of the state's authority. Groups that did not fit into a nation-state were assimilated, expelled or exterminated.

Fein uses the case of the Armenians to describe the process of placing people "outside the sanctified universe." The Muslim Turks regarded the Christian Armenians as *dimmis* or infidels. For many years the latter were tolerated and protected in exchange for their accommodation to discrimination, subordination, powerlessness, and oppression. Armenians were also labeled *rayah* or sheep who could be fleeced. The Young Turk movement before and during World War I attempted to establish power and authority in order to fulfill its ideal of forging a new Turkish identity and destiny. In their scheme there was no place for large distinct minorities like the Armenians.

The genocide of Jews and Gypsies during World War II was also based on this "formula." Nazism utilized a pseudoscientific, neo-Darwinian, racist ideology which identified the German people (*volk*) as possessing a distinct identity and destiny. This identity was based on "blood." Jews and Gypsies (as well as homosexuals) were formally defined as not *volk,* but aliens to whom the Germans or Aryans would owe no obligation at all. While the Germans belonged to the "greatest, highest race" of Aryans, the Jews and Gypsies belonged to no human race. By definition they were non human.

Jews were to be annihilated because they were "vermin," "lice," "bloodsuckers," "parasites," and "bacilli"; Gypsies, because they were "filthy animals," "rodents," etc. Both were seen as racial "polluters" because they were racially "deformed" and "degenerate" in the first place. Thus laws were passed making illegal sexual relations between Jews and Aryans.

In this ideological schema the Aryan *volk* had a messianic right to prevail over others and to use any means from war to political deception to do so. The *volk* demanded not only equality with other nations but room to expand and colonialize the concept of lebensraum). In its expansion it could justifiably subjugate and annihilate any "inferior" races who might "pollute" the *volk.* As Fein concludes about Armenians and Jews:

> . . . in both cases the victims had earlier been decreed outside the universe of obligation by Koranic injunction and by Christian theodicy. However, churches holding out the possibility of conversion to all must assume a common humanity and, therefore, may not sanction unlimited violence. But a doctrine which assumes people do not belong to a common species imposes no limits inhibiting the magnitude of crime permissible.

An ideology based on racism or the "new formula" that Fein describes is a prerequisite for genocide; it stigmatizes and isolates the victims while mobilizing the victimizers in their genocidal pursuits.

Technology

Once the victim is labeled by the prevailing propaganda as being outside the universe of moral obligations, the killing can take place. The technology of death has become more efficient as modern nation-states have become more technologically sophisticated. While primitive means like clubs, spears, and gun-butts have been used in poorly developed nations (for example, the genocide in Burundi-Rwanda in the 1960s), more sophisticated methods like the gas chambers, crematoriums, and "killing vans" were used by the Nazis to kill Gypsies and Jews. Today, of course, with modern nuclear systems we have the capacity to kill many more human beings in a shorter time than even the Nazi regime was able to do. Thus technology is an obvious component of genocide.

Bureaucracy

Hilberg (1961) has detailed the enormous state apparatus that was necessary to undertake genocide in Germany and the conquered territories. Just as technology has become more sophisticated, so too have organizational and logistic skills. The carrying out of genocide necessitates some minimum organization; optimally effective genocide such as in Germany necessitated an enormously complex organization. Coordination of various military and civilian groups, rail transportation, the courts, and the like is essential. Fein (1979a) and Horowitz (1976) have noted that modern premeditated genocide must first be recognized as organized state murder, and such murder requires a complex bureaucracy. The human victim is reduced to a non human entity and, like any merchandise, must be assembled, evaluated, selected, stores, and ultimately disposed of as efficiently as possible.

A Two-Step Sociological Theory of Genocide

Genocide is always performed by a state or other authority, not by an individual. We are not talking about serial killers or serial killing. Genocide always has an ideology, albeit crude. Genocide always has a bureaucracy or primitive social organization to carry it out. It is always a group thing, not an individual thing. Genocide always has a technology; as crude as machetes in Rwanda or knives in Bosnia, or a very sophisticated and complex system such as the crematoria and concentration camps with complex railway connections during the Holocaust.

There must be an identifiable group according to Chalk and Jonassohn, one placed outside the universe of moral obligation according to Helen Fein, and it must usually be intentional to kill this group.

The following is a schematic sociological theory of genocide consisting of a definition, component parts, a typology, and a two-step approach. (See charts I-IV for a visual outline of this theory.)

Definition

My definition is broader than the United Nations definition:

> Genocide is the **deliberate destruction,** in whole or in part, by a government, a state authority, or its agents—with intent to destroy—of a **racial, religious, tribal, ethnic, cultural, sexual, or political group.**

Components

It involves three major components: ideology (racism, anti-semitism, exclusivism); technology (crude or sophisticated techniques), and bureaucracy (crude or sophisticated social organization).

A Two-Step Theory

My theory is a two-step approach: ideology (racism, anti-semitism, exclusivism) is the animus that starts genocide, including the Holocaust, but then a second element kicks in—bureaucracy, obedience to orders, peer pressure, careerism, and all the myriad sociological, organizational, and psychological motivators take over; what Erich Goldhagen calls, the "foot in the door" theory: that once the killing starts, it takes on a momentum of its own. In short, it is Hannah Arendt's "banality of evil," ordinary human beings become ordinary killers. People can live together peacefully as neighbors for centuries and then suddenly become lethal killers, such as what happened in Bosnia.

Ideology can consist of sophisticated racial theories such as those in Nazi Germany regarding Jews, gypsies, and homosexuals; or it can be "pre-modern," and non-ideological as Helen Fein (1978) points out regarding the Turkish genocide of the Armenians. She coined the term "exclusivist" rather than racist to discriminate such ideologies since the Turks were not racist in the modern usage of that term.

One needs social organization (crude or sophisticated, simple or complex) as well as ideology to carry out genocide. One could also reverse the two-step process: that is, have a pattern of social organization (obedience to orders, for example) and then have ideology. In short, kill first, then rationalize later. Both steps are important but modernity has shown that social organization is more lethal than ideology.

Anti-semitism was a crucial element of the Holocaust but not the only element: the Holocaust showed that you could kill Jews without being an antisemite, simply by being a bureaucrat doing his job. In short, what are the cultural values and the social control mechanisms of a society that allows genocide to occur?

When Genocide Takes Place

Historically, genocide has taken place under three conditions: one, during war or following defeat in war; two, during internal colonialization or external imperialism; and three, during deep-rooted tribal or ethnic conflicts. (See Chart III.)

War

A situation leading to what Mendelson (1973: 189-198) calls victimity is common during wartime. Victimity, which he defines as the tendency or vulnerability to become victimized can involve many forms of collective violence including genocide. Of course one needs to be wary of tautologies—if one becomes a victim, then one must have been vulnerable.

There are structural and ideological reasons why some groups are targets of genocide. But the point I am making is that for several reasons, wartime is a specially favorable time for the commission of genocide and other atrocities. Minorities are more vulnerable during and after wartime. Why?

First, when armies are confronting each other, genocide against civilians can simply be considered an extension of military warfare.

Second, wartime provides an opportunity for utilizing propaganda effectively on a massive scale to label the enemy as traitors, to create hysteria leading to scapegoating, or worse to see human beings as inhuman, therefore as Helen Fein says "outside the universe of moral obligation."

Armenians and Cambodians are good examples of post-war stress leading to genocide. The Turks after World War I (1915) and the Cambodians (1975) after the war in Vietnam and the massive carpet bombings in Cambodia itself, both are examples of post-traumatic wartime stress leading to victimity and genocide.

Colonialization

Genocide has frequently been committed during periods of internal colonialization; for example, note the killing of North American Indian tribes in the United States and South American Indian tribes in Brazil and Paraguay. (See Dadrian, 1976; Savon, 1972; Arens, 1977, 1978.)

Small indigenous tribes are especially vulnerable. External colonialism has led to the death of aboriginal Indians such as the Tasmanians and Maoris in New Zealand and the near death of the Aborigines in Australia. One problem with this type of genocide is intent. Numerous Indian tribes have disappeared or are in the process of disappearing because of conquest, that is through outright murder, with an intent to kill every man, woman, and child of that tribe. Yet, other Indians have died indirectly, by the natural consequences of contact; for example, by handling blankets that transferred smallpox to victims without sufficient immunization.

Tribal or Ethnic Conflict

The third arena for acts of genocide to occur can simply be during inter-tribal conflict, the lethal hatred of the "other." Examples abound: the genocide of the Hutu-Tutsis in Burundi in 1972 and recently in Rwanda; the atrocities by Serbs against Croats and Muslims in Bosnia; against Hindus in East Pakistan and Buddhists in Tibet.

Mixed and Emerging Types

New and "creative" forms of genocide are emerging; humans are a continually creative species in finding new ways to kill themselves. Is it due to stress on the planet? overcrowding? a lethal "killing gene"? We don't quite know exactly why, but here are several new variations:

a) **Auto-genocide.** Killing one's own people or different strata of one's own people. Thus, the "other" in this case is one's "self." Best example: Khmer Rouge communist Cambodians under Pol Pot killing educated and upper-class Cambodians.

b) **Sexual genocide.** Killing people of a particular sexual orientation such as homosexuals in Nazi Germany and Austria during the Holocaust. While this turned out to be not a true genocide (intent was missing), it could be in the future.

c) **Politically-based genocide.** Killing based on one's political beliefs; for example the man-made famines in the Ukraine in the early 1930s or the killing of Communists in 1960 in Indonesia. This type was removed from the U.N. definition because of Soviet pressure by Joseph Stalin who was engaged in such "genocides" against the Ukrainians, and other ethnic groups.

The Prediction of Genocide

Sociological and historical research on the Holocaust and other genocides by Hilberg (1961), Horowitz (1976), Fein (1979a), Dadrian (1974, 1975a, 1975b, 1976, 1979) and Porter (1979a, 1982a), laid the foundation for not only a theory of genocide, but for a means of predicting genocide. Charny and Rapoport (1977) established the first genocide "early warning system" at the Henrietta Szold Institute in Jerusalem in the mid-70s.

By synthesizing the contributions of Fein (1979: 3-30), Horowitz (1976), and Dadrian (1974, 1975a, and 1979), I make the following predictive statements about when genocide will occur. In those nation-states where the following conditions are found, the likelihood for genocide increases exponentially:

a) The Existence of Minority groups (I use the term sociologically; they could be in fact numerically the "majority") have historically been outside the universe of moral obligation and placed there by the dominant group. Such groups have been labeled not simply "outsiders" but "bacilli," "vermin," and other non human epithets that precede their elimination. Their threat is considered so evil that they must be totally liquidated, not simply subjugated or, to use Daniel Goldhagen's term (1996: 469-471), "helotized." Slaves are at least useful. "Bacilli" must be destroyed. The Jews according to Steven Katz (1994) are an excellent example of this status; but I would also include Gypsies, Armenians, and homosexuals/ lesbians. They, too, are historical "outsiders." Other variables include:

b) The society holds deeply rooted and pervasive racial and biological ideologies.

c) Strong dependence on military security based on societal insecurity. "Outsiders" are considered threatening.

d) Powerful, monolithic, exclusionary political parties dominate the society and the state.
e) The leadership has strong territorial ambitions.
f) Defeat in war and/or internal strife has weakened the power of the state.
g) The possibility of retaliation for genocidal acts by kin of the victims or by intervention by neutral nations or NGOs (non-governmental agencies or organizations) is at a minimum.

Conversely, the following conditions will reduce the possibility of genocide exponentially:

a) Pervasive tolerance and respect for minority groups.
b) Temperate and controlled attitudes toward external military or political thereat.
c) Democratic political structures and governmental institutions.
d) Weak territorial and imperial ambitions.
e) Strong, healthy minorities with ready access to legal and human rights.
f) The possibility of retaliation and/or intervention by outside nations or NGOs (non-governmental agencies such as the U.N. or Amnesty International) or kin of the victims is at a maximum.

Other factors such as a healthy economy and non-involvement in war can also minimize genocide. Given the fact that the conditions cited can exist in most societies at least at some time in their. history, genocide is thus possible in any society. Still, some nation-states are more prone to genocide than others; but there are surprises in either direction. For example, the Union of South Africa only a decade ago seemed a highly likely place for genocide; but that threat seems to have passed as it moved into a democratic egalitarian state.

Yugoslavia seemed to be a tolerant haven for minorities yet exploded into genocidal acts, with neighbor pitted against neighbor. The Netherlands, Sweden, and Switzerland, of course, are much less likely to commit genocide. The so-called "third-world" countries, especially in Africa and Asia, have to be watched carefully as possible genocide sites.

The above are major variables leading to what Horowitz (1976) calls genocidal societies. I deal here with external variables; what is needed is more research on internal variables that can predict and describe genocide form within the society. I have used a systems approach, schematically showing major independent variables leading to genocide.

Conclusion

I have tried to sketch here the rudiments of a simple sociology of genocide. My "two-step" theory of ideology and social organization goes beyond Daniel Goldhagen's (1996) simplistic one-step approach that ideology (anti-Semitism in the case of the Holocaust) alone was the sole factor in the implementation of genocide.

What I have done here is only a beginning, a schematic, theoretical overview of some key variables that predict genocide. The sociological imagination that C. Wright Mills gave us in the 1950s can be applied to a scientific study of the Holocaust. Sociology can deal with unique events and it can bring a much needed and long-overdue perspective on genocide and other state-produced mass killings.

Porter's Theory of Genocide
Chart I. The Components of Genocide

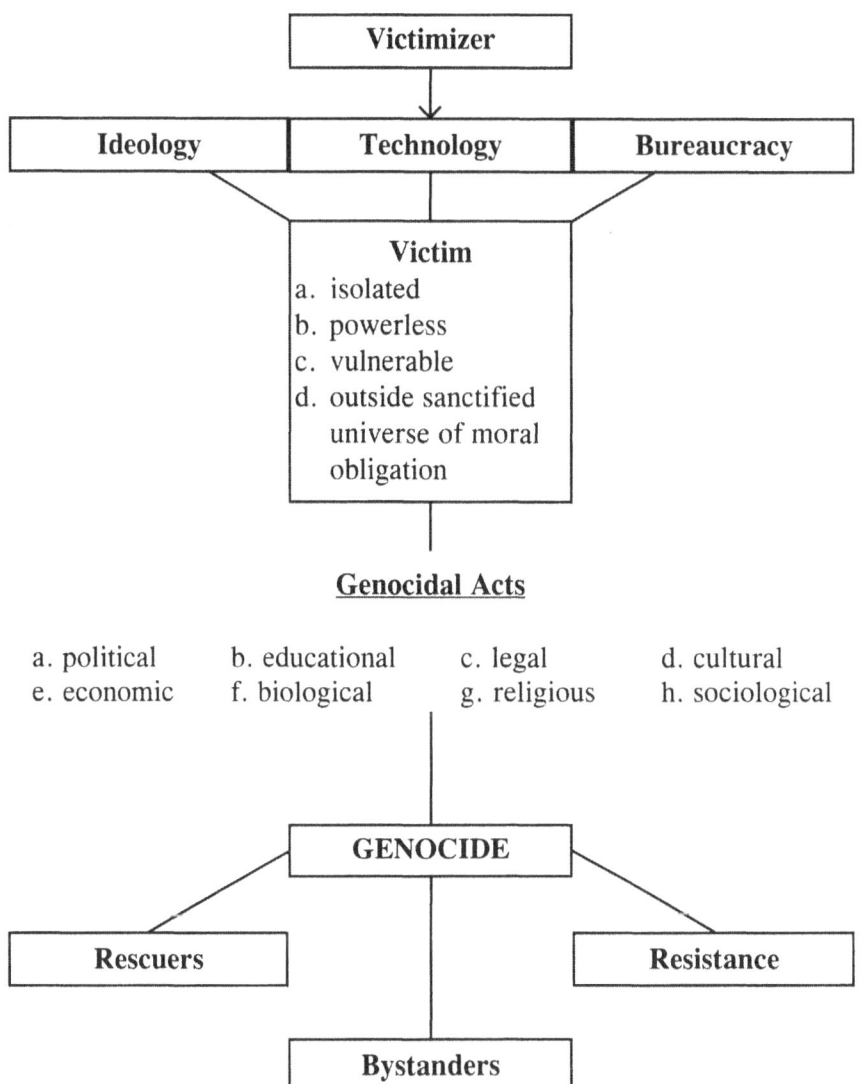

Chart II. The Three Major Factors in Genocide

I. Ideologists	Legitimization	Genocide
Agitators	Dehumanization	Sophisticated
Propagandists	Feralization	↑
Writers	Justification	↓
Teachers	Anti-Semitism	
Scholars	Racism	Crude

II. Technologists	Technology of Death	Genocide
Army Commanders	Shooting	Sophisticated
Concentration Camp Directors	Gas/poison	↑
Engineers/Chemists	Burning/cremating	
Doctors	Experimentation	
	Starvation	↓
Soldiers	Forced marches	
	Knives/spears/	
Guards	blunt objects	Crude

III. Social Organization	Bureaucracy	Genocide
Political leaders	Functionaries	Sophisticated
Inner Circle	Clerks	↑
Military Leaders	Railroad personnel	↓
	Guards	
	"Ordinary People"	Crude

Chart III. When Genocide Takes Place: A Typology of Genocide

I. During War or following a defeat in war
  A) Post-traumatic genocide
    • Armenians in Turkey during and after World War I
    • Jews before and during World War II
    • Cambodians following the Vietnam War in mid-1970s
  B) Ideological/racial genocide
    • Jews
    • Gypsies
    • Homosexuals
    • Disabled
II. During internal colonialization of indigenous people
  • Aborigines
  • Maoris
  • Tasmanians
  • Ache of Paraguay and Brazil
  • Certain North and Central American and Caribbean tribes
III. During deep-rooted tribal and ethnic conflict
  • Rwanda/Burundi
  • Bosnia
  • Hindus in East Pakistan
  • Buddhists in Tibet
  • Catholics/Protestants in Northern Ireland (to some degree)
IV. Mixed types
  • Cambodia—trauma of war *plus* ideology
  • Armenians—political threat *plus* war *plus* ideology
  • Burundi/Rwanda—political threat plus tribal hatred
V. New and emerging types/creative forms of genocide
  • Auto-genocide (killing segments of one's own people)—Cambodia
  • Sexual genocide (homosexuals in Nazi Germany)
  • Political genocide (man-made famine in Ukraine; communists in Indonesia)

Chart IV: Selected Genocides throughout History

Genocide	Location and date	Victims	Perpetrators	Bystanders/ resistance	Sophisticated ideology/ technology/ bureaucracy	Special Features
Biblical	Mideast 800 BC	Numerous	-----	All/ Yes	No/No/No	Controversy over intention
Bosnia "Ethnic Cleansing"	1941 to 1945	Serbs, Jews, & Roma gypsies	SS & Croatians; Muslims	World/Yes	Yes/No/No	First in Europe since WWII
	1992 to 1995	Muslims/Croats	Serbs	World/Yes	Yes/No/No	Controversy over intention
American Indian	Western United States 1492 to 1890	500 Indian tribes	Europeans in General	Americans/ Yes	No/Yes/Yes	Controversy over intention
Australian and New Zealander Indians	Australia and New Zealand 19th Century to present	Aboriginal tribes	Farmers, army colonizers	Australian people/ Yes	No/Crude/Yes	Often overlooked genocide
Ukrainian famine	Ukraine 1931 to 1933	Ukrainian people	Stalin, Soviet leadership	World/ very little	No/Crude/Yes	Induced famine; slow starvation
Tibetans	Tibet since 1960s	Tibetans	Communist Chinese	World/ No	No/Crude/Yes	Ethnocide: destruction of a culture and a religion but not a people

Chart IV: Selected Genocides throughout History (cont.)

Genocide	Location and date	Victims	Perpetrators	Bystanders/ resistance	Sophisticated ideology/ technology/ bureaucracy	Special Features
Homosexuals (but not lesbians)	Germany & Austria 1934-1945	Known homosexuals	SS under Hitler	German people/ none	Yes	First "sexual genocide" (Controversy over intention)
Women	World	Women	Men	World/none	Yes, not targeted	A new "genocide" (controversy over intention) (Not considered a true genocide)
Jews	Europe 1933-1945	Jews	Nazis	World/yes	Yes	The Holocaust
Gypsies	Europe 1944-1945	Senti and Roma Tribes	Nazis and collaborators	World/none	Yes	A true genocide
Jehovah's Witnesses	Germany/ Austria 1933-1945	Jehovah's Witnesses (non-violent)	Nazis	World/no	Yes	Ambivalent attitude; pacifists (Not a genocide)
Mormons	Germany/ Austria 1933-1945	Mormons	Nazis	World/no	Yes	Ambivalence (Not a genocide)

Chart IV: Selected Genocides throughout History (cont.)

Genocide	Location and date	Victims	Perpetrators	Bystanders/ resistance	Sophisticated ideology/ technology/ bureaucracy	Special Features
Disabled (euthanasia)	Germany 1933-1945	Mentally ill, deaf, blind	Nazi doctors and nurses	Germans/yes by families	Yes	The only Nazi genocide that was stopped
Armenians	Turkey 1894-1908 1915-1922	Ottoman Armenians	Sultan Abdul Hamid, Young Turks	The Allies/ very little	Yes/crude/Yes	Forgotten genocide; denial by Turks
Cambodians	Cambodia 1975-1979	Urban educated Cambodians	Communist Party of Cambodia	Americans, The "West"/No	Yes/crude/Yes	"Autogenocide" A self-inflicted genocide
Hutu-Tutsi	Burundi 1972-73 1993-96	Each other	Each other	The World/ very little	No/crude/Yes	Tribal Warfare
Hutu-Tutsi	Rwanda 1994	Tutsi	Hutu	The World/ very little	No/crude/Yes	Extremely fast and lethal genocide

References

Ainsztein, Reuben
 1974 *Jewish Resistance in Nazi Occupied Europe.* New York: Barnes and Noble.

Arens, Richard (ed.)
 1977 *Genocide in Paraguay.* Philadelphia: Temple University Press.
 1978 "Death Camps in Paraguay," *American Indian Journal.* 4:2-13.

Arendt, Hannah
 1963 *Eichmann in Jerusalem.* New York: Viking.

Bassiouni, M. Cherif
 1979 "International Law and the Holocaust," in Byron Sherwin (ed.), *Encountering the Holocaust.* New York: Hebrew Publishing Company, 146-188.

Becker, Ernest
 1975 *Escape from Evil.* New York: Free Press-Macmillan.

Bedau, Hugo
 1974 "Genocide in Vietnam?" in *Philosophy, Morality, and International Affairs.* Virginia Held et al. (eds.), New York: Oxford University Press.

Chalk, Frank and Kurt Jonassohn
 1990 *The History and Sociology of Genocide: Analyses and Case Studies.* New Haven, CT: Yale University Press.

Charney, I. W., and Rapoport, Chanah
 1977 "Innocent Odyssey," *Ararat: A Quarterly.* 18:13-18.
 1979 Personal Communication to the author.

Dadrian, Vahakn, N.
 1974 "The Structural-Functional Components of Genocide," in Israel Drapkin and Emilio Viano (eds.), *Victimology: A New Focus, Violence and its Victims.* Lexington, MA: D.C. Heath.
 1975a "A Typology of Genocide," *International Review of Sociology.* 5:2, Autumn, 201-212.
 1974b "The Common Features of the Armenian and Jewish Cases of Genocide: A Comparative Victimological Perspective," in *Victimology: A New Focus: Violence and its Victims.* Israel Drapkin and Emilio Viano (eds.) Lexington, MA: D.C. Heath.

    1976   "The Victimization of the American Indian." *Victimology: An International Journal.* 1:4, Winter, 517-537.

    1979   "A Theoretical Model of Genocide with Particular Reference to the Armenian Case." *The Armenian Review.* 31:115-136.

Dawidowicz, Lucy
    1975   *The War against the Jews.* New York: Holt, Rinehart, and Winston.

Des Pres, Terence
    1976   *The Survivor.* New York: Oxford University Press.

Dubro, Alex
    1977   "Methadone is . . ." *Liberation.* 20:2, January-February.

Ellerin, Milton
    1974   *The American Nazis* (Pamphlet). New York: American Jewish Committee.

Elliot, Gil
    1972   *The Twentieth Century Book of the Dead.* New York: Ballantine.

Epstein, Helen
    1979   *Children of the Holocaust.* New York: G. P. Putnam's.

Ervin, Sam
    1971   United States Senate Hearing. Washington, DC: Subcommittee on Genocide Convention of the Committee on Foreign Relations (Wednesday, March 10), Also in *Congressional Record,* May 25, 1970.

Fein, Helen
    1978   "A Formula for Genocide: Comparison of the Turkish Genocide (1915) and the German Holocaust (1939-1945)," *Comparative Studies in Sociology.* 1:271-293.

    1979a   *Accounting for Genocide.* New York: The Free Press.

    1979b   "Is Sociology Aware of Genocide? Recognition of Genocide in Introductory Sociology Texts in the United States, 1947-77," *Humanity and Society.* 3:3, August: 177-193.

1982 "On Preventing Genocide." *Worldview* and reprinted in Jack Nusan Porter, *Genocide and Human Rights*. 269-279.

1996 *Genocide: A Sociological Perspective*. Sherman Oaks, CA: Sage Publications.

Feingold, Henry
1978 "Four Days in April: A Review of NBC's Dramatization of the Holocaust." *Shoah: A Review of Holocaust Studies and Commemorations*. 1:15-17.

Fields, Rona
1976 "Psychological Genocide: The Irish Case." Paper Read at the American Sociological Association, New York City.

Fogelman, Eva, and Savran, Bella
1979 "Therapeutic Groups for Children of Holocaust Survivors." *International Journal of Group Psychotherapy*. 29 (April).

Friedlander, Henry
1973 *On the Holocaust: A Critique of the Treatment of the Holocaust in History Textbooks* (accompanied by an annotated bibliography). New York: Anti-Defamation League of B'nai Brith.

1978 "Towards a Methodology of Teaching about the Holocaust." *Social Education*. 42 (April): 21-25.

Goldberg, Arthur J.
1971 United States Senate Hearing. Washington, DC: Subcommittee on Genocide Convention of the Committee of Foreign Relations (Wednesday, March 10).

Goldman, Martin S.
1977 "Teaching the Holocaust; Some Suggestions for Comparative Analysis." *Journal of Intergroup Relations*. 6 (December): 23-30.

Goldhagen, Daniel Jonah
1996 *Hitler's Willing Executioners*. New York: Knopf.

Goodrich, H.
1977 "Uses and Abuses of the Terms 'Racism' and 'Racist'." *ASA Footnotes,* 5:4, April, 4,8.

Gould, Julius and Kolb, William L. (eds.)
1964 *A Dictionary of* the *Social Sciences*. New York: Free Press.

Hilberg, Raul
    1962   *The Destruction of the European Jews*. New York: Quadrangle.

Horowitz, Irving Louis
    1976   *Genocide, State Power and Mass Murder*. New Brunswick, Transaction Books.

Hoult, Thomas F.
    1969   *Dictionary of Modern Sociology*. Totowa, NH: Littlefield, Adams and Company.

Katz, Steven
    1994   *The Holocaust in Historical Context*. New York: Oxford University Press.

Lemarchand, Rene
    1975   "Ethnic Genocide," *Society*. 12:2, January-February, 50-60.

Levin, Nora
    1973   *The Holocaust*. New York: Schocken.

Lemkin, Raphael
    1973   *Axis Rule in Occupied Europe*. New York: Howard Fertig. (First published by the Carnegie Endowment for International Peace in 1944)

Lifton, R. J.
    1967   *Death in Life; Survivors of Hiroshima*. New York: Random House.

Lifton, R. J., and Olson, Eric.
    1975   *Living and Dying*. New York Bantam Books.

Mendelson, Binyamin
    1973   "Victimology and the Needs of Contemporary Society," *The Israel Annals of Psychiatry and Related Disciplines*. 11-3, 189-198.

Milgram, Stanley
    1975   *Obedience to Authority*. New York: Harper and Row.

Morse, Arthur
    1975   *While Six Million Died: A Chronicle of American Apathy*. New York: Hart.

Naral
    1979   Literature from National Abortion Rights Action League. Washington, DC.

Nowitch, Myriam
    1968   *Le Genocide des Tziganes sous le Régime Nazi.* Paris: Comité pour l'érection du monument en memoire des Tziganes assassinés à Auschwitz.

Patterson, William L. (ed.)
    1961   *We Charge Genocide; The Crime of Government against the Negro People.* New York: International Publishing Company.

Peson, Yves
    1979   "D'un genocide à l'autre." *Pluriel.* 19:89-94.

Porter Jack, Nusan
    1977   A Nazi Runs for Mayor. *Present Tense.* 4 (Summer): 27-31.
    1979a   "Some Social-Psychological Aspects of the Holocaust; Obstacles to Military Resistance during Genocide" in Byron Sherwin and Susan Ament (eds.), *Encountering the Holocaust.* Chicago: Impact Press, 1979, 189-222.
    1979b   "On Therapy, Research, and Other Dangerous Phenomena." *Shoah: A Review of Holocaust Studies and Commemorations.* 1:3 (Winter): 14-15.
    1981   "Is There a Survivor's Syndrome? Some Social-Psychological and Political Implications." *Journal of Psychology and Judaism.* 6:1 (Winter).
    1982a   *Genocide and Human Rights: A Global Anthology.* University Press of America.
    1982b   *Jewish Partisans: Memoirs of Jewish Resistance During World War II.* University Press of America, 2 vols.

Robinson, Jacob
    1971   "Holocaust" and "Genocide" Convention" in *Encyclopedia Judaica.* Jerusalem: Keter Publishing Company, vols. 8 and 7.

Roth, John K.
    1978   "Difficulties Everywhere: Sober Reflections on Teaching about the Holocaust." *Shoah: A Review of Holocaust Studies and Commemorations.* 1 (Spring): 1-3.

Savon, H.
    1971   *Du cannibalisme au genocide.* Paris: Hachette.

Seligman, E. R, A., and Johnson, Alvin (eds.)
    1933   *Encyclopedia of the Social Sciences*. New York: Macmillan.

Sherwin, Byron
    1978   "The Spertus College of Judaica Holocaust Studies Curriculum" *Shoah: A Review of Holocaust Studies and Commemorations*. 1 (Spring): 9-10.

Sherwin, Byron and Ament, Susan (eds.)
    1979   *Encountering the Holocaust*. New York: Hebrew Publishing Company, and Chicago: Impact Press. (See Porter's essay in this book.)

Sills, David (ed.)
    1968   *International Encyclopedia of the Social Sciences*. New York: Macmillan.

Steinitz, Lucy Y. and Szonyi, David M. (eds.)
    1975   *Living after the Holocaust*. New York: Block Publishing Co.

Strom, Margo Stern and Parsons, William S.
    1977   *Facing History and Ourselves: Holocaust and Human Behavior*. Brookline, MA: Brookline Public Schools.

Suhl, Yri (ed.)
    1975   *They Fought Back*. New York: Schocken Books.

Theodorson, G. A. and Theodorson, A. G.
    1969   *Modern Dictionary of Sociology*. New York: Thomas Crowell.

The Crime of Genocide
    n.d.   "New York: United Nations Signed the Genocide Treaty?" Paper read at the American Sociological Association meeting, Chicago, IL.

Weisbord, Robert G.
    1975   *Genocide: Birth Control and the Black American*. Westport, CT: Greenwood Press.

Wrong, Dennis
    1976   Personal communication to author.

Part I

Toward a Sociology of the Holocaust

Chapter 1

The Meaning of the Holocaust for Sociologists

"A plea for the survivors? I know, it seems insane. It is not. Because they are decreasing in numbers and because they themselves feel misunderstood and unloved, and also because they have locked themselves into their sorrow, I thought it important to make this plea for them—for all of us. And for our children. So that they shall know. So that they shall remember."[1]

—Elie Wiesel, Nobel Laureate

I lost 25 members of my family in one night. They were machine-gunned by Ukrainian police and SS *Einsatzgruppen* in front of mass graves that they dug themselves. It was a Sabbath day, September 25, 1942, the town of Maniewicze, western Ukraine, near Kovel, north of my birthplace, one year later, of Rovno. I lost all my aunts and uncles, all my grandparents, but most especially my two darling little sisters, age 4 and 2, sisters I never knew. I don't even know what they looked like. They died before a photo could have been taken of them.

My father and mother miraculously escaped. He was saved by a Ukrainian mayor who respected him; my mother hid in a barn, then crawled out of the ghetto, and into the deep forests of Volynia. Later, they both joined the Jewish Partisan unit *Kruk Otryad*. My mother became a cook; and my father became a unit commander, later won a medal from the Soviet Army for his heroism. I was born while the guns still raged on December 2, 1944—a miracle child, my mother called me—a "special" child with a "special mission" in life.

On April 22, 1993, I along with hundreds of other survivors and their children dedicated the US Holocaust Memorial Museum in the nation's capital before the President of the United States and the heads of state of Israel, Poland, Croatia, and many other countries. I "thanked" Bill Clinton for coming. I welcomed him to "my" museum. He was very gracious. He understood.

Back in Milwaukee in 1964, I took my first sociology course with a charismatic teacher Karl Flaming and because of him I became a sociologist. But I wish to also thank all my University of Wisconsin-Milwaukee teachers who helped Americanize this refugee boy—Irwin Rinder, Lakshmi Bharadwaj, Donald Noel, J.J. Palen, Hugo Engelmann, Robert Silverberg, and Sidney Greenfield.

One day Flaming asked us to interview our grandparents for a sociology project. He asked how many of us had grandparents? Nearly all the hands shot up. I thought that was funny. To me, NOT having grandparents, aunts, uncles, cousins was "normal." It was then that my "sociological imagination" emerged.

When I was fifteen I watched the Eichmann Trial on TV; my parents sat transfixed. This was the Holocaust. I was stunned. Being a child of survivors isolated me from my peers. I agree with Professor Mona Weissmark of Harvard University, with whom I was involved in discussion groups with children of Nazis, that it made us different. It was so morbid, no one wanted to hear about it, and no one could understand it, so you feel different, separate. Even my own former professors will be surprised to learn that I am a child-survivor of the Holocaust. They never knew. My only friends were other children of survivors and sensitive Jewish kids who understood us refugee families. It was my "secret."

Yet, I became a sociologist because of it. Of that I am certain. In order to find meaning in this absurdly different life that I led, I had to find some handle. I was drawn to sociology because sociologists were what Robert K. Merton called "insiders-outsiders." We understood the deviant, the outcast, the weird. Evil. That I understood well. Furthermore, sociologists could enter the most dangerous situations and armed only with their professionalism, could remain untouched. It was very much like being a survivor. To emerge whole. To bear witness/ The sociologist as survivor. I had been to a strange and monstrous planet, had lived intimately among its inhabitants and I had to tell the tale. Could I describe that planet to the outside world? I started by interviewing my parents.[2]

Is it any wonder that I saw myself as a stranger, the ultimate "outsider"?[3] Is it any wonder that I was drawn to the works of Erving Goffman, C.W. Mills, Howard S. Becker, Ernest Becker, Karl Marx, Jacques Ellul, and other "outsiders"? Yet, ironically, sociology ignored the Holocaust and thus, ignored me.[4] Today, everything reminds me of the Holocaust—total institutions, modernity, gay rights, ecology, black-Jewish tensions, medical experimentation. The Holocaust is always on my mind—while I read or drive, look out a window or play baseball with my son or daughter. Never once do I forget these tender, loving, gentle people who died in the *shtetlach* and ghettos of the *tremendum*.

As the years pass, the losses become more poignant. My own children ask: where is our family? My former wife is also a child of survivors. We had few relatives at our *bar mitzvahs*. But you can't tell from looking at us. We can "pass" as "ordinary human beings." Yet, as the years go by, my status as a "survivor" becomes more and more unique. An ascribed trait, I am given respect just for being a child of survivors.

* * * * *

"Not all victims were Jews but all Jews were victims."
—Elie Wiesel

But what is the meaning of this museum to sociologists? Well, I urge them to see it and to take their parents, spouses, children, students, and colleagues. Put away your theories, your "political correctness", and your expectations. You will find mentioned other victims besides Jews—gays, Poles, the disabled, gypsies (Roma).[5] In fact, on the very next day after seeing the Museum, on April 23, I was honored to have been asked to join the leadership team of the massive March on Washington for Gay, Lesbian and Bi-Equal Rights and Liberation for a special tour of the Museum with me acting as a "consultant." I walked the corridors arm-in-arm with Pat Hussain of the Executive Committee, a proud and beautiful black lesbian. She was my "soul sister" on so many levels as we took this tour.

* * * * *

Regarding the interesting question of whether the Holocaust is unique or not, Wiesel gave the following response:

Question: History is replete with genocides, mass imprisonments, unmentionable horrors. Why do you argue that the death of six million Jews was an unparalleled tragedy?

Wiesel: The uniqueness of the Jewish tragedy must be respected. This does not mean others have not suffered. The Cambodian experience was a civil war; there was an ideology there, communism and so forth. Cambodians killed Cambodians. The Gypsies? Not all Gypsies were destined to die; Hitler exempted two tribes. Homosexuals? This involved something people practiced. Only Jews were destined to die solely for being Jews.

Being became a crime, and for this there is no parallel in history.

* * * * *

The Museum is so authentic it is unnerving. There is even a special section called "Daniel's Story" that portrays the Holocaust from a child's point of view. I urge parents to take their children.[6] You are given a "passport" upon arrival, and at the end you are told whether they lived or were deported and executed. The Wexner Learning Center is also a must-see for the teacher. The entire Holocaust, an encyclopedia of knowledge, is at your fingertips. Press a button on any topic, and the screen conjures up photos, films, songs, articles . . . awesome. Every college should be hooked up to this computer.

I looked up "mobile killing units" and up came a rare film of Jews killed in pits—the way my sisters were executed. I played the film over and over again. It wasn't my family or my region, but it was the only thing I have on film. I sat mesmerized, I also found the names of my parents in the official registry. Finally, it is all so real to me. My family has not been forgotten. They are in this museum.

The tour starts with the history of racism and the rise of Nazism. Good sociology all of it. They have copies of the actual books burned by the Nazis, including the works of Magnus Hirschfeld and his work on *sexualität*. Next, the ghettoization process. Righteous gentiles, including my good friend Stephanya Bruzminski, who saved 13 Jewish lives in her attic and then later married one of them and moved to Boston. The Death Camps. A recreation of Auschwitz—a cattle car that brought crazed and thirsty Jews to the camp. The wooden bed bunks where inmates slept. I wanted to climb inside and feel what it was like to be in Auschwitz even for a moment. The piles of shoes. Toothbrushes. Eyeglasses. The Partisans of the Forest. Think of my father and mother, Irving and Faye, when you see the partisan rifles and documents. The DP Camps. Liberation by General Eisenhower and the Allied Troops. The desire to go to Israel. The illegal *aliyah*.

* * * * *

From a sociology of evil to a legacy of evil. It is difficult for sociology's tools to fathom the Holocaust—objectivity, scientific precision, controls, these all break down when confronted by the Holocaust.[7] Perhaps that is why we need our Nobel Laureate Elie Wiesel with his mystical, Talmudic, ambivalent, God-centered approached.

In the following quote, Wiesel grapples with this legacy of evil in the personification of Franz Stangl, Kommandant of Treblinka, Sobibor, and Belzec.

> How was he able to spend his free time with his wife, whom he loved, and their child away from Belzec and Treblinka? How could he love his wife and help murder half a million innocent people at the same time? How is it conceivable? How did he manage to distance the corpses towering like walls between himself and other human beings? . . .
>
> Do not expect to find answers to that in this book. There are no such answers, neither in this book nor anywhere else. But you will find the questions, and they will haunt your nights.[8]

Stangl was the only *kommandant* of an *extermination* camp who had been brought to trial. There were, extraordinarily enough, only *four* men who specifically filled that function. One was dead at the time (1970 Germany) and two had disappeared. There were many concentration *lager* and work camps or combination camps (like Auschwitz-Birkenau) but only four whose sole purpose, from cattle-car to gas chamber, was only death: Treblinka (where 900,000 Jews died), Sobibor, Chelmno, and Belzec.

Stangl was a man of keen intelligence and charm and Gitta Sereny spent 70 hours interviewing him in Remand Prison in Dusseldorf. She describes this evil in her book *Into That Darkness*.[9] Stangl only received a life imprisonment and since he was only in his early 30s when he was *kommandant,* he lived until 1974, long after his victims perished.

* * * * *

April 22, 1993 was a great day for me and my "family" of survivors. Aside from President Clinton, I also met Lech Walesa, the President of Poland, Chaim Herzog, the President of Israel, and the President of Croatia. The Holocaust certainly makes strange bedfellows. Croatian Uztashi killed Serbs, Jews, and Roma during the war, including members of my wife's Sephardi family in Belgrade and Sarajevo. That day, however, we welcomed the Croat leader but the Serbian President was not invited, even though Serbs saved many Jewish lives during the war.

Bill and Hillary looked fit, tanned, and ebullient. Walesa was solemn and in a bit of a hurry to catch a plane. As I walked the Museum with the Polish President, I told him the story of how my father was aided by a Polish man Casimir Slovik and his son Yazenty. He listened well but said nothing. I told the same story to Jerzy Wroblewski, director of the Auschwitz Museum. He listened better. The Polish press that flocked about us duly noted it. It is good PR for a Jew to say good things about Poles. I was happy to do so. My father taught me to hate no one. I guess that's the greatest sociological lesson of all, isn't it?

* * * * *

I suppose being a child of Holocaust survivors makes me, in some eyes, "emotional" and "subjective," and therefore not very "objective" about this issue. So be it. My subjective experience and the culmination of extensive objective studies have led me to believe the following:

1. Sociology should concentrate on the Holocaust and the phenomenon of genocide; in short in "comparative genocide" but using the Holocaust as a unique touchstone and case history to compare the others. Politicide, democide, and nuclear omnicide are secondary issues and often confuse and cloud the analysis. I do, however, like the term "ethnocide" which describes the destruction of a culture (Black, Indian, Irish Catholic) without it turning into actual physical genocide.

2. The Holocaust (of the Jews in Europe from 1933-1945) is unique in history in bureaucratic and technological scope. There have been mass murders and deaths (native Americans, blacks in the Middle Passage) that have far exceeded the Holocaust in sheer numbers, but none before nor since have duplicated its ferocity, lethalness, and sophistication in terms of modernity (what I define as a tripartite framework of advanced ideology, technology, and bureaucracy).
3. The Holocaust was the culmination of some of the most significant political, moral, religious, and demographic tendencies of Western Civilization in the 20th century. (See Richard Rubenstein, *The Cunning of History*, New York: Harper & Row, 1975). I do not believe we will ever see another holocaust like "the Holocaust."
4. Sociologists are uncomfortable with unique events. Professor Grimshaw in his report to the ASA on war and genocide does not once mention the term Holocaust (however he has added it in subsequent reports). It disappears under the rubric of "genocide, politicide, and democide." Of course, all historical events are unique, but the Holocaust was a "tremendum," one of the defining events of our civilization. Hiroshima was also unique. But because something is unique does not mean that it cannot be comparable and generalizable to other genocides. We sociologists, unlike historians, are afraid of unique events, and especially of "uniquely unique" events such as the Holocaust.
5. I do not, however, take a strictly exclusionist view of the Holocaust as do scholars such as Professor Steven Katz of Boston University (Jewish Studies) or Professor Daniel Goldhagen (Assistant Professor of Government at Harvard University and their Center for European Studies), who feel that the only real genocide was the Holocaust because it was the only state-sponsored genocide that had as its intent the destruction of every Jew on earth. In all other genocides (against Indians, blacks, witches, homosexuals, even Armenians, Cambodians, and Gypsies) there was never an intent to kill *every* single member of the targeted population, according to Katz. This is quite a provocative statement. (See

Volume One: *The Holocaust in Historical Context,* New York; Oxford University Press, 1994.)

But to discuss Katz and Goldhagen is beyond the scope of this small space. Suffice it to say, Katz is convincing regarding homosexuals, blacks, Indians, witches, and "women" (misogyny) as genocidal targets, but not about Gypsies or Armenians. The latter two were definitely genocides. The former were not genocides, but then again, most scholars never thought of them as genocides anyway. However, most of our students think of them as such.

6. There is a problem of Holocaust denial and definitional abuse. Misapplying and abusing the term genocide is very common in sociology. *To make everything genocide is to make nothing genocide.* Massacres, mass murders, "oppression", "atrocities", nuclear attack, aerial bombardment (such as the firebombing of Dresden), Hiroshima, My Lai, Maalot, black slavery, abortion, the treatment of women and witches, even the "suppression" of American Indians are not examples of genocide. (I have discussed this in the introduction to my book *Genocide and Human Rights,* Lanham, MD: University Press of America, 1982, reprinted 2002.)

7. To overlook the uniqueness of the Holocaust is also a form of Holocaust denial, though a very subtle form. To see the Holocaust as just another genocide is to deny its uniqueness and its profound ability to be used as the *key case study of our era* of universal comparability to other genocides. This is not to gainsay or to underestimate other genocides. I do not believe in "comparative suffering." Just because something is not a "genocide" does not mean it is not a heinous act. Just call it something else (massacre, mass murder) but not genocide.

8. With access to insightful educational material on the Holocaust, I believe we can persuade sociologists to teach courses in the Sociology of Genocide or to use such concepts as war, mass murder, and genocide in many of their other courses. I have developed a learning guide *The Sociology of Genocide and The Holocaust* (Washington, DC: American Sociological Association, 1999) that addresses many of these questions of uniqueness and universality, plus it has useful mate-

rial on several historical and ethnic/racial genocides. It contains many syllabi and teaching material for teachers. This and other texts like it can help sociologists teach courses in the Holocaust and the phenomenon of genocide. I also recommend my curriculum guide on American and European Jews, *The Sociology of Jewry* (ASA, 1722 N Street NW, Washington, DC 20036, 1999) as well as Frank Chalk and Kurt Jonassohn's, *The History and Sociology of Genocide*, New Haven, CT: Yale University Press, 1990).
9. But the key point is not to lock ourselves into rigid frameworks, definitions, and paradigms. There must be respect for a multi-paradigmatic approach. Mine could be called the "uniqueness-comparability" approach. It sees the Holocaust as unique yet comparable to others. Others may have a more "inclusivist" or "exclusionist" approach. Some will label events genocide where others would not call them genocide at all (i.e., blacks in the Middle Passage or the treatment of Native Americans or homosexuals). Some will attempt to expand the boundaries of genocide by inventing new concepts such as "politicide" (the killing of groups for political reasons), "ethnocide" for the destruction of a culture but not a race or tribe, "democide" (state-sponsored killings of any targeted group) or "nuclear omnicide" (mass death through nuclear attack).

So be it. Let a hundred flowers (and typologies) bloom! Let us respect our differences and learn from them by listening to each other and learning from each other. I have noticed a great deal of incivility lately both in academia and in the general society (note the Goldhagen scandal) and this too must end. Human beings are finding more creative ways to kill each other every day as we enter the 21st century, but not every killing is a genocide. The following is an example of ways of teaching genocide in a university setting:

Alan Wolfe (1991) recently urged sociologists to resurrect the "moral tradition" in social theory. What better subject to do that with than to grapple with the moral and theoretical issues of the Holocaust? I did just that in a course I taught several years ago at Boston University. The following provides an introduction to the Holocaust literature for theorists who wish to follow suit.

The Holocaust is an oddly overlooked topic in sociological teaching, although a few brave souls have tackled it, Zygmunt Bauman (1989) and Helen Fein (1979) among them. As Fein (1990) suggests in a review of the comparative genocide literature, this neglect is due to sociology's self-image as a generalizing science. Wary of the unique, it has little to say of the most dramatic events which have shaped our age, events like Vietnam, Hiroshima, and the Holocaust. Fortunately, historical sociologists have been less intimidated in this regard.

Drawing on Max Weber's comparative sociology, historical sociologists depict the Holocaust (or *Shoah* in Hebrew) as one culmination of the process of modernization. Without bureaucratic controls, impersonal criteria of efficiency, and divided responsibilities, Auschwitz and Treblinka would be impossible. Bauman has taken this point the furthest. "When the modernist dream [of a perfect arrangement of human conditions] is embraced by an absolute power able to monopolize modern vehicles of rational action, and when that power attains freedom from effective social control," he writes, "genocide happens" (1989: 93-94).

Richard Rubenstein's *The Cunning of History* (1975) and Raul Hilberg's *The Destruction of European Jewry* (1985, three volumes), were greatly influenced by Weber's sociology. They show the *Shoah* as the culmination of a process of intergroup conflict that began in the middle ages and came to fruition with the rise of fascism in the twentieth century.

Rationalization and Modernity

Following the standard Weberian account of the rise of modernity, Rubenstein and Hilberg show how the *Gemeinschaft* of medieval feudalism gave way to the *Gesellschaft* of the highly complex, mobile, bureaucratic society of the early twentieth century. As markets and the monetarization of economic activity replaced manorial institutions and obligations, a new emphasis on the individual emerged. New ideologies—in particular the trans-national, abstract humanism of liberal intellectuals—developed to support these changes. Jewish intellectuals in the European diaspora promoted the new humanism, even as emergent nationalist movements attacked these "strangers within" for their economic mischief, ideological subversion, and sexual "depravity."

Rationalization also produced a new form of social control called bureaucracy. Weber recognized the awesome efficiency of the modern bureaucratic organization. But he also warned that the subordination of values to calculation which it fostered could destroy the liberal-humanist order itself. The bureaucratic apparatus of the "final solution" realized a nightmare of inhumanity worse than anything Weber could have foreseen.

How can we explain the *end* to which the bureaucratic machinery of the Holocaust was put? Here we must go beyond the critique of rationalization and modernity, perhaps further than Alan Wolfe's moral sociology wishes to go, to a theory of evil. Along with modern scientific racism (Bauman), the disenchantment of the world (Weber), and greedy institutions (Coser), we need a better understanding of the human capacity for evil (the non-rational desire to harm others without respite).

(1994)

Notes

1. All Wiesel quotes are from the collection of his speeches and writings *Against Silence: The Voice and Vision of Elie Wiesel,* selected and edited by Irving Abrahamson, New York: Holocaust Library, 1985, three volumes; see especially "A Plea for the Survivors" from *A Jew Today,* New York: Random House, 1978; and see Volume 1, page 194 and Volume 11, pages 329-330. See also: Carol Rittner (ed.), *Elie Wiesel: Between Memory and Hope,* New York: New York University Press, 1990.

2. I collected these interviews in my two volumes of *Jewish Partisans,* Lanham, MD: University Press, 1982. See also my collection of essays *Confronting History and Holocaust,* Lanham, MD: University Press of America, 1984. It contains a bibliography of my writings up to 1984. For my views on the so-called "survivor's syndrome" see my long essay "Social-Psychological Aspects of the Holocaust" in *Encountering the Holocaust.* Edited by Byron L. Sherwin and Susan Ament. Chicago: Impact Press, 1979.

3. Not surprisingly, I called one of my first collection of essays: *The Jew as Outsider: Historical and Contemporary Perspectives, Collected Essays, 1974-1980,* Lanham, MD: University Press of America, 1981. But others have discovered the Holocaust as well. See, for example, Zygmunt Bauman, *Modernity and the Holocaust,* Ithaca, NY: Cornell University Press, 1992; William B. Helmreich, *Against All Odds: Holocaust Survivors and the Successful Lives They Made in America,* New York: Simon and Schuster, 1992.

4. Sociology seems to handle the concept "genocide" better than Holocaust. See the works of I.L. Horowitz, Vahakn Dadrian, Helen Fein, and oth-

ers. For example: Helen Fein, "Genocide: A Sociological Perspective," *Current Sociology*. Vol. 38, No. 1, Spring 1990 and the first "textbook" on genocide compiled by sociologist Kurt Jonassohn and historian Frank Chalk, *The History and Sociology of Genocide: Analyses and Case Studies*, New Haven, CT: Yale University Press, 1990. See especially Gerald Markle, *Meditations of a Holocaust Traveler*, Albany, NY: SUNY Press, 1995; and Harold Kaplan, *Conscience and Memory*, Chicago: University of Chicago Press, 1994.

Non-sociologists have made good use of Weber and other classic sociological work in their analysis of the Holocaust. Aside from Bauman, see the works of Leo Kuper, *Genocide: Its Political Use in the Twentieth Century*, New Haven, CT: Yale University Press, 1981 and his other important works; the political scientist and Holocaust scholar Raul Hilberg, *The Destruction of the European Jews*, New York: Franklin Watts, 1973 and his latest *Perpetrators, Victims, Bystanders*, New York: Harper Collins, 1992; and the theologian Richard. L. Rubenstein, *The Cunning of History*, New York: Harper, 1978.

I would be amiss if I did not mention a few other sociologists who have worked on the Holocaust and/or genocide: Nechama Tec, Samuel Oliner, Vera Laska, Ernest Becker, Theodore Abel, Henry L. Tischler, Troy Duster, Elmer Luchterhand, Isidor Walliman, and Anna Pawelczynska. Social psychologists and political scientists, our brothers and sisters in cognate fields would include: Erwin Staub, Robert J. Lifton, Stanley Milgram, Bruno Bettelheim, Hanuch Arendt, Israel Charny, Joel Dimsdale, and Herbert C. Kelman. Forgive me if I have left someone out.

Several other books should be mentioned: Lyman Legters (ed.), *Western Society After the Holocaust*. Boulder, CO: Westview Press, 1983. Jack Nusan Porter (ed.), *Genocide and Human Rights: A Global Anthology*, Lanham, MD: University Press of America, 1982; Jack Nusan Porter, *The Sociology of Genocide/the Holocaust: A Curriculum Guide*, Washington, DC: American Sociological Association, 1992; Ervin Staub, *The Roots of Evil*, Cambridge: Cambridge University Press, 1989; Helen Fein, *Accounting for Genocide*, New York: The Free Press, 1979; Tom Segev, *The Seventh Million: The Israelis and the Holocaust*, New York: Hill and Wang, 1992; and for a discussion of why sociology finds it hard to deal with the Holocaust, see Jack Nusan Porter, "Moral Sociology and the Holocaust." *Perspectives: The Theory Section Newsletter of the ASA*, 15:4, 1992 and "The Holocaust as a Sociological Construct" in *Contemporary Jewry*, Volume 14, 1993.

5. This issue has been a point of concern. How extensive should the treatment of non-Jewish victims be? I feel the museum handles the issue well and is very sensitive to it. In fact, the Project Director of the Museum Michael Berenbaum has edited a book on the subject called: *A Mosaic of Victims: Non-Jews Persecuted and Murdered by the Nazis*, New York and London: New York University Press, 1990. See also Bohdan Wytwycky, *The Other Holocaust: Many Circles of Hell*, Washington, DC; The Novak Report, 1980. Based

on Dante's *The Divine Comedy,* the title means the many circles of damnation, with the Jews in the center of the most desperate circle of Nazi hell with many other groups in concentric circles around them.

The gay victims have increasingly become prominent in the literature. See my work: "The Jewish Homosexual" (on Magnus Hirschfeld and his life). Pp. 139-152 in Jack Nusan Porter, *The Jew as Outsider,* op. cit.; *Sexual Politics in the Third Reich* (pamphlet), Montreal: Concordia University, Montreal Institute for Genocide Studies, 1991; Frank Rector, *The Nazi Extermination of Homosexuals,* New York: Stein and Day, 1981; Richard Plant, *The Pink Triangle: The Nazi War Against Homosexuals,* New York: Henry Holt & Company, 1986; and Erwin J. Haeberle, "Swastika, Pink Triangle, and Yellow Star—The Destruction of Sexology and the Persecution of Homosexuals in Nazi Germany," *The Journal of Sex Research.* Vol. 17, No. 3, August 1981, pp. 270-287.

6. Children over 10 should be taken to the Museum. Under 10, it may be a bit too violent though there are barriers to some of the graphic photos such that only adults can peer over. But the Museum is a learning center. This hit home when my ten-year-old daughter brought home from school her *Scholastic News* (Vol. 55, No. 23, April 30, 1993) and the front page story dealt with the Museum with a headline that read: "Museum Shows the Danger of Hate."

7. See Bauman (1992), Porter (1992), and Fein (1990) for more on this. Modernity, bureaucracy, perhaps a new sociology of evil is needed and it will come.

8. Abrahamson, op. cit., Vol. II, pp. 329-330. The book that Wiesel refers to is Gitta Sereny's interview with Franz Stangl, *Into That Darkness: From Mercy Killing to Mass Murder,* New York: McGraw-Hill, 1974.

9. See Sereny, op. cit. This is a book that all sociologists should read in order to understand the mind of a Nazi killer.

Selected Bibliography

For spurs to theoretical thinking on the Holocaust, see Jeffrey Herf, *Reactionary Modernism* (Cambridge, UK: Cambridge University Press, 1984); Frank Chalk and Kurt Jonassohn, *The History and Sociology of Genocide* (New Haven: Yale University Press, 1985); and Leo Kuper, *Genocide: Its Political Use in the Twentieth Century* (New Haven: Yale University Press, 1981) and *The Prevention of Genocide* (New Haven: Yale University Press, 1985).

For sociological accounts of the concentration camps, see Anna Pawelczynska, *Values and Violence in Auschwitz: A Sociological Analy-*

sis (Berkeley: University of California Press, 1979); and Eugene Kogon, *The Theory and Practice of Hell* (New York: Berkeley Books, 1984). For sexual and gender issues, see Rudiger Lautmann, Erhard Vismar, and Jack Nusan Porter, *Sexual Politics in the Third Reich: The Persecution of Homosexuals during the Holocaust* (forthcoming); and Vera Laska, *Women in the Resistance and in the Holocaust* (Westport, CT: Greenwood Press, 1983).

On the idea of evil in social and moral theory, see Ervin Staub, *The Roots of Evil: The Psychological and Cultural Origins of Genocide and Other Forms of Group Violence* (Cambridge, UK: Cambridge University Press, 1989); Joel E. Dimsdale (ed.), *Survivors, Victims, Perpetrators: Essays on the Nazi Holocaust* (Washington, DC: Hemisphere Publications, 1980); . Robert Jay Lifton, *The Broken Connection: On Death and the Continuity of Life (New* York: Basic Books, 1984); and Jack Nusan Porter, *Genocide and Human Rights* (Washington, DC: University Press of America, 1982).

Realistic novels are often helpful in the classroom. Consider Elie Wiesel, *Night* (New York: Pyramid Books, 1961); Primo Levi, *Survival in Auschwitz* (New York: Collier Books, 1959); Tadeusz Borowski's short stories, *This Way for the Gas, Ladies and Gentlemen* (New York: Penguin Books, 1967); and Jerzy Kosinski, *The Painted Bird* (New York: Bantam Books, 1972).

For curricular development and teaching tips, see the special issue of the *Social Science Record* edited by Samuel Totten (vol. 24(2) 1987); Samuel Totten and William S. Parsons (eds.), "Teaching About Genocide," *Social Education 55(2)* (1991); Gideon Shimoni (ed.), *The Holocaust in University Teaching* (Oxford: Pergamon Press, 1989); and Jack Nusan Porter, *Sociology of Genocide/the Holocaust: A Curriculum Guide* (Washington, DC: American Sociological Association, 1992, 2nd ed., 1999).

References

Abel, Theodore. *Why Hitler Came to Power.* Cambridge, MA: Harvard University Press, 1986 (1938).

Bauman, Zygmunt. *Modernity and the Holocaust.* Ithaca, NY: Cornell University Press, 1989.

———. *Thinking Sociologically.* London/Oxford, UK and Cambridge, MA: Blackwell Publishers, 1992.

Berenbaum, Michael (ed.). *A Mosaic of Victims: Non-Jews Persecuted and Murdered by the Nazis.* New York: New York University Press, 1990.

Chalk, Frank, and Kurt Jonassohn. *The History and Sociology of Genocide.* New Haven, CT and London: Yale University Press, 1990.

Charny, Israel (ed.). *Genocide: A Critical Bibliographic Review.* Two volumes. New York: Facts on File, 1988 and 1991.

Fein, Helen. *Accounting for Genocide: National Responses and Jewish Victimization during the Holocaust.* New York: The Free Press, 1979, reprinted by the University of Chicago Press, 1984.

———. "Genocide: A Sociological Perspective," *Current Sociology,* vol. 38, no. 1, pp. 1-126.

———. *Genocide: A Sociological Perspective.* Sherman Oaks, CA: Sage Publications, 1996.

——— (ed.). *Genocide Watch.* New Haven, CT: Yale University Press, 1992.

Fein, Helen, and Joyce Freedman-Apsel. *Teaching About Genocide.* Ottawa: University of Ottawa, Human Rights Centre, 1992.

Hilberg, Raoul. *The Destruction of the European Jews.* Second edition. Three volumes. New York: Holmes and Meier, 1985.

Horowitz, I. L. *Genocide, State Power, and Mass Murder.* New Brunswick, NJ: Transaction Books, 1976.

Kershaw, Ian. *The Nazi Dictatorship: Problems and Perspectives of Interpretation.* London: Edward Arnold, 1990.

Kuper, Leo. *Genocide: Its Political Use in the Twentieth Century.* New Haven, CT: Yale University Press, 1981.

Porter, Jack Nusan. "Social-Psychological Aspects of the Holocaust," pp. 189-222 in *Encountering the Holocaust: An Interdisciplinary Survey,* Byron L. Sherwin and Susan G. Ament, eds. Chicago: Impact Press, 1979.

——— (ed.). *Genocide and Human Rights: A Global Anthology.* Lanham, MD: University Press of America, 1982.

———. *Jewish Partisans: A Documentary of Jewish Resistance in the Soviet Union During World War 11. Two* vols. Lanham, MD and London: University Press of America, 1982; reprinted by The Spencer Press, 1999.

———. *Sexual Politics in Nazi Germany: The Persecution of Homosexuals during the Holocaust: A Bibliography and Introductory Essay.* Montreal, Quebec, Canada: Concordia University, Montreal Institute for Genocide Studies, 1992.

———. *The Sociology of Genocide/the Holocaust.* Washington, DC: American Sociological Association, 1992.

Rubenstein, Richard. *The Cunning of History.* New York: Harper Perennial, 1978.

———. *The Cunning of History: Mass Death and the American Future.* New York: Harper & Row, 1975.

Staub, Ervin. *The Roots of Evil.* Cambridge, UK: Cambridge University Press, 1989.

Wolfe, Alan. "Revitalizing the Moral Tradition in Sociology." *Perspectives: The Theory Section Newsletters, vol.* 14, no. 2, 1999, pp. 1-2.

Chapter 2

The Holocaust as a Sociological Construct

> *"The task is important not because of any . . . renewed triumph of fascism in the foreseeable future, but in the hope of strengthening the awareness that democratic, humanitarian values are not an inevitable, or necessarily lasting property of modern industrial society, but that they must constantly and repeatedly be fought for and defended against all inroads—some quite new in form of modern authoritarianism."*
> —Ian Kershaw, *The Nazi Dictatorship*.
> London: Edward Arnold, 1989, p.191.

Sociology has had the greatest difficulty handling unique events like Hiroshima, the Vietnam War, or the Holocaust. This, it has left to the historians. Sociology is best with stable, recurring, non-provocative, normative events.[1] Aside from a few brave souls (Irving Louis Horowitz, Helen Fein, Theodore Abel, and Vahakn Dadrian as well as this author), sociology has abandoned the Holocaust to others; yet it does not mean that these "others" have abandoned their "sociology." The theologian Richard Rubenstein in his book *The Cunning of History* applies a Weberian framework to the Holocaust, and Rubenstein, best known for his "death of God" theology is not a sociologist, but a rabbi! Why did he find sociology, Weberian sociology—modernity, bureaucracy, authority—so laden with riches and we sociologists have not?

Raul Hilberg, a professor of political science and the pre-eminent historian of the Holocaust from the German point of view—Lucy

Dawidowicz would be his counterpart from the Jewish perspective—is well known for his monumental three-volume *The Destruction of the European Jews,* recognized as the definitive work on the subject, and it uses a Weberian framework—the role of bureaucratic rules, roles, and regulations in the systematic annihilation of nearly every Jew in Europe. And Hilberg is no sociologist.

Finally a sociologist, and not surprisingly a non-American—Professor Zygmunt Bauman, Emeritus Professor of Sociology at the University of Leeds (UK)—has written the definitive *sociological* treatment of the Holocaust. Bauman, however, goes beyond bureaucracy to a study of the very nature of modernity. He writes:

> Hilberg is a historian. Rubenstein is a theologian. I have keenly searched the works of sociologists for statements expressing similar awareness of the urgency of the task posited by the Holocaust; for evidence that the Holocaust presents, among other things, a challenge to sociology as a profession and a body of academic knowledge. When measured against the work done by historians or theologians, the bulk of academic sociology looks more like a collective exercise in forgetting and eye-closing. By and large, the lessons of the Holocaust have left little trace on sociological common sense. . . . I do not know of many occasions on which sociologists, qua sociologists, confronted publicly the evidence of the Holocaust. (pp. 9-10)

Bauman continues with a short description of one such occasion—a symposium on "Western Society After the Holocaust" convened in 1978 by the Institute for the Study of Contemporary Social Problems and the debate there between Rubenstein and the eminent Weberian scholar and sociologist Guenther Roth.[2] We desperately need another symposium on just such a subject.

Bauman goes beyond Roth and Rubenstein and expands sociology's xenophobic attitude toward the Holocaust and explains it on several levels. If at all discussed in sociological texts, the Holocaust is at best defined as a sad example of man's "untamed innate human aggressiveness"; or as a form of "privatization"—the private, parochial, particularistic experience of the Jews, a matter simply between Jews and their anti-Semites; or as a defense of Israel or as a rationalization for Zionist persecution of the Palestinians. This is especially worrysome to Bauman, as it should be to all sociologists, that the Holocaust can happen on such a massive scale elsewhere, it could happen again anywhere. It is within the range of human possibility. It is human, not inhuman. It is social; not asocial. It is a laboratory study in a non-laboratory setting. It is a rare yet significant and reliable test of the hidden possibilities of modem society.

Tom Segev, in *The Seventh Million,* has written a controversial book on the impact of the Holocaust on Israeli society, from the first immigration of survivors in the 1947-1949 wave of immigration through Ben Gurion's use of the Eichmann Trial to "educate" the Israelis and the distorted and confusing messages of the Demjanjuk Trial. Is the Holocaust simply a rationale for a healthy state of Israel; a refugee for Jews facing genocide anywhere? Is the Holocaust justification for the "Masada Complex"? Will Israelis go down dying or commit suicide to defend Eretz Yisroel? Or, is there a new, more mature approach forming? One a little less "sabra," less *macho*, one concerned with the deeper spiritual and sociological implications of the Holocaust? Something on this order is thankfully emerging in Israel as it confronts its historic demons. Benno Weiser Varon confronts some of these demons with grace and wit. Varon—raconteur extraordinaire, peripatetic ambassador at large for Israel, ardent Zionist, Boston University professor on fin-de-siécle Vienna, a Mittle-European intellectual—is a man whose kind will not pass on this earth again. Varon's *Professions of a Lucky Jew* should be read in the context of the Segev book with the Holocaust as background, and it is a joy to read. Varon has seemingly been everywhere, met everyone, said all that had to be said, and he, at over 80, is still writing reviews of plays and movies, a kind of modern-day Herzl-like master of the bon-mot and the feuillonton. He was especially important in gaining support for Israel during the Eichmann Trial among Central and South American countries.

He has survived assassination attempts by Palestinian terrorists, coups in South America—all "in the service of the Jewish people." Biographies are difficult to write well and Varon writes very well. Your students will love this book.

Finally, I come back to Hilberg's *Perpetrators, Victims, Bystanders*. This book is the capstone of his professional life. Even the title has influenced the Holocaust Museum in Washington, DC with its neat divisions of participants—victims, bystanders, and perpetrators. Yet, I am unhappy with the title. A separate category is needed for the righteous gentiles who saved Jewish lives. They were neither victims nor bystanders, but took the same risks as Jews. And a special category is needed of course for the resistors—the partisans, the ghetto fighters, the organizers of death camp revolts, and the soldiers in the Red Army.

This is an old argument against Hilberg's work. He and Hannah Arendt were both taken to task in the wake of the Eichmann Trial when they and Bruno Bettelheim talked of Jews who walked like "sheep to slaughter." This time, however, Hilberg does mention the Jewish partisans in his book, and I am honored that he quotes from my two-volume collection *Jewish Partisans* (p. 202, footnoted on p. 312) but again he places the discussion under the section of "bystanders."

Resistance was more than simply "by-standing." Sociologists will like this book though few will use it in their courses. First, the style. It is written, like the film *Shoah* by Claude Lanzmann, in a dry, almost laconic style, never emotional, always unflinchingly calm and clear. Second, his approach to methodology. These are "case studies" that sociologists can relate to: the "establishment", functionaries, zealots, physicians, lawyers, refugees, men and women, the dispossessed, the unadjusted, the survivors. To a sociologist, the pages resonate with the echoes of C. Wright Mills *(White Collar, The Power Elite)*, Hans Gerth, Karl Mannheim, Louis Wirth, and George Simmel. It is chilling to place these sociological classics in the context of the Holocaust and yet they fit like a seamless glove. They anticipated, experienced, or reacted to the Holocaust, and only now do we see how much of the fabric of sociology is based on the *tremendum* of the Holocaust. But no one ever told us until now.

(1993)

Notes

1. See Jack Nusan Porter, 1992. "Moral Sociology and the Holocaust." *Perspectives: The Theory Section Newsletter of the ASA [American Sociological Association].* 15:4

2. This symposium was collected in Lyman Legters (ed.). 1983. *Western Society After the Holocaust.* Boulder, CO: Westview Press.

References

Raul Hilberg, *Perpetrators, Victims, Bystanders*. Harper-Collins, Aaron Asher Books, hardcover, $25/$35 Canada, 1992, 340 pp.

Zygmunt Bauman, *Modernity and the Holocaust*. Cornell University Press, soft cover, $15.95, 1992, 238 pp.

Tom Segev, *The Seventh Million: The Israelis and the Holocaust*. Hill & Wang/Farrar, Straus & Giroux, hardcover, illustrated, $27.50, 1992, 593 pp.

Benno Weiser Varon, *Professions of a Lucky Jew*. New York: Cornwall Books, hardcover, $24.50, 1992, 431 pp.

Chapter 3

Comparative Aspects of the Holocaust and Other Genocides

The route of normal science is to move to higher and higher levels of abstraction and theoretical construction. Holocaust and genocide studies have moved through the first stage, simple observation and description, which we have a great deal of, to the next level, list-building, stages of killing, types of genocides, conditions favoring genocide, etc. (See Fein, 1990: 32-50).

But now we are ready for level three and beyond: comparative, contextual, and theoretical research. (See Fein, 1990: 51-91). If sociology is to grow as a discipline, we need to move to a higher level of abstraction and theory-building without, and this is the trick, losing the basic humanity and sensitivity embedded in the victims. This has always been the fear of Holocaust scholars to sociology—that our methods and theories are so abstract and so abstruse that they may de-humanize the very people we talk about. This is a danger that sociologists must be wary of. In this short essay, I try to lay out an outline of various areas of comparative research between and among genocides. Comparative analysis is crucial to the growth of genocide and Holocaust studies.

When we begin to move onto this third level of comparative analysis, we will not diminish the "uniqueness" of any one genocide but we will instead see the basic commonalities of all genocides and genocidal acts. We will see that people at various times in history and throughout various parts of the world, regardless of race, religion, or national origin, act quite the same way when confronted with genocide. If and when there is an exception, it may prove the rule, as the saying goes, and it may act to prompt further investigation.

Usually, in the past, most research has been what we call the "two-case" analysis, usually comparing the Holocaust and another "lesser" genocide, such as the Armenians or American Indians. The best and earliest examples here have been the work of Vahakn Dadrian (1974) where he analyzes the common features of the Armenian and Jewish genocides from a "victimological" perspective and Helen Fein (1978) where she compares the Turkish genocide of 1915 to the German Holocaust of 1939-1945. Helen Fein, the preeminent scholar in comparative sociology of the genocide, has extended and strengthened this comparative approach in two ways: first, between European countries in her analysis of the Holocaust in her ground-breaking book *Accounting for Genocide* (1979) and between and among genocides in a special issue of *Current Sociology* (Volume 38, Number 1, Spring 1990: 51-91), later in her book *Genocide: A Sociological Perspective* (1996).

Even the nasty debates about Holocaust "uniqueness" inadvertantly serve the comparative sociological and historical approach. See, for example, Alan S. Rosenbaum's book *Is the Holocaust Unique? Perspectives on Comparative Genocide* (1998) and Ward Churchill, *A Little Matter of Genocide* (1997).

There are other examples of such a comparative approach that need more comparative analysis and theory building. For example:

I. Stigma

   A. The Yellow Star of the Jews vs. the Blue and Yellow Kerchiefs used in Cambodia vs. the facial characteristics and body shapes of the Hutu and Tutsis vs. the stigmatas placed upon Armenians. The methods which victims are demonized and placed outside the realm of a moral universe, to use Helen Fein's felicitous phrase, are important to contrast.

   B. The presentation of self in various genocides. Not only the way victims respond—with acquiescence, retreat, depression, or resistance—but how one internalizes the threat to one's self posed by genocide, is important to study.

II. Reaction of Victims

   A. *Passivity*—a common reaction of victims, not just during the Holocaust or Turkish genocide of the Armenians but among later genocides is passivity. For example, see Porter (1974: 341) in his chapter in a sociology textbook published in the mid-70s *The Study of Society,* wherein for reasons that are unclear, Hutus apparently accepted their deaths with awesome apathy—some even showing up voluntarily for their own executions when told to do so. I am speaking here of Burundi in 1972. This terrifyingly echoes Jews showing up at the *umshlagplatz* in Warsaw for shipment to Treblinka and the many other examples of marching like "sheep to slaughter" throughout Europe. What psychological and sociological mechanisms come into play to make this so common?

B. *Resistance.* Rare yet important in most genocides. Why? Compare Musa Dagh to the Warsaw Ghetto. Such research will bring out hitherto rare instances of resistance among Aborigines, Cambodians, Gypsies, homosexuals, and others. In short, if you don't ask the question, you don't get the answer. For too long, victims have seen themselves as victims, not active actors in this drama. Why don't people fight back until it is too late?

C. *Going into Hiding.* Is this an example of passivity or of resistance? Is it an act of cowardice or of bravery? Hiding leads to the next section—rescuers and bystanders.

III. Rescuers

A comparison of "good" Turks who helped Armenians; "good" Germans or Poles who helped Jews and Gypsies; "good" colonizers who saved Aborigines or American Indians. The altruistic personality. Why do some people help and most do not?

IV. Bystanders

Again, common to most genocides. Why do individuals and nations stand by and do nothing? Elie Wiesel calls "bystanders" as guilty as perpetrators.

V. Perpetrators

This past half-decade has seen a great interest in the motives and actions of the perpetrators rather than the victims. The Goldhagen thesis vs. the Milgram and Zimbardo experiments. How and why do people commit such evil? Is there a common thread among Turkish, German,

Hutu, Cambodian, colonizer, and other perpetrators? See my essay on why men kill in this book.

VI. Factors Leading to Genocide
A. Societal
B. Political
C. Economic
D. Military (wartime conditions)
E. Colonialization and De-colonialization
F. Tribal Conflict
G. Others
See Porter, 1982: 2-24; Fein, 1979, 1990; and Horowitz, 1976, 1982.

VII. Post-Traumatic Stress
Commonalities of response to victimization and brutality and torture—depression, anger, resignation, transference, avoidance, and sublimation to higher goals.

VIII. Compensation
Why and how some groups (the Jews) were compensated while others (Armenians, Cambodians, homosexuals, Gypsies) were not? What does that tell us about political clout or other factors of compensation?

IX. Tribunals
Comparison of Nuremberg Tribunals of post-World War II and the more recent tribunals at The Hague regarding Pol Pot of Cambodia, Milocevic of Bosnia, and Rwanda.

IX. Legacies
Comparisons of children, grandchildren, and later generations of survivors. Is there a survivors syndrome that is passed on? What legacies are passed from family to family, from generation to generation? How do these legacies differ by genocide?

X. Remembrance/Memorialization
How do Armenians, Cambodians, Gypsies, Hutus, Tutsis, Bosnians, homosexuals and lesbians, and Jews differ in the remembrance of their genocides? How do their respective governments memorialize them? What

about Holocaust/Genocide deniers such as David Irving? What impact does form of denial have on the victims, the perpetrators, and the rest of the world. What acts of reconciliation, such as those of Pope John Paul, can help avert future acts of genocide?

Conclusions

Debates on uniqueness are sterile. More important for our students and our theories is research of a comparative nature. The above is only the beginning. Comparative research is good and exciting not only for theory-building but in order to prevent future genocides. Frank Chalk and Kurt Jonassohn (1990: 32) make this point explicit:

> . . . the major reason for doing comparative research on genocides is the hope of preventing them in the future. Such prevention will pose difficult applied problems, but first it must be based on an understanding of the social situations and the social structures and processes that are likely to lead to genocides. Only by acquiring such knowledge can we begin to predict the likely occurrence of genocides and direct our efforts toward prevention.

(2000)

Sources

Chalk, Frank and Kurt Jonassohn, *The History and Sociology of Genocide: Analyses and Case Studies,* New Haven, CT and London: Yale University Press, 1990.

Churchill, Ward, *A Little Matter of Genocide: Holocaust and Denial in the Americas 1492 to the Present,* San Francisco, CA: City Lights Books, 1997. (I would like to acknowledge Ward Churchill for bringing my attention to the Chalk and Jonassohn quote above.)

Dadrian, Vahakn, The Common Features of the Armenian and Jewish Cases of Genocide: A Comparative Victimological Approach," in Israel Drabkin and Emilio Viano (eds), *Victimology: A New Focus: Violence and its Victims,* Lexington, MA: D.C. Heath, 1974.

Fein, Helen, "A Formula for Genocide: Comparison of the Turkish Genocide (1915) and the German Holocaust (1939-1945)," *Comparative Studies in Sociology,* Volume 1, pp. 271-293.

——, *Accounting for Genocide,* New York: The Free Press, 1979.
——, "Genocide: A Sociological Perspective," *Current Sociology,* Volume 38, No. 1, Spring 1990, pp. 1-126.
Genocide: A Sociological Perspective, Sherman Oaks, CA: Sage publications, 1996.
Horowitz, Irving Louis, *Genocide: State Power and Mass Murder,* New Brunswick, NJ: Transaction Books, 1976, 1982.
Porter, Jack Nusan, "Race and Ethnic Relations," Unit 15, in *The Study of Society,* Guilford, CT: The Dushkin Publishing Group, 1974, pp. 338-356.
——, (ed), *Genocide and Human Rights,* Lanham, MD: University Press of America, 1982.
——, with Steve Hoffman, *The Sociology of the Holocaust and Genocide,* Washington, DC: American Sociological Association, 1999.
Rosenbaum, Alan S. (ed), *Is the Holocaust Unique? Perspectives on Comparative Genocide,* Boulder, CO: Westview Press, 1998.

Chapter 4

Toward a Sociology of National Socialism

I must admit that when I was going to graduate school at Northwestern University from 1967 to 1971, Talcott Parsons was considered by my cohort to be a distant, grandfatherly-type figure overshadowed by C. Wright Mills and other radical sociologists.

In fact, in 1969 when he came to campus to speak on family ties and kinship relations, it was at the behest of a Professor Francis Hsu, an anthropologist who specialized in the Chinese family. The sociology department, for the most part, was cool to his coming.

But it is clear that in our youthful certainty, we were too hard on him, thinking that he was another Sorokin or Pareto—forlorn and nearly forgotten figures except for a concept or two. Parsons has not been forgotten. In fact, he seems to have increased in visibility, having been "rediscovered" by a new generation of theorists.

A strong interest has also emanated from Germany. Uta Gerhardt is a medical sociologist and Director of the Medical Sociology Unit at Justus Liebig University in Giessen. The present volume came out of a recent sabbatical she spent as a Research Associate of the Minda de Gunzburg Center for European Studies at Harvard University. Her research into the Parson papers at the Harvard University Archives is archival and oral history at its best, particularly since Mrs. Helen W. Parsons granted permission to re-publish previously published and unpublished works.

The book consists of 14 articles, radio broadcasts, speeches, addresses, and position papers dealing with Germany, National Socialism, fascism, or the Jews. It contains 270 pages of Parsons' work, Gerhardt's

60-page introduction, and 18 pages of astonishing and extremely valuable footnotes.

During the years between the publication of his two major works *The Structure of Social Action* (1937) and *The Social System* (1951), Talcott Parsons was primarily engaged in political activity through the OSS (Office of Strategic Services) in its efforts to bring about the defeat of the Third Reich and to set the stage for a democratic reconstruction of Germany in the postwar period.[1] These essays, as the dust jacket notes, are the by-products of that period of intense commitment. They reflect a single dominant theme: National Socialist Germany as a tragically flawed social system that required the same rigorous analysis Parsons brought to other social systems. Since virulent authoritarianism and even more virulent anti-Semitism were the dominant traits of that system as he saw it, Parsons dedicated many pages to each aspect, although he did not know the full scope of the "war against the Jews." Very few in fact did, or if they did know, did not believe it. This collection takes its rightful place in the growing body of Holocaust literature and the sociology of genocide.

Far from being the "reactionary" that 1960s antiwar activists thought of him as during the years of Vietnam, this book makes it clear that Parsons was a strong supporter of human rights in the fight for democracy against the onslaught of Nazism.

One reads this book with a newfound respect for Talcott Parsons as an activist an ardent organizer, radio speaker, talk-show host, and antifascist organizer. Gerhardt discovered an entirely different Talcott Parsons from the one imagined by many youthful 1960s sociologists. In this fascinating and well-documented book, a very sympathetic Parsons emerges.

Gerhardt's introduction is packed with insights and unknown nuggets of information. The sad fact is that few will read this book A less expensive paperback edition for professors and students is needed.

Between 1937 and 1951 Parsons was busy helping to rescue emigre German and Austrian refugees, countering German propaganda, and working tirelessly for the antifascist cause. His years in the OSS under Major-General William "Wild Bill" Donovan have not been known until now, There is clearly need for further research into sociology's role during World War U. The irony is that after the tragic death of a young colleague Edward Yarnall Hartshorne, Jr. (1912-1946), he rarely wrote a paper or gave a speech on the subject of Germany or National Socialism again.

Hartshorne was shot in the head and killed on the *Autobahn* near Nuremberg, Germany by the occupant of another car. It was a bizarre "drive-by" shooting. Was Hartshorne a CIA agent killed by the KGB? by Nazi sympathizers? We may never know. Gerhardt does not say who did it and it remains a mystery.

On the occasion of Parsons's farewell dinner at Harvard in May 1973, he paid tribute to their friendship by saying that Hartshorne was "one of our real stars." Hartshorne had successfully masterminded the reopening of German universities in the American occupation zone in 1945-1946, and had deeply influenced Parsons's thinking on Germany going back to the late 1930s. Parsons wrote an obituary for him in the *American Sociological Review* 1946.[2]

He also wrote very little on Jews after this period, and in fact his major contribution on the subject "The Sociology of Modern Anti-Semitism" (see pages 131-152 in the book) also has a controversial and contorted history. It was probably the only essay ever written by Parsons where an editor (a colleague), Isacque Graeber, unilaterally changed his writing and distorted his thought so as make Parsons seem like an anti-Semite. The tale is too long and cumbersome to tell here, but happy to say, the entire essay is restored as it should have appeared in the original. Parsons's essay is important for the study of the sociology of Jewry. He saw anti-Semitism as a manifestation of social disorganization and societal insecurity. Heavily influenced by Freud and Erich Fromm (especially *Escape from Freedom,* 1941), he describes the "free-floating aggression" of the "emotionally unstable." But where Parsons becomes controversial is when he wrote,

> Finally, the Jews, owing to their peculiar position in the world, undoubtedly suffer to a much larger extent than any other group, excepting the American Negroes, from a sense of insecurity; consequently they are more likely to be aggressive. This again is resented by Gentiles and becomes a further source of friction and ill feeling toward them. . . . The main consequences or this wide-spread psychological insecurity among Jews are the closely related tendencies to over-sensitiveness to criticism, on the one hand, and "abnormal" aggressiveness and self-assertion, on the other. This is particularly true of the more successful of the Jews who are usually those who have become more or less assimilated and who are in closer contact with the Gentile world. Gentiles in contact with them often get irritated and, as a rule, are ready to accuse the whole group as sharing what they think obnoxious qualities.

Out of context, it is easy to see how Parsons could have been labeled as "insensitive" to Jews. However, the full knowledge and impact of the Holocaust was *not known to the West at the time he wrote this essay.* Parsons' discussion of Jewish insecurity and aggression is understandable *if* debatable.[3]

But what was Parsons' contribution to theory building as it relates to National Socialism? In fact, he developed *a sociology of National Socialism* that other sociologists who have worked in this field such as Helen Fein, Zygmunt Bauman, I.L. Horowitz, and Porter could usefully incorporate into their own theory building.[4]

Parsons' essays in this book are full of insights into the sociological aspects of fascist movements, the social structure of both pre-Nazi and Nazi Germany, propaganda and social control, and memoranda for political and military intervention. These are rich veins of sociological insight for our students to apply to research on social structure, economic elites, family and kinship patterns, class structure, even romantic love and feminine roles. Beyond Weber, we see the deep impact that Sigmund Freud made on Parsons aggression, fixation, introjection, and hostile impulses. Parsons was then in many ways a "social psychiatrist," ready to put all of Germany on the couch in order to understand its structure of evil. Parsons's use of psychoanalytical concepts predates the psychohistorical approach 20 to 30 years later and is reminiscent of Erich Fromm and Wilhelm Reich.

His April 25, 1942 presidential address before the Eastern Sociological Society (pages 203-218 in the book) thoughtfully but turgidly makes the theoretical connections between the structural and the psychological levels of society and the variables of class, tradition, and social access as important consequences of both. Parsons even began to gingerly touch on the issue of "evil," what he called the "nonlogical" aspects of human behavior in society, the sentiments and traditions of family and informal social relationships, the refinements of social stratification, the peculiarities of regional, ethnic, or national culture—perhaps above all, of religion. The "antiintellectualist" reaction of fascism fascinated Parsons. He asked, Why were so many intellectuals enthralled with Nazism and Italian fascism?

Parsons cared deeply about the issue of how aggression and evil were embedded into the Nazi social structure. He even had a feminist interpretation of the Nazi "fear of feminization" and of and of the "feminine" admiration of the "heroic." He was fascinated by the "he-man" image of Nazi leaders even though some of them like Hitler and Himmler were in fact effeminate, and how such patterns played a major role in the spread of the Nazi movement for example, the attraction of women and the lower middle class to such feminized leaders (see page 346, note 8).

Not only was Parsons' ahead of his time with regard to feminism, he predated some of C. Wright Mills' sociological imagination by 35 years in 1921 by absorbing Alexander Meiklejohn's teachings at Amherst. (From 1912 to 1923 Meiklejohn was president of Amherst.) Meiklejohn's dismissal from Amherst came in 1923, just before Parsons' senior year.

Parsons was also deeply influenced by Edward Yarnall Hartshorne's book *The German and National Socialism* (London: Allen and Unwin, 1937). Hartshorne's sociological analysis of Nazi destruction of liberal learning alerted Parsons to the seriousness of the Nazi threat. National Socialism, according to Hartshorne was a revolution aimed at totalitarianism in a double sense—in political power monopolized by one group of agents and in the second place by this group or clique extending its sphere of influence over the entire society, seeping into every pore of society, infecting all aspects of social structure. Such was the nature of National socialism that Parsons was obsessed to understand it in those short 15 years of work from 1937 to 1951.

It was true that Parsons wrote in somewhat of a vacuum. He and the world were unaware of the full implications of evil during the Holocaust, that is, of the Final Solution. But he tried. He merits our intellectual and moral respect for that.

Uta Gerhardt discovered this aspect of Parsons while studying his sociology of the professions and his use of medical practice to demonstrate how social science could become an antidote for fascism and authoritarianism.

The irony is that we are in the midst of a major scandal in America in discovering how professions such as medicine and engineering were involved in nuclear radiation experiments. The works of Robert J. Lifton *(The Nazi Doctors)* and Robert N. Proctor *(Racial Hygiene)* come to mind. All professions, including sociology, were perverted by National Socialism. Careerism, scientism, eugenics—all led science, law, medicine, the courts, as well as academia to sell out to Nazi Germany. We see this in the example of the physician Dr. Josef Mengele, "the angel" of Auschwitz, in other Nazi doctors and scientists, in Prof. Martin Heidegger, in Paul Du Man, Mircea Eliade, and others selling out to the cause of "Science" or "Career" in the service of "Society."

Professor Gerhardt should be applauded for opening up an exciting area of research, and now with a new U.S. Holocaust museum and research institute, we should see many years of productive relations between sociologists and Holocaust scholars. Recent events in Bosnia, Rwanda, and other parts of the world show that the message of the Holocaust still resonates and demands our attention.

(1994)

Notes

1. He was not in the OSS but involved with it. Harvard colleagues, such as William Langer and Clyde Kluckhohn were however in the OSS.
2. Parsons (146). See also Parson's retirement speech (1973).
3. The original article was published in an abbreviated and unauthorized version in Graeber and Britt (1942). The version in Gerhardt's book was reconstructed from manuscripts and notes found in the Harvard University Archives (42.41, box 2: "Unpublished Manuscripts"). In 1979, Parsons, troubled by the original article, wrote a postscript to the article that addressed the problem of Germany's change since 1945 and noted that the horrendous scope of Nazi atrocities had become known only *after* his article had been published. According to footnote 106 in Gerhardt's book, the manuscript carried a handwritten note by Victor Lidz, Parson's literary executor, that the essay should be "edited and prepared for publication by S.Z. Klausner after T.P.'s death." That essay, along with Samuel Klausner's commentary, did in fact appear in *Contemporary Jewry* (1980).
4. See Porter (1981, 1982, 1984); Bauman (1991); Fein (1979, 1993); Horowitz (1980).

For spurs to theoretical thinking on the Holocaust, see Herf (1984); Chalk and Jonassohn (1985); Kuper (1981, 1985).

For sexual and gender issues, see Porter (1992b); Laska (1983); Rittener and Roth (1993).

On the idea of evil in social and moral theory, see Staub (1989); Porter (1992a); Lifton (1984).

For curricular development, see Totten (1987); Totten and Parsons (1991); Shimoni (1989); Freedman-Apsel and Fein (1992).

For sociological accounts of the Holocaust, especially the concentration camps, see Pawelczynska (1979); Kogon (1984).

References

Bauman, Zygmunt
    1991   *Modernity and the Holocaust*. Ithaca, NY: Cornell University Press.

Chalk, Frank and Kurt Jonassohn
    1985   *The History and Sociology of Genocide*. New Haven, CT: Yale University Press.

Fein, Helen
    1979   *Accounting for Genocide: National Responses and Jewish Victimization During the Holocaust*. New York: Free Press.
    1993   *Genocide: A Sociological Perspective*. London: Sage Publications.

Freedman-Apsel, Joyce and Helen Fein, eds.
    1992   *Teaching About Genocide: A Guidebook for College University Teachers*. Ottawa, Ontario: Human Rights International.

Fromm, Erich
    1941   *Escape from Freedom*. New York: Holt, Rinehart, and Winston.

Gerhardt, Uta, ed.
    1993   *Talcott Parsons on National Socialism*. New York: Aldine de Gruyter.

Graeber, Isacque and Steuart Henderson Britt, eds.
    1942   *Jews in a Gentile World*. New York: Macmillan.

Harshorne, Edward Yarnall
    1937   *The German Universities and National Socialism*. London: Allen and Unwin.

Herf, Jeffrey
    1984   *Reactionary Modernism*. Cambridge and New York: Cambridge University Press.

Horowitz, Irving Louis
    1980   *Taking Lives: Genocide and State Power*. New Brunswick, NJ: Transaction Books.

Klausner, Samuel
    1980   *The Theory and Practice of Hell*. New York: Berkeley Books.

Kuper, Leo
    1981   *Genocide: Its Political Use in the Twentieth Century.* New Haven, CT: Yale University Press.
    1985   *The Prevention of Genocide.* New Haven, CT: Yale University Press.

Laska, Vera
    1983   *Women in the Resistance and in the Holocaust.* Westport, CT: Greenwood Press.

Lifton, Robert J.
    1984   *The Broken Connection.* New York: Basic Books
    1986   *The Nazi Doctors: Medical Killing and the Psychology of Genocide.* New York: Basic Books.

Parsons, Talcott
    1937   *The Structure of Social Action.* New York: McGraw-Hill.
    1946   "Edward Yarnall Hartshorne 1912-1946," *American Sociological Review.* 11:877-878.
    1951   *The Social System.* Glencoe, IL: Free Press.
    1973   "The development of sociology at Harvard." Retirement Address, Retirement Banquet for Talcott Parsons at Harvard University, May 18, Parsons papers, 42.8.8, box 12.
    1980   "The Sociology of Modern Antisemitism," (essay) *Contemporary Jewry.* 5:31-38.

Pawelczynska, Anna
    1979   *Values and Violence in Auschwitz: A Sociological Analysis.* Berkeley, CA: University of California Press.

Proctor, Robert N.
    1988   *Racial Hygiene: Medicine under the Nazis.* Cambridge, MA; Harvard University Press.

Porter, Jack Nusan
    1981   *The Jew as Outsider: Collected Essays.* Lanham, MD and London: University Press of America.
    1982   *Genocide and Human Rights: A Global Anthology.* Lanham, MD and London: University Press of America.
    1992a   "Moral sociology and the holocaust," *Perspectives: The ASA Theory Section Newsletter.* 15(October):4.

1992b   *Sexual Politics in the Third Reich: The Persecution of Homosexuals During the Holocaust: A Curriculum Guide.* Washington, DC: American Sociological Association.

Rittner, Carol and John K. Roth, eds.
    1993   *Difference Voices: Women and the Holocaust.* New York: Paragon House.

Shimoni, Gideon, ed.
    1989   *The Holocaust in University Teaching.* Oxford: Pergamon Press.

Staub, Ervin
    1989   *The Roots of Evil.* Cambridge and New York: Cambridge University Press.

Totten, Samuel, ed.
    1987   [special issue]. *Social Science Record.* 24(2).

Totten, Samuel and William S. Parsons, eds.
    1991   "Teaching about Genocide" [special issue], *Social Education.* 55(2).

Part II

The Holocaust and Western Civilization

Chapter 5

The Role of the Holocaust in Western Civilization

Introduction

While this title sounds like a good senior's honors thesis or a speech before the Library of Congress, it signifies a real problem for scholars, teachers, and citizens at all levels of society. It is ironic that the Shoah, one of the preeminent events of not only the 20th Century but the entire millennium, has had great difficulty being placed in the canons of history. Why has it been so difficult to persuade professors and intellectuals to place the Shoah firmly into the structure and history of Western Civilization?

We find ourselves at a time where rampant revisionism is taking place, where people are denying the Holocaust even happened. We are seeing the sales of the forgery *The Protocols of the Elders of Zion* sold around the world by Amazon.com, and barnesandnoble.com. We have witnessed the recent verdict, a successful verdict, in May of 2000, of the David Irving-Deborah Lipstadt trial in London. We are seeing hundreds of hate-sites on the world wide web.

We even saw blatant anti-semitism emanating from the most prestigious schools in the world. Note the embarrassment at Harvard University over the comments of Biblical scholar John Strugnell in the early 1990s or the case of Nazi collaborator Paul Du Man at Yale University in the 1980s.

It took a long time for artists, writers, and intellectuals to come to grips with the Holocaust. Writers such as Leslie Epstein and William

Styron, when asked why they never wrote about the Holocaust before said it was too painful, too awesome an event to approach. They needed distance; they needed time. The Shoah lay neglected for decades until recently but now, you cannot stop the flow of material.

The Failure of Sociology

The Holocaust seems to be one of the last of the *nova,* arguably one of the major epochal events of the 20th Century, and yet sociology was late in coming to grips with it. As Spencer Blakeslee (1999) points out in *The Sociology of the Holocaust and Genocide*, sociology stands out for its absence of scholarship on the Holocaust when compared to other disciplines.

Helen Fein (1990: v), in an excellent trend report and overview of genocide theory, notes how happy she was that editors invited her to review a "question that few sociologists or other social scientists (excluding historians) have explored": why such absence of scholarship on the Holocaust and genocide in general? And she attributes this avoidance to several factors: the tenacity of collective denial, the rigid proscriptions of modern sociology, and most especially she quotes from a review by Yale sociologist Kai Erickson (1989: 475) of a book by Neil Smelser, *Handbook of Sociology*:

> (Readers) would find nothing at all in the pages of the *Handbook* about happenings that the rest of the world called "historic," events that helped shape the character of our age. Nothing about Hiroshima and Nagasaki, the Holocaust, Vietnam, Bhopal and Chernobyl. That should not surprise them, considering how deeply American sociology has invested in the study of the "general" as opposed to the study of the "particular." . . .

In other words, because sociology is a generalizing-type of discipline, it is most uncomfortable with unique events like the Holocaust and was thus blind to it for decades. The debate, however, about its uniqueness continues unabated. However, few will quarrel with the fact that, unlike other genocides of the 20th Century, the Holocaust is the *tremendum* (to use Arthur A. Cohen's phrase)—unique, powerful, not unprecedented, but uniquely awesome in its sway over our imagination. It had a formative impact on the 20th Century and beyond.

The Failure of Modernity

To understand the Holocaust we need to understand modernity and its failure. Modernization signifies the historical transformation of the Western world; modernization was the way the world emerged from feudal Europe. Medieval society, with its sacred values and its rural, agricultural culture, emphasized community at the expense of individuality, superstition at the expense of reason. As market institutions and the monetization of economic activity gradually replaced feudal and manorial institutions and obligations, a new emphasis on the individual emerged. New ideologies and values developed to support these social changes.

When one studies the process of modernization in Western Civilization, one studies the wholesale transformation of political and economic institutions and their far-reaching impact on family life, stratification (class) systems, religious (church) structures, and ideological systems. The French Revolution, the Enlightenment, and the Industrial Revolution were key elements in this historical process.

Modernization was good in many ways. It lifted us out of the "Dark Ages" so to speak. But some, like Bauman (1989), see the failure in modernity or, conversely, the "uncontrollable success of modernity" (Blakeslee, 1999). And the Holocaust with a fifty-five year hindsight, could be called a form of *diseased modernization*—modernity gone haywire.

We can see the Holocaust as a rejection of all that was noble in Enlightenment thinking and progressive Western action. Jeffrey Herf (1984) calls it "reactionary modernism," meaning the ability to reject the rationalism of the Enlightenment (the good humane stuff) and yet embrace the modern technology (the technology that could build death camps and gas chambers capable of killing 20,000 humans per day). Herf describes this as an uneasy fusion of *Kultur und Technik* (culture and technology) and *Zivilization und Wirtschaft* (civilization and economy).

The Three Pillars: Technology, Bureaucracy, and Ideology

I laid out a tripartite theory similar to this as early as the late 1970s in my book *Genocide and Human Rights* (1982) and later in *The Sociology of the Holocaust and Genocide* (1999): namely that the Holocaust was carried out by rational actors utilizing the highest levels of technology, bureaucracy, and ideology known to them at the time. These three components are the three major pillars of Western Civilization but they were used by diseased minds for diseased purposes, thus the perversion, the failure, and the ultimate destruction of modernity, and the need for new postmodern theories to help explain this seeming contradiction between modernity and evil. Rubenstein (1975) and Hilberg (1985) also make these points about rationalization, bureaucracy, and modernity.

Three New Directions for Research

Postmodern Theory

What are some new directions to take to explain genocide? It is not only the Holocaust that has threatened our thinking but all of modern society. If we look around us: the violence, the dysfunctionality of our families, the impact of modern technology (computers, cell phones, beepers), the loss of spiritual values in our lives and in the lives of our children, and all the destructive forces surrounding us—one sees what I mean. We do not understand it. We need new directions, and we have them in the vast field of postmodern theory.

Ironically, though sociologists overlooked and avoided the Holocaust, they have been, interestingly enough, in the forefront of post modern theory. Names like Jurgen Habermas, Jean Baudrillard, Daniel Bell, Jean-Francois Lyotard, Jacques Derrida, Michel Foucault, and many others come to mind. Most sociologists have been deeply influenced by postmodern thinking. The literature is vast and beyond this short entry to enumerate but see Powell, 1998), Cahoone (1996), Dickens and Fontana (1994), Lemert (1999), and Palmer (1997).

Feminist and Gay Theory

As Blakeslee (1999) points out we need to explore the Holocaust from the perspectives of gender theory, feminist methodology, and the implications that this analysis carried for explaining the "other" in society. Many aspects of the Holocaust will become explicable—the sociology of work, family, the use of force and violence—when we analyze women's role in the Holocaust and comparative genocide. Furthermore, the use of gay theory will open up many areas of research hitherto taboo. It must be understood that Nazism was a perversion not only of race and religion (that is, of Jews) but a perversion of sex and gender (women and gays). There was a great fear and ambivalence, even a tolerance for a while, of the gay culture, but this subculture was destroyed when it no longer proved useful to the Nazis.

Marxian Theory

Marxism is over and we can mourn the end of the world's great project of social transformation (see Aronson, 1995). It is over as a political system and as a way of life; however as a means of understanding modernity and the postmodern condition, it may still be useful as a philosophy and as a sociology. Meaning, that an economic and/or class-based analysis of the Holocaust would be extremely provocative yet extremely useful. Even using the words "Holocaust" and "Marxism" in the same sentence is anathema to some scholars and to many survivors. Yet early post-World War II books such as *Behemoth* by Franz Neumann were Marxian in their examination of the Nazi state. Marxian analysis, and I mean by that, sober, scientific analysis, not Soviet nor Communist-inspired propaganda, might help us understand the class differences among victims, perpetrators, and bystanders; it would help us, for example, understand the many forms of resistance. For example, there were Ukrainian Communists who fought alongside Polish and Soviet Jewish partisans and should be seen as allies, not enemies or collaborators. In short, many things would become clearer if we saw them in terms of class and ideological categories rather than ethnic or religious categories.

Conclusion

We are finally seeing, after fifty years, the important role that the Holocaust played and continues to play in Western Civilization. However, it brings to mind whether the West is truly civilized or whether the idea of "western civilization" may really be an oxymoron. What indeed is so "civilized" about western culture? We will need new theories such as postmodern, feminist, neo-Marxian, and multicultural perspectives to help guide us and we will need to redefine "civilization" in light of the Holocaust.

(2003)

Sources

Aronson, Ronald, *After Marxism*. New York and London: The Guilford Press, 1995.

Bauman, Zygmunt, *Modernity and the Holocaust*. Ithaca, NY: Cornell University Press, 1989.

Blakeslee, Spencer, "Sociological Perspectives on the Holocaust" in Jack Nusan Porter with Steve Hoffman (ed), *The Sociology of the Holocaust and Genocide*. Washington, DC: American Sociological Association, 1999, pp. 84-88 and found also in this volume.

Cahoone, Lawrence E. (ed), *From Modernism to Post Modernism: An Anthology*. Cambridge, MA and Oxford: Blackwell Publishers, 1996.

Dickens, David R. and Andrea Fontana (eds), *Post modernism and Social Inquiry*. New York and London: The Guilford Press, 1994.

Erickson, Kai, "Symposium—Smelser's Handbook: An Assessment," *Contemporary Sociology*. Vol. 18, No. 4, 1989: pp. 511-513.

Fein, Helen, "Trend Report: Genocide: A Sociological Perspective," *Current Sociology/La Sociologie Contemporaine*. Vol. 38, No. 1, Spring 1990, entire issue. It is the journal of the International Sociological Association and was published by Sage Publications.

Herf, Jeffrey, *Reactionary Modernism*. Cambridge, UK: Cambridge University Press, 1984.

Hilberg, Raul, *The Destruction of the European Jews*. second revised edition, three volumes, New York: Holmes and Meier, 1985.

Kaufman, Debra, "Sociology and the Holocaust: Why So Little Research," *Contemporary Jewry*. 1996. This is a journal of the Association for the Social Scientific Study of Jewry and is now an annual journal.

Lemert, Charles (ed), *Social Theory: The Multicultural and Class Readings*. Boulder, CO and Oxford: Westview Press, 1999.

Palmer, Donald, *Structuralism and Poststructuralism for Beginners*. New York: Writers and Readers Publishing, Inc., 1997.

Porter, Jack Nusan (ed), *Genocide and Human Rights: A Global Anthology*. Lanham, MD and London: University Press of America, 1982. Reprinted by The Spencer Press of Newton, Massachusetts, 2002. It was the first anthology of its kind ever published.

———, "Moral Sociology and the Holocaust," *Perspectives: The ASA Theory Section Newsletter*. Vol. 15, No. 4, October 1992, page 4.

———, with Steve Hoffman (eds), *The Sociology of the Holocaust and Genocide*. Washington, DC: American Sociological Association,

1999. This is the revised edition of the 1992 edition, which was also the first teaching and learning guide in sociology of its kind ever published.

Powell, Jim, *Post Modernism for Beginners*. New York: Writers and Readers publishing, 1998.

Rubenstein, Richard L. *The Cunning of History: Mass Death and the American Future*. New York: Harper and Row, 1975.

Chapter 6

What is Evil? Some New Post-Modern Theories to Explain the Post 9/11 Era

> *"Western civilization? It's a good idea."*
> —Albert Einstein

Reflexive Statement and Abstract

My aim quite simply is to apply quantum physics and mathematics to sociological and political phenomena; to apply chaos theory, uncertainty theory, and postmodern theories to such phenomena as terrorism, genocide, suicide bombing, anti-Semitism, and other acts of random hate and violence as well as to understand past genocides such as the Holocaust in light of these theories. I believe this is the first time someone has applied these two separate entities, one to the other. As the late Marshall Mcluhan said, this is a *probe*. Not a final answer or even any answer at all. The application may even fail. It is only a probe. The old answers are inadequate; the old theories have failed to give us answers.

Naturally, we will as humans never be able to fully predict such phenomena. Why? Because if we could, we would have to control nearly all events in a closed system, such as totalitarian state. We are complex human beings, not molecules, atoms, or electrons. It would be totally unacceptable ethically to have such total control. As I note below, Bronowski has emphasized: if things are totally "certain," we have a total institution. we need some uncertainty in order to be human. One of the prices of freedom is the "freedom" to be killed randomly.

However, even if we are unable to be totally certain of our theories and applications; at least we will be able to predict or at best, understand the random evil that has befallen us as we enter the 21st Century. There is enough work here to fill out the entire century. Some definitions:

What is chaos theory? Chaos theory is a theory that says that small changes in part of a system can make for large changes in another part of the system. It is the "famous butterfly effect', that the flapping of the wings of a small butterfly in China can cause a hurricane patterns (we can't forcast longer than five days because of such fluctuations) to predicting traffic patterns (It doesn't pay to jump lanes since all traffiic will meet at the same point anyway) High hopes had been placed on chaos theory over the years but it has not panned out as predicted. But we should keep trying, especially in the area of predicting evil such as terrorism or genocide. We will define postmodem and chaos theories next.

Introduction

Evil exists. In various forms. But why does it exist? Traditional political (power) theories haven't enlightened us, neither have social, psychological (group pressure) or ideological (racism, anti-Semitism, tribalism, xenophobia, fundamentalism) theories. Perhaps the far more complex and encompassing cluster of theories known as postmodern, uncertainty, and chaos theories, can help us understand the basis of random violence terrorism, Holocaust, and genocide—in short to understand where evil develops and how it grows. This short essay is the basis for what will be a book on the subject. It only touches the surface.

What was Heisenberg's Uncertainty Theory? Essentially, he stated that we can never know the location and speed of an electron at the same time. In other words, there will always be some kind of uncertainty in the world. Heisenberg's genius, like Einstein's, was that he *quantified* that uncertainty into mathematical terms. For our discussion here, it means, there will always be uncertainty in this universe and that the orderly world that Einstein dreamed of never really existed.

I say "uncertainty" in the same way that Albert Einstein reacted to Werner Heisenberg's Uncertainty Principle and Niels Bohr's and Max Planck's Quantum Theory when he said, "God does not play dice with the universe," but, as Einstein's colleague Abraham Pais responded, "How does he [Einstein] know what God does? Perhaps, God does indeed play dice with the universe." (PBS "Nova" special, "Einstein Revealed," WGBH-TV, Boston, Massachusetts, 1996). Perhaps, violence is random and we need to delve deeper into "God's world" with more sophisticated theories and approaches. (For more on the life of Heisenberg, see Cassidy, 1992 and Dawidoff, 1994. For more on the life of a physicist, see Weisskopf, 1989.)

The orderly world of Einstein's special and general theory of relativity and his lifelong search for a unified theory was based on an orderly and certain faith in the laws governing the universe, but what if the world is not orderly but chaotic and random?

Can the laws "governing" evil in this world conform to universal laws? Is evil part of this "orderly" universe, or an aberration of that universe? The "uncertainty theory" of evil tells us that evil arises out of nowhere from seemingly ordinary people. Hannah Arendt said the same thing: the Nazis were terribly and terrifyingly normal. Thus, evil emerges from normal and natural, not supernatural, people and events.

Uncertainty theory is one possible probe; chaos theory is another. What is it? Chaos theory says that a slight change in one part of the universe ultimately makes a ripple effect so that change of a much larger scale occurs much further down the road. Chaos theory had its start with Lorenz's work on weather. He found that a slight weather pattern change in one part of the country can make for massive changes a few days later. What it showed is that weathermen could only predict patterns that are accurate for only 2-3 days; then prediction deteriorates. (For more on chaos theory, see Alligood et al, 1997; James Gleick, 1987, Hao Bai-Lin, 1984, and Gutzwiller, 1990.)

However, could uncertainty and chaos theory help us predict terrorist acts, terrible tragedies, and even genocide? Electrons and precipitation patterns are physical elements and can be predicted to some degree. Human behavior, on the other hand, is vastly more complex. To manipulator and predict such behavior would practically be an act of god, like puppets deux ex machina. Sadly, we don't have such powers . . . yet. Evil is not ineffable; it is terrifyingly quite understandable. The evil of the killing may be irrational, but the prediction that men will kill is fairly easy to do. (See Porter, 1982) Genocide, for example, is easy to predict, but stopping it, intervening, is fraught with geographical and political difficulties.

Because evil is so "normal," we need new theories to explain it, and the new postmodern theories that have come ironically from Europe, mainly France, are a possible answer. I saw ironically given that Europe has seen and is now seeing a major upswing in anti-Semitism and racism and xenophobia. Thus, out of that sad cultural milieu may come some answers.

Definition of Postmodernism and Postmodern Theories

Postmodernism is a complex, multifaceted, and often misunderstood field. In fact, there are universities such as Boston University under President John Silber, that have tried to outlaw postmodern teaching. (He failed.) Why do people feel so strongly about postmodern theory?

First, some feel it is "insensitive" to a-subject such as the Holocaust. Some feel not only that postmodern theorists such as Foucault, , because of their radicalism and "obsession" with violence and sex, demean issues. but that purveyors of these theories may even be anti-Semites, including, for example, Paul DuMan.

Second, they do not trust the sociological approach of postmodern theorists, most of whom tend to be French sociologists or philosophers, there is fear that such sociologists will only turn the Holocaust into a 2x4 statistical table, further demeaning the victims or that deconstructionists such as Jacques Derrida and Paul Du Man have destroyed proper academic discourse with their emphasis on the structure and underlying meaning of the text and not with the text itself.

As with all prejudices, there is a nugget of truth to all of these criticisms. I, too, cringe when a sociologist or philosopher begins work in any field with little or no historical, literary or language training. I shudder at the possible consequences. It is not surprising, for example, that the two most controversial books of the past few years in Holocaust studies were written by two social scientists, Daniel Jonah Goldhagen (1996) and Norman G. Finkelstein (2000), neither of whom could be publicly known (though privately they may be known) as postmodern theorists, while historian Peter Novick (1999), who writes about issues very similarly to both social scientists but in a more prudent and sober manner, is not castigated at all.

Part of this is, of course, due to the conservative bias of most Holocaust scholars such as Raul Hilberg, Yehuda Bauer, and Deborah Lipstadt, who rarely welcome any new ideas on "their turf," and rightfully so; the

Holocaust is a holy issue and these people have devoted their entire lives to it; they fear outsiders entering the field with their newfangled ideas. Even though I see myself still as an outsider (though some might disagree), I, too, am upset when outsiders, including respected academics, come into Holocaust and genocide studies with their new ideas.

Novick (1999: 270) even suggests that Deborah Lipstadt's book *Denying the Holocaust: The Growing Assault on Truth and Memory* (1992) claimed that the willingness of campus editors to run deniers' advertisements were evidence of the strength of postmodernism and deconstructionism! This theme was eagerly picked up by conservative commentators. See Michiko Kakutani (1993) in *The New York Times;* David Singer (1993) in *The New Leader;* Edward Norden (1993) in *Commentary;* and Robert Eaglestone (2001).

This view, of course, is preposterous. In fact, as Novick pointedly emphasizes, the student leaders in question had not been immersing themselves in such postmodern thinkers and French sociologists, by the way, as Foucault or Derrida, but instead ". . . reading, somewhat carelessly, those 'dead white males' Thomas Jefferson and John Stuart Mill, and concluding that their principles required making a place in the marketplace of ideas for the deniers."

But we come back to the original question: what exactly is postmodern theory? *The Cambridge Dictionary of Philosophy*, second edition, edited by Robert Audi (1999: 725-726) defines "postmodern" as:

> of, or relating to, a complex set of reactions to modern philosophy and its presuppositions. . . . Although there is little agreement on precisely what these presuppositions are, postmodern philosophy typically opposed foundationalism, essentialism, and realism.

Based on the theories of Nietzsche, Heidegger, and Sartre, as well as later philosophers such as Foucault, Derrida, and Lyotard, postmodernism is seen as a complex cluster concept that includes the following elements: an anti- (or post-) epistemological standpoint; anti-essentialist; anti-realist; anti-foundationalist; opposition to transcendental arguments; rejection of knowledge as accurate representation; rejection of truth as corresponding to reality; rejection of canonical descriptions; rejection of final vocabularies, of what are called "grand narratives."

One can see why postmodernism can be so threatening. In plain language, postmodern thinking rejects any metaphysical theory that sees objects as simply "essences"—having an intrinsic or fundamental property—but a shifting, flowing nature. Postmodernism rejects the view that knowledge is non-inferential or foundational and accepts the premise that knowledge is inferential, can be concluded from evidence or premises leading to a result or conclusion. Postmodernism rejects grand canons and grand narratives such as Marxism (so it is anti-Marxist in part), Liberalism, Conservatism, and even what we could call "Holocaustism"—that is, turning the Holocaust into an untouchable and holy narrative immune from all criticism, akin to the canon of the Catholic Church.

Sociologists have expanded postmodern theories in a most wide-ranging way. Building on the works of Jean-Francois Lyotard, Michel Foucault, and Jean Baudrillard, as well as Zygmunt Bauman, Richard Rorty, Cornel West, Donna Haraway, and Judith Butler, as well as some more conservative or apolitical thinkers such as Daniel Bell and Erving Goffman, sociologists have made some very interesting forays into sex and gender issues, media's impact on youth, especially film and music and combinations of film and music such as music videos and MTV (in fact, the classic postmodern film is Ridley Scott's *Blade Runner* with Harrison Ford), and the question of power and evil. (See Steve Seidman, 1994)

What Is Postmodernism?

MODERNISM	POSTMODERNISM
Form (closed)	Anti-Form (open)
Purposeful	Play
Design	Chance
Hierarchy	Anarchy (Chaos—JNP)
Art Object/Finished Work	Process/Performance/Happening
Presence	Absence (also Silence—JNP)
Centering	Dispersal
Genre/Boundary	Text/Intertext
Root/Depth	Rhizome/Surface

And I have added the following:

Focused Violence	Random Violence
Conviviality/Cheerfulness	Depression/Nihilism
Optimism	Cynicism

Hope	Despair
Socialism	Barbarism
Grand Narratives	Sound Bytes
Reality	Simulation/Simulacra
Mono-Sexual Identities	Multi-Sexual Identities
Monogamy	Serial Monogamy
Male	Female/Transsexual
Sex	Gender
Love	S&M

See Ihab Hassan (University of Wisconsin-Milwaukee)
Probably the best synopsis of postmodernism that exists is Powell, 1998

What Does Postmodernism Mean?

Postmodernism is many things to many people and is quite complex. Much of it is useful; some of it is verbal garbage; all of it is fascinating, even Talmudic, in that first readings are difficult. It may take years to understand the material.

Cahoone (1996: 14-19) and Powell (1998) give several meanings, with my interpretations added:

1. Postmodernism studies the "*representation*" of something instead of the thing itself. That does not mean that there is no real world, only that we encounter real referents through texts, representations, and mediations. In that sense, postmodernism is "talmudic," even Kabbalistic, seeing hidden meanings in acts and words. Deconstructing the text or the definition is paramount since it will uncover the underlying power arrangements, meaning that minorities such as blacks, women, gays, and colonized people will be shown to be oppressed. One readily sees here then the sociological and radical agenda.
2. Postmodernism is obsessed with the power of *simulation* and what is called *hyper-reality*; that is, simulation is more "real" than the real. Main Street in Disney World is more real to most people than the "real" Main Street. Many teenagers can no longer distinguish reality from simulated reality or fantasy. The recent murders at Dartmouth University, the

killings at Columbine High School, and other plots such as in New Bedford, Mass., are only a few of many cases of this issue. Even the events of September 11, 2001, are examples of confused reality. The movie *Blue Velvet* by David Lynch is another good example. It juxtaposes the quiet world of small-town, middle-class high-school romance with the world of sickos, druggies, S & M, random violence, unruly, chaotic behavior, and simple craziness in such a way; that we do not know which world is real anymore. A less well-known film dealing with postmodernism is Wim Wenders' *Wings of Desire* on Berlin and its anomie and multiple identities. Ridley Scott's *Blade Runner* with Harrison Ford, Daryl Hannah, and Rudiger Hauer is a cult classic in postmodern circles. Everything in the film is double-coded. There are not only human replicants; everything is a replicant, even some say, the Harrison Ford character, which will come as a shock to many people. The main question in the film and in postmodern theory is: what is the difference between a machine and a human being? Replicants and human beings are so much alike that it is very difficult to tell the copy from the "real" thing. Plus, the replicant burns himself out quickly; his/her life span is short. Can Nazis or terrorists be seen as "replicants"?
3. Postmodernism is obsessed with *power* and power fantasies. For example, Madonna had the ability to produce images of rebellion against established powers and yet do so in a winsome way. She also deconstructed gender, sexuality, and race.
4. Along with power, postmodernism is obsessed with *sexuality and S & M*, especially in the works of the late French sociologist Michel Foucault, who ironically died of AIDS after a lifetime of S & M practices. One can better understand Nazism and other fascisms by looking at their sexual perversities and their connection to power.
5. *Chaos Theory*. Random acts of violence based on uncertainty are becoming more and more common.

These are just a few ways that postmodern theory can help explain the present reality. As for Holocaust and genocide studies, postmodernism can be useful in new ways to look at:

- the role of propaganda and media (what was real and what was unreal in Nazism?);
- the role of sex and gender;
- the role of power relations;
- the role of "grand narratives" in history;
- the role of plural meanings, rather than unity;
- the difference between a human being and a machine; and
- the denial of the transcendence of norms. Norms such as truth, goodness, beauty, rationality, are no longer regarded as independent of the processes they serve to govern or judge, but are rather products of these processes. For example, where most philosophers might use the idea of justice to judge a social order, postmodernism regards the idea itself as the product of certain social relations that need to be understood within the context of time and place. Thus, most things are relative. (See Cahoone, p. 15 and Alvesson, p. 150-151, 177-179)

The Areas of Postmodernism

Surprisingly, as we will see, postmodern thinkers, rather than being insensitive to the Holocaust, have made some important contributions. I will examine Zygmunt Bauman, Lyotard, Foucault, and others soon, but now I will capitulate what are the main areas of postmodernism for our concerns. There are six:

1. As noted, a mistrust of "grand narratives" and "final vocabularies." In essence, this came out of a mistrust of these thinkers with the uprisings in Paris, Berlin, and the USA in 1968 and their infatuation with Marx, Stalin, and leftist dogma. Postmodernism is surprisingly anti-Marxist.
2. Postmodernism tries to understand our confusion between reality and simulacra (simulation), as well as postmodern nations' gift of developing "hyperreality" (Disneyland, *The Truman Show*, hip-hop, most video games) that, in a way, confuses our young people into a neurotic disassociation from reality (e.g., the recent Zantop-Dartmouth College killings and the many other killings by young people) who can no

longer differentiate between what is real and what is a game or a "show."
3. Our obsession with fame, scandal, media, movies, TV shows, and pomp and celebrity itself is a subject about which postmodern theorists, especially Baudrillard, have written.
4. Sex and gender issues. Again, coming out of the 1960s, these topics have dominated sociology and other fields in recent times.
5. The hidden meaning of texts (deconstructionism). Of course, one can go too far with this, to the point of ridicule and satire, but deconstructionism contains some useful nuggets.
6. Finally, an interest in the origins of violence, death and evil—in short, an "archaeology of death," to paraphrase Foucault.

As one can see, postmodernism and Holocaust Studies have much in common. It is, in fact, the new frontier, the cutting edge of research, despite some obvious dangers, but who were some of the early postmodern thinkers in Holocaust Studies, and how can postmodernism help us explain the Holocaust and other genocides?

Major Figures in the Field of Postmodernism and Holocaust Studies

Two major gaps in the field are the "uniqueness issue" best represented by Jewish philosopher Steven Katz and the "ineffability issue" best represented by Elie Wiesel. They have both, in their own ways, caused a conflict between Holocaust and genocide scholars and, more precisely, between historians and theologians on the one hand and sociologists/social scientists on the other, and their new theories, one of which is the postmodern cluster.

However, certain thinkers, unbeknownst to them at the time, have bridged these gaps. First, Raul Hilberg (1961), a political scientist, wrote the first "sociological" account of the power structure and decision-making structure of the Nazi apparatus of killing. Then, Hannah Arendt (1964) wrote what I call the first postmodern text—a muckraking classic that criticized in true postmodern style all prevailing theories, even going so far as to blame the Jewish victims themselves, not for resisting but more for over-aiding and abetting their own killers.

A third person who, though he does not think of himself as a postmodern thinker but is in his distrust of his faith's "grand narratives," is the theologian and "death of God" writer Richard Rubenstein, whose *The Cunning of History* (1975, 1987) is based on the German sociologist Max Weber's thinking on rationalism and how the Holocaust was the "rational" outcome of modernity's obsession with bureaucracy, ideology and technology. In short, modernity can and did lead to great and humane works, and it also led to Auschwitz. Rubenstein, unbeknownst to himself, influenced me and many other sociologist, in this "postmodern" interpretation.

However, the man who was most influential to postmodernism, yet is relatively little known in the USA, is the Polish-British sociologist Zygmunt Bauman, author of *Modernity and the Holocaust* (1992). I have laid out his theories in two places (Porter, 1992, 1998) as well as in many of my other essays in this book.

Despite opposition for many years among Holocaust scholars to postmodernism, we are seeing a few provocative and important books emerging, and there will be more to come. Soon everyone will call himself or herself a postmodern.

Elizabeth J. Bellamy's book *Affective Genealogies: Psychoanalysis, Postmodernism, and the "Jewish Question" after Auschwitz* (1997) is a contribution to the current reassessment of postmodern culture and theory. Bellamy examines how the Holocaust and Jews have been represented in a wide range of French poststructuralist thinkers.

* * * * *

Alain Finkielkraut, a French philosopher, in *The Wisdom of Love* (1997), examines the seemingly contradictory claims of Universalism and partisanship for the ethnic or racial "Other."

Norman G. Finkelstein, in *The Holocaust Industry: Reflections on the Exploitation of Jewish Suffering* (2000), contends that the main danger posed to the memory of Nazism's victims comes not from the distortions of deniers but from self-proclaimed guardians of Holocaust memory who have turned the Shoah into an "industry" and who have undertaken a "shakedown" of European countries. It is a most disturbing and provocative book, to say the least, and Finkelstein is wrong in many ways, yet his critique deserves attention.

How Can Postmodern Theory Explain the Holocaust and Other Genocides?

Uncertainty Theory

Because the Holocaust is so bizarre and so difficult to understand, it will take some of the new postmodern theories to help us understand it. One of these is what I call "The Uncertainty Factor," that is, why bizarre behavior happens—the unpredictability of human relations, the disorder that lies hidden beneath the surface. Perhaps even "chaos theory" may help. If more research on "uncertainty theory" takes place, we may have some answers.

"Uncertainty" has another meaning: that any group that has no puzzlement, no questioning, no uncertainty in its ideology (such as Nazism, Stalinism, or most fascisms) is extremely dangerous. If such groups are totally certain of its "uncertainty" and its "illogical" logic, said ideology can and will lead to genocide or other forms of severe human misconduct.

Ironically, the basis for this theory lies in physics, in the theories of Werner Heisenberg, a German scientist who himself was a collaborator of the Nazis (though not a party member). Heisenberg's Uncertainty Principle posited that no one could know both the speed and location of electrons at the same time. Dr. Jacob Bronowski, in *The Ascent of Man*, his famed television series on western thought, applied the Uncertainty Principle to fascism.

Rational Choice vs. Symbolic Meaning Theory

Rational choice theory, a prevailing orthodoxy in both political science and sociology, holds that political actors make rational decisions after weighing all the pros and cons. However, opposed to rational choice was the pioneering work of the University of Illinois political scientist Murray Edelman, whose work predated postmodern and deconstructionist theory in the fields of literary and cultural studies, with its emphasis on subjective interpretation, and could be called "postmodern political science."

Edelman, who passed away on January 26, 2001, at age 81, believed that public political developments often act as what he called symbols with meanings or purposes that can be determined only by careful investigation. He once said, "A fact is always embedded in a theory and has to be interpreted." (Lewis, 2001) His best-known books were *The Symbolic Uses of Politics* (1964) and *Politics as Symbolic Action: Mass Arousal and Quiescence* (1971). Virginia Shapiro, a political science professor at the University of Wisconsin, said, "He looked under manifest institutions to see the hidden shadow plays."

It is this approach that will prove useful in studying the Nazis and the Holocaust. As I show in my essay on Erich Goldhagen, Nazism without ritual and show would not have been Nazism, and when all the rituals and showmanship ended, Nazism ended. Postmodern theories tell us that if we "deconstruct" the symbols of Nazism and other genocides, we may learn important lessons, which leads to the next subject.

The Role of Propaganda and Media

Nazism was the most visual of genocides, full of pomp and pageantry. It was in a sense the first modern (or even postmodern) genocide with its reliance on propaganda, radio, film, and other media. To understand the Holocaust, we need to better understand the role of media. Other genocides, such as in Rwanda, also in a much cruder, simpler manner, used the radio to dehumanize the victims and place them "outside the moral university," to use Helen Fein's fine phrase. Thus, you could kill them with impunity.

Sex and Power

A major influence of postmodern theories has, of course, been on the spate of sex and gender studies in Holocaust and genocide research. See, for example, the essays by many scholars on "Holocaust Women," articles on rape as a genocidal weapon, and essays on how sociology has incorporated sex and gender issues in dealing with the Holocaust. Of course, one danger is to turn the Holocaust into two genocides, one for men and one for women; one for gays and one for straights. However, if one does not turn sex and gender studies into a new doctrine, much new data and insights can be gained.

Modernity and Postmodernity: A Conclusion of Sorts

Michael Freeman, in an influential essay that originally appeared in the respected *British Journal of Sociology* in June 1995 (the previous classic essay on the Holocaust and modernity was by Zygmunt Bauman in 1989), argues with Bauman about the issues of modernity, civilization, and genocide. He calls into question the thesis of Zygmunt Bauman, a British sociologist, that the modernity of the Holocaust challenges orthodox approaches to the sociology of morality and politics. While the Holocaust indubitably manifested distinctive features of modem society, it also, he notes, reproduced ancient motivational and structural sources of genocide. If modernity produced the Holocaust, it also produced the sociological and moral critique of genocide.

Furthermore, Bauman, according to Freeman, is misleading in three ways. First, although Bauman is correct to associate genocide with the process of civilization, he is incorrect to equate civilization with modernity. Second, although he is correct to associate genocide with the bureaucratic state and the incapacity of civil society to constrain the state, Bauman overlooks the association between genocide and warfare, especially modern warfare. Third, although he draws correct and important lessons from the Holocaust about the dangers inherent in modern society, in concentrating his attention on a single albeit exceptionally important case of genocide, namely the Holocaust, and by associating it with problems of modernity, he misses other important lessons of the Holocaust.

These lessons are to be learned from what was not modem in that genocide. They required us to do what Bauman does not: to locate the Holocaust in the more general theoretical consideration of comparative genocide. (Freeman, 1995: 207-209 and this book)

Still, I concur with Richard Rubenstein (1975) that the Holocaust was an expression of some of the most significant political, moral, religious and demographic tendencies of western civilization in the 20th century. The Holocaust could not have occurred except in the 20th century, and it could not have occurred without modernity and modern civilization. Bureaucracy is closely related to other tendencies in western civilization: secularization, disenchantment with the world (Max Weber), rationalization, and technological industrialization. In essence, the

Holocaust was the "modernization of slavery," often white-on-white slavery, according to Rubenstein.

Postmodern theories, built on the shoulders of Weber, Durkheim, Simmel, Marx and others, can help us understand the old forms of "industrial killing" as well as the newer forms of technologically "clean" killings that we may see in the future. These and other ideas should spur new research in the field of Holocaust and genocide studies, a field that has been stagnant and torpid. Postmodernism will stir things up a bit, but hopefully in a positive and constructive way.

(2004)

Sources

Alligood, Kathleen T. et al, *Chaos: An Introduction to Dynamical Systems*. New York: Springer, 1997.

Alvesson, Mats, *Postmodernism and Social Research*. Buckingham, UK and Philadelphia, PA: Open University Press (Routledge Press), 2002.

Arendt, Hannah. *Eichmann in Jerusalem: A Report on the Banality of Evil*. New York: Viking Press, 1963.

Audi, Robert (ed). *The Cambridge Dictionary of Philosophy*. second edition. New York, NY, and Cambridge, UK: Cambridge University Press, 1999.

Bai-Lin, Hao, compiler and editor, *Chaos*. Singapore: World Scientific, 1984.

Bauman, Zygmunt. *Modernity and the Holocaust*. Ithaca, NY: Cornell University Press, and Cambridge, UK: Polity Press, 1989.

Bellamy, Elizabeth J. *Affective Genealogies: Psychoanalysis, Postmodernism, and the "Jewish Question" after Auschwitz*. Lincoln, NE: University of Nebraska Press, 1997.

Bennett, Deborah J., *Randomness*. Cambridge, MA and London, UK: Harvard University Press, 1998.

Cahoone, Lawrence (ed). *From Modernism to Postmodernism: An Anthology*. Cambridge, MA, and Oxford, UK, 1996, pp. 14-19.

Cassidy, David Charles, *Uncertainty: The Life and Science of Werner Heisenberg*. New York: W. H. Freeman, 1992.

Dawidoff, Nicholas, *The Catcher was a Spy: The Mysterious Life of Moe Berg*. New York: Vintage Books, 1994.

Eaglestone, Robert. *Postmodernism and Holocaust Denial*. New York: Totem Books, 2001.
Finkielkraut, Alain. *The Wisdom of Love*. Lincoln, NE: University of Nebraska Press, 1997.
Finkelstein, Norman G. *The Holocaust Industry: Reflections on the Exploitation of Jewish Suffering*. London and New York: Verso, 2000.
Freeman, Michael. "Genocide, Civilization, and Modernity," *British Journal of Sociology*. vol. 46, no. 2, June 1995, pp. 207-223.
Gleick, James, *Chaos: Making a New Science*. New York: Viking Penguin, 1987.
———, *Genius: The Life and Science of Richard Feynman*. New York: Vintage Books, 1992.
Goldhagen, Daniel Jonah. *Hitler's Willing Executioners*. New York: Knopf, 1996.
Gutzwiller, M. C. (Martin C.), *Chaos in Classical and Quantum Mechanics*. New York: Springer-Verlag, 1990.
Hilberg, Raul. *The Destruction of the European Jews*. Chicago: Quadrangle Books, 1967, with later editions.
Kakutani, Michiko. "When History is a Casualty," *The New York Times*. April 3, 1993, p. Cl.
Lewis, Paul. "Murray Edelman, 81, Professor and Pioneer in Political Science (obituary), *The New York Times*. January 28, 2001.
Lipstadt, Deborah. *Denying the Holocaust: The Growing Assault on Truth and Memory*. New York, 1993.
Norden, Edward. "Yes and No to the Holocaust Museum," *Commentary*. vol. 96, August 1993.
Novick, Peter. *The Holocaust in American Life*. Boston and New York: Houghton Mifflin, 1999.
PBS, *Nova* special, "Einstein Revealed." Boston, MA: WGBH-TV, 1996.
Porter, Jack Nusan. *Genocide and Human Rights*. Lanham, MD: University Press of America, 1982. Reprinted by Lanham, MD and London: University Press of America, 2002.
———, review of Zygmunt Bauman's *Modernity and the Holocaust* in Antony Polonsky, *Polin: Studies in Polish Jewry*. vol. 11. London and Portland, OR: The Littman Library of Jewish Civilization, 1998, pp. 355-357.
Powell, Jim. *Postmodernism for Beginners*. New York: Writers and Readers Publishing, Inc., 1998.

Rubenstein, Richard L. *The Cunning of History: The Holocaust and the American Future*. New York: Harper Torchbooks, 1975, 1987.

Seidman, Steven (ed). *The Postmodern Turn: New Perspectives on Social Theory*. New York, NY, and Cambridge, UK: Cambridge University Press, 1994. Contains essays by Jean-Francois Lyotard, Michel Foucault, Richard Rorty, Judith Butler, Cornel West, Donna Haraway, Charles Lemert, Zygmunt Bauman, Joan Scott, and Steven Seidman.

Singer, David. Review of "Denying the Holocaust," *New Leader*. vol. 76, May 17, 1993.

Weisskopf, Victor F., *The Privilege of Being a Physicist*. New York and Oxford, UK: W. H. Freeman and Company, 1989.

Chapter 7

The Genocidal Mind: The Contribution of Erich Goldhagen to Holocaust Studies

Reflexive Statement

Sociology, as Zygmunt Bauman (1988) has shown, has only recently dealt with the Holocaust. The purpose of this essay is to show that one major "sociological" contribution has been heretofore overlooked and recently discovered and introduced to sociologists, namely the contribution of Erich Goldhagen of Harvard University. While his son Daniel Jonah Goldhagen is much more famous and his book *Hitler's Willing Executioners* (1996) has become the most controversial book on the subject in 40 years, ever since Hannah Arendt's *Eichmann in Jerusalem* (1963), it is important to note the influence on the son by the father.

One reason why the son is so much better known than the father is because Erich Goldhagen has published very little over the years, only a few essays. His renown in Holocaust circles comes mainly from being a longtime lecturer at Harvard University, teaching undergraduates and evening adult "extension school" students for over twenty years and from his few public lectures.

It is from his course "The Holocaust and the Phenomenon of Genocide" that most of the information in this essay appears. Thus, this is "oral history" or "oral sociology" since that is the only venue to find his ideas expressed because he has never published any of this before. I understand that this is a unique approach—the oral rather than the written approach.

This is also, I believe, the first time any one has outlined and described Erich Goldhagen's thoughts on the Holocaust. Unless otherwise stated, all ideas expressed in this essay are from Goldhagen's lectures in the fall of 1994 at Harvard University. I hope this outline proves useful to teachers and scholars and I hope they will integrate Goldhagen's ideas and imagery into their own work and teaching.

One of his greatest contributions is his brilliant use of language in describing what has long been considered indescribable and ineffable.

I see Goldhagen's work in basically five areas: first, the ideological roots of Nazi genocide, of anti-semitism, racism, and the Nazi *weltanschauung*; second, his description of the "genocidal mind" including what he calls a "Nazi decalogue"; third, a sociology and ethnography of Nazi institutions (ghettos, death camps, mobile killing units); fourth, the mind of Adolf Hitler; and fifth, the mind and spirit of the Eastern European Jew during the Holocaust. I will only be able to deal with a few of these issues in this essay; the others will have to await future articles.

In all cases, my point is that Goldhagen writes, not so much as a historian but as a *sociologist*, and thus his ideas will prove fruitful to sociologists and social psychologists as they examine the genocidal mind and the sociological and social psychological aspects of Nazism during the terrible time known in history as the Shoah, 1933-1945.

Brief Overview of Goldhagen's Life and Writings

He was born on August 3, 1930 in Roznow, Poland, Bukovina on the Ukrainian-Hungarian border, and nearly lost his life to the Nazi mobile killing units. The story he told his Harvard class was that just as he was about to be shot by an Einsatzkommando officer through the head with a pistol, Soviet shots were heard and the Germans posted a hasty retreat but not before the SS kicked the young boy in the head. It is with great historical irony that not only would he and his son Daniel write and teach so influentially about the Holocaust but that Erich Goldhagen would be called upon to testify in Germany at SS mobile killing unit trials.

He came to Canada after the war and lived in Montreal. He received his B. A. from Sir George Williams College (today known as Concordia University) in 1952 and his M. A. in 1954 from McGill University. In 1955 he came to America to be a Russian Research fellow at Harvard. He came with his wife and had two sons and a daughter. He stayed at

Harvard until 1957 and then began teaching at Brandeis University where he was appointed an Assistant Professor of Politics and then at age 35, Director of the Institute of East European Jewish Studies in 1965. He remained at Brandeis until 1969.

Perhaps he left Brandeis because he saw no future there due to two personal weaknesses: no Ph.D. and very little published works; two traits that would hinder him his entire career.

After a stint at the University of Berlin, he returned to Harvard in the 1970s as a University Lecturer with year to year appointments, again possibly due to his lack of a Ph.D.

He was, however, a very popular teacher. He taught Harvard undergraduates in his popular course "General Education 136—The Holocaust and the Phenomenon of Genocide, " probably the first course taught at Harvard on the Holocaust and one of the first in the country.

He has bounced about to many departments and milieus at Harvard, teaching as a lecturer in the divinity school, in the evening division extension, under "government" courses, and as an associate of the Russian Research Center. Surprisingly, never at the sociology department. He has taught other courses aside from his popular Holocaust course: "The Nature of Prejudice," "Political Ideologies," and "Ethnic Minorities in the Soviet Union."

What is not usually known about Goldhagen is that he began his career not in Holocaust studies but in Russian research. His first and only book is actually an anthology *Ethnic Minorities in the Soviet Union* (1972), a by-now dated book, containing about a dozen essays including one by Goldhagen on the various non-Soviet minorities in the former Soviet Union.

The book is among his first writings to emphasize the evil of Soviet Communism, which he sees as not much more pernicious than Nazism. It is a theme that runs like a vein throughout his career as a writer and teacher: he equates Communism as simply another form of fascism.

The emphasis on the Soviet Union is important. Goldhagen is a conservative or at best, a liberal moderate. He has as much distaste for the Communists as he does for the Nazis. He constantly emphasizes Russia's anti-Semitism, anti-Zionism, and Judeophobia. In fact, the erasure of Jews from Soviet historiography of the Holocaust is simply another example of their anti-semitism.

His opus, sadly, is quite small and fits easily onto one page. A search at the Widener and Pusey libraries at Harvard University shows eight articles, one source book, and three sound cassettes, aside from the above book. Not surprisingly, a Hollis search brought up more reviews and responses to his son Daniel than to the father.

Also, interestingly, the Pusey stacks (Stack No. 2) find Goldhagen's source book in a section dealing with "criminology," "terrorism," and "organized crime," and not very far from "Social Sciences" and "Sociology." This is fitting because Goldhagen is, I will show, more of a sociologist and a criminologist than a historian, and combined with the mind of a lawyer and the phrasing of a poet, he is one of the most poetic and eloquent lecturers in academia.

The source book is quite interesting. Used in his General Education 136 course for students and called "Explaining the Holocaust and the Phenomenon of Genocide," it is 269 pages long and has rarely been seen by scholars. It contains fifteen articles, three by Goldhagen himself, nearly all of them by sociologists and social psychologists, people like Gordon Allport, Albert Bandura, Hans Gerth and C. Wright Mills, Herbert Kelman, Philip Zimbardo, and Stanley Milgram—as well as essays by Sigmund Freud, Erich Fromm, Ruth Benedict, Marjorie Housepian, and Raul Hilberg.

What is so interesting about this source book is that it emphasizes a social psychological explanation of Nazi motives, an explanation that his son Daniel Jonah Goldhagen rejects. I will go into this later in my article but it shows that Erich Goldhagen has a more nuanced and complex explanation of the "genocidal mind" than simply attributing it to anti-semitism.

I. The Ideological Roots of Nazi Genocide: Anti-Semitism, Racism, and the Nazi Weltanschauung

According to Erich Goldhagen, the Nazi outlook emphasized racial doctrines. They believed the Jews to be satanic, evil incarnate, bearers of multiple evil, sexual perverters, a race bent on undermining the world. Killing them was thus a rational necessity; annihilation, a moral imperative, a logical step in eliminating a people who seek harm to the world.

He goes onto differentiate the Germany of the last quarter of the 19th century in which the attack against the Jews was mostly "verbal violence" from the 20th Century, where it went far beyond words. Physical violence against Jews in the 19th Century was rare and when it did occur, the government would intervene and punish the offenders.

Jews felt anxiety but did not expect a great catastrophe. They were certain that reason and love would triumph over bigotry and hate. This hope in the past was vindicated by the first decade of the 20th Century. Anti-semitism seemed to abate.

World War I reinforced this hope; all were united against a common enemy. Jews were zealous in the war effort; they wished to dispel anti-Semitic sentiment and hoped that enmity toward them would be weakened. Ninety thousand Jews served in the Gereman army and 12,000 were killed. Jews were later expelled from the army and Jewish war veterans were delivered to extermination camps.

Here, he seems to depart from his son somewhat in that he shows how the Jews were assimilated and accepted into German life in the 19th Century and early 20th Century. His son implies Jews were never accepted into German society.

Let us now look more closely at this Nazi ideology:

Nazi Ideology

To comprehend Nazi ideology, one must, Goldhagen says, quoting Coleridge, "suspend disbelief." That such inconceivable absurdities could come from a nation of poets and thinkers is beyond belief. There is at first a temptation to laugh at such nonsense yet we know today the consequences.

In fact, Goldhagen gives the example that there are German comics at work in Berlin today who read portions of Hitler's Mein Kampf and gales of laughter greet them from the audience.

Goldhagen's makes us bear in mind that Nazi ideology was genocidal, independent of anti-semitism. If Jews had never existed, Nazism still would have been the greatest assault ever on European civilization. Nazism seemed to go beyond traditional anti-semitism; it came from some far-off mystical plain. It invented a Jew that never existed except in one's imagination.

In some of his most beautifully poetic and brilliant passages, Goldhagen describes nazi ideology as "multi-purposeful, polyphonous, kaleidoscopic." One can read almost anything into it. It was "richly variegated, like a glittering Christmas tree, a gift for everyone, for every hatred, for every purpose." It was "manna-like"; it tasted like anything you wanted. Every fear, every hate, every love was contained in it.

The Nazis promised to restore Germany to greatness. The ideology had to be vague to appeal to many. Goldhagen called it a "fragrant fog of obfuscation." Nazi language was both vague and emotive. It had incantatory and hypnotic power, a "suggestive indefiniteness," inchoate, filled with whatever one wants to hear. The sympathetic listener hears whatever he/she wanted to hear.

Nazism coopted everything. The Nazi flag, a red background with a white circle and swastika inside, was taken from the red flag of the Bolsheviks, the socialist workers. Even the name "Nazi," National Socialism" was a cynical device to win workers away from Marxism. However, the Nazis pretended to be socialists. They usurped socialism and communism in order to win over adherents. Those Nazis who represented a worker's position and wished to continue the socialist revolution such as Ernst Roehm's SA were done way with when they proved dysfunctional and a stumbling block to Hitler's consolidation of power.

Nazi ideology, according to Goldhagen needs "deconstruction." Deconstruction, a term used in literary criticism, states that there is no such thing as "meaning" in a text; the reader *invests* meaning into the words. The meaning of the text is in the mind of the reader. It's all in how we interpret it. (In that sense plus Nazi emphasis on form and sound and vision, that I call Nazism, the first "post-modern" ideology.)

Some examples: Phrases like "Blut und Erde," "Blood and Soil." Blood stands for "purity" and *erde* for "stability, security." "Nacht and Nebel," "night and fog," a place where people disappear in the camps.

We are "socialists of the deed." The other socialists simply talk; we do! We will build a "1000-year old Reich." "When we hear the word culture, we reach for a gun." To outsiders, it sounds like gibberish, ludicrous nonsense but to true believers, to use Eric Hoffer's term, this was "oscillating, exulting, execrations."

The Nazis, according to Goldhagen, had no canonical text. They preferred the spoken word to the written word. Mein Kampf, while selling well, was read by few. Germans preferred non-verbal symbol and gesture to the spoken word. See for example, the pageantry of Olympia and Triumph of the Will.

Nazism was theater-like. Nazism became dependent on the conductor. When the symbols and the conductor were destroyed, the ideology evaporated. That's why Nazism is so difficult to resurrect, except in small, marginal deviant groups. No pageantry, no leader, no Nazism. Nazism was a theatrical, emotional movement. Walter Benjamin said that communism politicizes art and fascism aesticizes politics, turns politics into art or theater.

One positive appeal to the movement was that it drew from a deep well of European culture. The promise of Nazism was to build a "people's community" (a *Volks Gemeinschaft*) that would reconcile all classes into one harmonious community. All inequities were to be abolished. The German people would speak with one voice. Nazis would make society whole, healthy, harmonious. It would blossom under the Fuhrer. It would end all class war, create social justice, and satisfy an ancient quest for community.

The Nazis' aims were quite noble, and most Germans voted for the regime because it promised salvation. Instead, what they got was Auschwitz. Why?

Because, these noble ideals concealed what Goldhagen calls the "junk ideas":

- The rejection of the Judeo-Christian tradition
- The erasure of the Ten Commandments, which are the roots of Western culture
- The reinvention of a new opposite ideology, far more radical than Communism, an apostasy that consciously rejected the Judeo/Christian tradition.

Nazi ideology wished o "smash the tablets of Mt. Sinai" and write a new set of commandments. Nazi ideology, radical in the extreme, had to be defeated. It could not function rationally. The Nazis were incapable of rational pursuits of self-interest. It was a self-destructive movement, not an Armeggedon but a Gotterdammarung (how appropriately Wagnerian), bringing down the entire world with it.

II. The Genocidal Mind/The Nazi Decalogue/ The "Nine Commandments" of Nazism

Since it was a the goal of Nazism to erase the old tablets and put up new ones, Goldhagen describes the nine (anti-) commandments of Nazi ideology:

First Commandment: Race is Everything

Goldhagen here gives an interesting reverse example of reverse racism. The case of Benjamin Disraeli, Lord Beaconsfield, a Jew who became a baptized British Christian, who was looked down upon by British aristocrats. His belief was that Jewish blood was superior to British "blood." His ancestors wrote the Bible and built great temples in Jerusalem while the British were painted blue and naked, living in swamps or like monkeys, dwelling in the trees.

However, Nazism was different from racism in the United States or England. It was not just what Goldhagen calls "narcissistic self-exultation"; it was not rooted in culture but came from some far-off mystical place. It tried to waken some hitherto non-existent race consciousness. It was contrived and manufactured by pseudo-intellectuals. It had be taught and inculcated. It was not merely an assertion of superiority as in America or England, but a "program for action," a call for biological eugenics, a form of racial engineering.

In essence, there were two Nazi racial theories: one, most Germans were superior to others. I may be a janitor, a German would say, but I am superior to a Jew. This was the general form of racial superiority. Two, there was a more esoteric form wherein not all Germans were superior but only those with Nordic blood (tall, symmetrical, blond, blue-eyed). Thus, certain Swedes, Danes, and Dutch were Nordic while some Germans were inferior to true Nordic-looking types. Only Nordics, not just any German, were admitted into the SS. Color hair had to be approved. No darkness, only shades of blonde. Eye color had to be approved; even spouses.

But what about Nazi leaders? Goldhagen relates a popular underground joke in Germany: Who is a true Nordic? One who is as "blond" as Hitler: as "tall" as Goebbels; and as "lean" as Goering.

Yet, in the pseudo-scientific world of the Nazis, there was a hierarchy of races and racial types and the were as follows:

> Nordic (the ideal type)
> Westich (tall, straight, blondish)
> Ostich (round but blond)
> Slavs
> Mongols and Asians
> Blacks
> Animals
> [Jews]

Nordic aryans were at the highest levels and they need not have been Germans. The Nazis combed Europe looking for blond, blue-eyed, slim, symmetrical "aryans" among the Slavs, Swedes, Dutch, and other European countries. "Westich" and "Ostich" are pseudo races, and lower levels of Aryan raceology. Even Germans themselves could have been lower than other ethnic groups racially if they did not look "aryan." One could ask how Nazi propagandists put the spin on questions from foreign press that asked how Hitler and other top Nazi leaders could be Aryan when they were dark-haired and swarthy and crippled (like Goebbels) and overweight (like Goering). The answer: they were Aryans "in their heart."

Slavs came next in the hierarchy, to be used as slaves, worked to death, but not systematically annihilated. Mongols and Asians (including Japanese, their Axis allies) were next in line, and then came "Blacks"—Africans, Afro-Americans, and Caribbean blacks—with mulattos being of a higher ranking. Animals made up the lowest rung, one rung below blacks and yet higher than Jews.

Jews are not on the list of races technically because they were seen as a "counter-race"; they lie "outside" the usual racial categories, and thus, did not deserve to live at all. They were in a sense a "higher" race, but one so powerful and satanic, that they threatened all other races.

The goal was to maximize Nordic blood by eugenics. The Nazis stole children of Slavic and Polish people who looked Nordic and reared them in special SS homes as Germans. The goal was to "Nordify" Germany as much as possible, or in Goldhagen's poetic phrase, to "sieve" Europe and gather its "golden Nordic nuggets."

In 1936, during the Olympic Games in Berlin, an assistant to foreign minister Von Ribbentrop went further and was quoted: "Blacks are animals . . . they can't be in the Olympics. They shouldn't be allowed to race against humans." Germans were shocked when Jesse Owens won. Hitler walked out. He couldn't conceive that a Black could win against a Nordic.

An important Nazi doctrine was that there was no such thing as "humanity." There was in fact no such thing as a "human" race since that implied racial intermarriage and mixing and all such race mixing was dangerous and lead to decay. There were in Nazi eyes such enormous differences between the races that no *one* single human race could emerge.

Second Commandment: Reject Christianity

While it was not possible to be a Nazi and a total atheist, still, the Nazis were profoundly anti-Christian. Hitler purposely deceived Christians about his "positive" Christianity. Privately, Hitler was cynical about Christianity. He did not trust Christians. After the war, he planned to destroy them all. Many Christians fell for it and supported Hitler, not knowing he was the greatest enemy Christianity ever had. Nazism was far more dangerous to Christianity than Communism. He fooled the Christians just as he fooled the socialists and the workers.

To Hitler, Christianity was a mistake; people were not equal. He rejected all meekness, humility, love of humanity, and equality. It was Himmler's dream to hang the Pope in St. Peter's Square upside-down in full tiara. Christianity was furthermore thought to be of Jewish origin. The Nazis hated St. Paul, calling him the "spiritual circumcizer of the world." To them, Christianity was simply a Jewish invention and a mask for Judaism itself.

The Nazis believed the whole of Christianity was a vast mistake and even a violation of nature, for nature was hard and only the fittest survived. Human equality was absurd; the virtues of peacefulness and meekness were enfeebling and humility and love were debilitating.

Third Commandment: Do Not Love Thy Neighbor Not of the Same Racial Stock

The Nazi regime determined who shall live and who shall die. Pity was a temptation to resist. Heydrich was the perfect Nordic—tall, blond, with great physical stamina. He was assassinated by British Intelligence agents. Hitler delivered the ovation at his funeral: "He was the greatest of Nazis; he had a heart of stone." The role model was to be ruthless, hard-heartedness. In fact, the name "Hartman" which means "tough guy," was very popular with the SS to name their boys.

Fourth Commandment: Preserve the Purity of Race

Racial mixture is original sin; violators will be punished with death. Sex is to be controlled by the state. He who sleeps with Jews pollute themselves. Before the war, you got a long prison term; during the war, you could be hanged. If an SS officer slept with a Jew, but not a black, he was sentenced to death. The SS was considered a "priestly" order. They were subjected to great rigors. Over 400 SS men were sentenced to death for all sorts of transgressions.

Fifth Commandment: Be Fruitful and Multiply

Sex was de-eroticized according to Goldhagen. It's chief function was for procreation, not recreation. Anything that stood in the way of demographic incubation was rejected. Abortion on Germans was a capital crime, but not for Poles or Jews. For them it was legal, even mandatory in most circumstances. Virginity, monogamy, homosexuality—all were dismissed. In the name of procreation, all laws and restrictions were set aside and all taboos relaxed. It was a curious anti-bourgeois conservatism.

In 1940, Himmler issued orders to SS troops: German women with husbands at the front must see to it that they bear children, even while husbands were away. Meaning: that SS officers should have sex with such wives. It was received with such incredulity that Hitler had to rescind the order.

Germans were fined if not married by age 25. Homosexuals were considered "effeminate," did not propagate the race. Lesbians were invisible to the Nazis because they were good incubators. A homosexual group tried to persuade Himmler that they had rights too. They were taken out and shot.

The SS were charlatans who tried to induce German women to have twins and to bear children after menopause. Much of Mengele's work on twins was based on this commandment.

Sixth Commandment: Do Not Always Follow Reason and Intelligence

Be anti-intellectual. Jews created intellectualism. Be wary of it. Rely on "racial intuition." Science was deprecated as "shulc" knowledge; a higher racial knowledge was better than "shule." Hitler was always suspicious of reason, science, intelligence, interestingly all "Jewish" contributions. Goebbels called Freud that "Jewish know-it-all." Nazis toyed with astrology, divination, theosophy, Steinerism, the occult. Both Himmler and Hitler employed astrologers, and Hitler's greatest military victories were, at the early stages, based on astrological signs. Nature is elevated to scientific medicine. Higher knowledge is acquired through racial ability. SS men and Nordic types had greater susceptibility to this higher knowledge.

Himmler had a recipe how to make sexual intercourse result in a boy—walk ten miles a day, drink no alcohol, do 30 pushups.

Hitler wanted to mandate boxing and javelin throwing in the schools and abolish Latin and Greek. He desired only housing with flat roofs to be built in Berlin.

To the Nazis, war was unavoidable, even desirable, munificent, invigorating, ennobling. Peace causes nations to become flabby. The Nazis elevated war and violence to a supreme maxim.

Their favorite slogans were: "When I hear the word culture, I reach for my gun." Our goal is "education for death." "We are intellectual beasts."

Nazi school books discussed killing with poison gas as an arithmetic problem: If it takes two kilos of poison gas to kill 2,000 people, how much would it take to kill a city of 200,000?

In summary, according to Goldhagen, the Nazis had an "erotic affair with death."

Seventh Commandment: Kill All Life Unworthy of Living

Change your sensitivities. Curb your inhibitions. Conquer all feelings of pity. The biologically inferior must be killed. Conscience, like circumcision, is unGerman. As Shakespeare says: "Conscience is a word that cowards use."

Example of a child of the SS thrown into a pool because it was born too dark. If it lives, it is worthy; if it dies, it is its fate. The baby was saved by its mother.

These ideas were radically opposed to Western culture. According to Goldhagen, it was actually easier to create a Fascist or a Nazi than to create a Christian or a Communist. (Thus, the influence of Milgram and Asch here.)

Eighth Commandment: Honor They Father & Mother Conditionally

Your first duty is to the State and to the Fuehrer. In essense the state has become your family. The gesellschaft of society and state has become your gemeinschaft. If your father or mother are disloyal, denounce them. It is a characteristic feature of totalitarian states when children are more feared than adults. Youth was the ideal. Young leaders like Speer and von Shirach were the norm.

Ninth Commandment: Be Firm in Thy Faith

Brave the laughter that will greet you. The world is off-course, try to set it on-course. The world is degenerate, we are alright; We Nazis are called upon to restore the racial purity of the world. We must cleanse the world of satanic Jews. We are not crazy. We have carte-blanche to make it right, almost a religious mission to make it right. Our goal is to produce a perfect world and a perfect race. People in the future will thank us for this thankless task but we must carry it through as onerous as it is. Nordic man must rule. Slavs are to be enslaved. Jews are to die. It was a form of Western messianic escatology in Goldhagen's eyes. Usually, political cults such as these pass harmlessly by but not this time.

All the Nazis did was to combine all these elements into a lethal program for action.

Conclusions

One of the great ironies of this brilliant man's "work" is that it is almost entirely "oral" and therefore inaccessible to most scholars. I hope I have made his work a bit more accessible. He wanted to write a book based on his Harvard lectures called "The Genocidal Mind" but writer's block stopped him.

Interestingly, his son Daniel Goldhagen wrote the book that his father *wanted to write* but couldn't. The father's analysis is much more nuanced, much more complex, and spends much more time on such social psychologists as Herbert Kelman, Philip Zimbardo, and Stanley Milgram, that is, on the "obedience-following--orders" thesis, a thesis that his son rejects. Does the father spend time on these subjects simply for pedagogical reasons, to present all sides in class, or does he truly believe in these men's theories? I think he believes them.

Thus, the son uses most of his book rejecting that part of the father's conclusions. The father also spends considerable time on the "inbred" anti-semitism of Germans—the part that the son was influenced by—but the father balances it with discussions of social-psychological theories.

So, who is right? Father or son? Is it one (anti-semitism) or the other (peer pressure/obedience) that makes men kill, or is it, as I believe—

both? (See my "two-step theory"—anti-semitism and then peer-group pressure, Porter, 1998 and my essay on Daniel Goldhagen called "The Goldhagen Controversy" in this book).

We are seeing an increased number of controversial genocide and Holocaust theories as we enter the second millennium. The case of Goldhagen, father and son, is one of these mysteries. The irony is that the son's controversy has overshadowed the father's brilliant contributions to sociology and Holocaust studies.

(2002)

Sources

Arendt, Hannah, *Eichmann in Jerusalem*. New York: Harcourt Brace, 1963.

Bauman, Zygmund, *The Holocaust and Modernity*. Ithaca, NY: Cornell University Press, 1988.

Finkelstein, Norman G. and Ruth Bettina Birn, *A Nation on Trial: The Goldhagen Thesis and Historical Truth*. New York: Henry Holt (An Owl Book), 1998.

Goldhagen, Daniel Jonah, *Hitler's Willing Executioners*. New York: Knopf, 1996.

Kelman, Herbert and V. Lee Hamilton, *Crimes of Obedience: Toward a Social Psychology of Authority and Responsibility*. New Haven, CT: Yale University Press, 1989.

Klee, Ernst, Willi Dressen, and Volker Riess (eds.), *"The Good Old Days": The Holocaust as Seen by its Perpetrators and Bystanders*. New York: The Free Press-Macmillan, 1991.

Littell, Franklin H., *Hyping the Holocaust: Scholars Answer Goldhagen*. Merion Station, PA: Merion Westfield Press International, 1997.

Milgram, Stanley, *Obedience to Authority*. New York: Harper and Row, 1974.

Porter, Jack Nusan, "Impaired Memories/Distorted History," *Genocide Studies Newsletter* (McQuarie University, Australia). Vol. 4, No. 1, September-October, 1997, pp. 5-8.

———, "Genocide is a New Word for an Old Crime: Toward a Social Scientific Study of the Holocaust and Other International Crimes," the introduction to *The Sociology of Genocide/the Holocaust*, with Steve Hoffman, Washington, DC: American Sociological Association, 1998.

———, "Holocaust Controversies: A Point of View," in Israel W. Charny (ed), *Encyclopedia of Genocide*. Santa Barbara, CA: ABC-Clio, 1999, pp. 307-311.

Rubenstein, Richard, *The Cunning of History*. New York: Harper and Row, 1978.

Weiss, John, *The Ideology of Death*. Chicago, IL: Ivan R. Dee, Inc., 1996.

Bibliography of Erich Goldhagen's Work

Note: Prof. Goldhagen's opus is quite small. There are only four items of his listed in Widener Library and cognate libraries in the Harvard University system and only a few articles in such journals as *Midstream*, a Zionist magazine published in New York City, *Patterns of Prejudice* (a British journal based in London), and in various European scholarly journals. Several of his essays can be found in the *Sourcebook* mentioned below.

Goldhagen, Erich (ed), *Ethnic Minorities in the Soviet Union*. New York: Praeger, 1968. Published for the Institute of East European Jewish Studies of the Philip W. Lown School of Near Eastern and Judaic Studies at Brandeis University. Essays were first read at a symposium held in the fall of 1965 at the above institute. Includes bibliographies, xiv, 351 pp., 22 cm. Hollis Number 001269023. Book is located in Gutman, Lamont, Russian Research Center, Social Relations-Sociology Department, and Widener libraries at Harvard University.

———, *General Education 136 Sourcebook: Explaining the Holocaust and the Phenomenon of Genocide*. Cambridge, MA: Harvard University, Pusey Library, Stack No. 2, 269 pp. 28 cm. Widener LC HV632.7 .G44, 1988. A sourcebook of readings used by Goldhagen in his Harvard course on the Holocaust. Several of his essays, "Nazi Sexual Demonology," "Obsession and Realpolitik in the Final Solution," and "Albert Speer, Himmler, and the Secrecy of the Final Solution" can be found in this book.

———, *The Mind and Spirit of East European Jewry During the Holocaust*. sound recording, 1978. Introduction by Krister Stendahl, Widener Library, Harvard depository, 3 sound cassettes. JDSC 4 {Consult Judaica Division}.

———, *The Mind and Spirit of East European Jewry During the Holocaust* (pamphlet). Cambridge, MA: Widener Library, Judaica Division, 1979. Introduction by Krister Stendahl. The Beiner-Citrin Memorial Lecture, delivered November 21, 1978. Harvard Archive. HUC 5201.78. Hollis Number 009138127.

———, "Albert Speer, Himmler, and the Secrecy of the final Solution," *Midstream: A Monthly Jewish Review*. Vol. XVII, No. 8, October 1971.

"Erich Goldhagen: 25-Year Honorand," *The Harvard Lamplighter: The Harvard University Extension School Newsletter*. Fall, 1996. A profile of Goldhagen when he was honored for 25 years of service to the school. Contains several interesting anecdotes about students at Harvard and about teaching a course on the Holocaust at Harvard.

———, "More Than Enduring," *Alumni Bulletin*. Harvard Extension School, 1997. Goldhagen shares his views on teaching at Harvard "The Holocaust and the Phenomenon of Genocide" and "Modern Political and Social Ideologies" at a dinner banquet in his honor. His insights into the differences between adult learners in the evening division Extension School and the more youthful and inexperienced Harvard undergraduates are quite interesting as are his anecdotes of their diverse political philosophies.

Part III

Social and Sexual Deviance

Chapter 8

Genocide of Homosexuals in the Nazi Era

"The pink triangles died like flies in a few weeks. There was never any society of homosexuals in the camps, or a society of gays in the camps. They were never organized like the politicals or some of the other groups. They were isolated. They died quickly. They were starved to death or worked to death. There was no big deal made about them. They entered as pink triangles and they died. Where there was homosexuality in which there was some pleasure were the guards, the soldiers, the Ukrainians, the Estonians, Roumanians and Hungarian SS, even the Germans. Yes, there was homosexuality among the guards. They were the 'real' homosexuals.

"They used little children. They kept the little boys in cages. Later they killed them like chickens when they were finished using them. Yes, there was a lot of homosexuality but not many homosexuals. Maybe I was an ugly little kid and that's why they didn't choose me. I wish they had chosen me to be their homosexual because then I could have gotten food and I would have survived."

—Interview with a Jewish survivor of ten Nazi camps including Auschwitz, Dachau, Budzin, Krasnik, Radom, Nikaresulm, and Grossazanheim
December 17, 1988, Massachusetts

I.

Research on homosexuality and sexual rights gained momentum after a memorable international conference on genocide and the Holocaust held in Oxford and London, England in July 1988. Some of the most eminent authorities on genocide and the victims of genocide were there, including Yehuda Bauer, Frank Chalk, Kurt Jonassohn, Gabrielle Tyrnauer, and Vahakn Dadrian. I was happy to have been part of that panel and to have discussed those who wore pink triangles as forgotten victims of the Holocaust.

There were many kinds of victims in the Nazi camps. Different groups wore different triangles, and different triangles denoted different "crimes." Jews wore yellow stars but also red triangles—political triangles. One of the biggest groups consisted of Germans who were made to wear black triangles, meaning saboteurs. Green triangles were worn by murderers. There were other triangles or strips for Jehovah Witnesses, vagrants, emigrants, gypsies, special markings for Jews, inmates of punishment battalions, "race defiler" (male), race defiler (female), escape suspects, special inmates, repeaters (those who were incarcerated more than once), and members of armed forces. A bewildering array of stigmatization.

Because of language barriers (knowledge of German, Polish, Yiddish is needed) and access to archives, holocaust research in general is difficult, but for research on homosexuals the problems multiply. First, the data that exist are often unreliable, and primary data are scant and inadequate. Many records were lost or destroyed. Complete reports are hard to find.

Even after the war, "homosexual" was still a dirty word; Paragraph 175 and 175a of the 1935 Nazi revision of the ancient German law proscribing homosexual acts remained in force until June 1969, when much of Paragraph 175 and all of 175a were abolished. Gay men (and women) were thus stigmatized for many years after the war. Unlike Jews and other victims, they could not receive *wiedergutmachung* (restitution) payments, since West German courts decreed that gays had been criminals under the Nazis and thus not eligible for such payments.

Furthermore, under the Nuremberg Laws in which genocide was defined after the war, the killing of homosexuals was not considered a crime against humanity or a war crime. In addition, gay men and women who wished to emigrate from Europe after World War II had to keep their sexual identity secret because many nations, including the United

States, enforced laws that forbade homosexuals from immigrating or even visiting those countries. Gays who fled Germany after the war feared that their new citizenship would be jeopardized if their homosexuality was discovered. (Nearly all gays who were killed or persecuted were German or Austrian citizens). Finally, employers and neighbors might shun someone who was openly gay. For all these reasons, it was very difficult to find and interview gay survivors of the Holocaust. Prof. Rudiger Lautmann of the University of Bremen was one of the very few sociologists to have done so, and there is a publisher in Milwaukee, Wisconsin (of the gay newspaper *Wisconsin Lights*) who says he has tapes of 25 such interviews but he has not made them available, and there is a serious question about their very existence. In short, there are very few gay respondents to interview.

Scholars, too, have been homophobic on the subject, either overlooking homosexuals or simply dismissing them. Prof. Steven Katz of Boston University does not think that the gay genocide should even be called a genocide. Persecution, yes, but not with the intention for genocide. Lucy Dawidowicz and Raul Hilberg, major Holocaust scholars, put gays into the same category as criminals, perverts, and deviants.

It is a difficult question to answer. On a political level, I would call it a genocide, but if pressed as a scholar with a duty for precise definitions, I would have to admit that this was not a genocide for several reasons. First, the killings were only limited to gays in Germany and Austria. Also, very few lesbians were effected. Secondly, anyone who could conceal his sexual identity or remain celibate was spared. Thirdly and most importantly, there was no intention on the part of Himmler to kill every homosexual in Europe.

Gay men could be "reeducated" or at worst castrated. Castration is painful but people can live a long life in that condition. For Himmler, who was the central figure to any policy, homosexuality was a pathology, not an immutable biological fact. At the very least, gay men could escape criminal prosecution and death if they agreed to abandon their sexual practices and remain celibate.

Work them until they dropped, yes. But as for a planned, systematic genocide, I have reluctantly come to the conclusion that there was none. They were, however, victims of the Third Reich and therefore belong in any holocaust museum. Still, I would conclude that gays were victims of a genocidal mentality.

Most references on the Nazi era however omit any mention of homosexuals or treat the subject superficially, usually in connection with the homosexual tendencies of Hitler or certain SA leaders murdered under Hitler's order. Thus, because research builds upon prior research, there are almost no well-traveled roads in this field until this past decade when we have seen a profusion of books from Germany.

The persecution of homosexuals during the Third Reich has emerged out of the shadows only during the past few years. Several books and monographs, an Italian movie *One Day* (with Sophia Loren and Marcello Mastroianni) about two people left by themselves, the rest went to hear Mussolini speak—she, an abused wife; he, an aging homosexual); a Broadway play and some say a future movie (Bent) about a homosexual caught in the Nazi dragnet and sent to a concentration camp; and the revival of *Cabaret*, based on the Berlin stories of Christopher Isherwood. The new Holocaust Museum in Washington, DC has not overlooked the gay persecution and even had a consultant on gay issues (Claus Muller) on the staff of the Holocaust Research Institute affiliated with the museum.

This forgotten "genocide," some have called it a "homocaust,"can now come out of the closet, so to speak, not only historically but also sociologically. Thanks must go to Professor Rudiger Lautmann of the University of Bremen and his colleagues for leading the way. Other people supportive of this research over the years include Vern Bullough, Erwin Haeberle, James Steakley, Erich Goldhagen, Richard Rubenstein, Israel Charny, Bill Percy, George Mosse, Gunter Grau, Claus Muller, and Richard Plant.

Some of the files in Germany have been closed to the public since Prof. Lautmann did his research, but he is revising and bringing out material, and many new books have emerged in the past decade dealing with this "genocide."

II.

In the 1930s there began in Germany a persecution of male homosexuals that was like that of Jews, the worst in their respective history. Lesbians, since they could continue to breed children, presented no practical reproductive problems to the Nazi state. There were only two or three lesbians arrested by the Germans over the period 1933-1945. The modern plague of AIDS heightens interest in this "gay genocide." In fact, AIDS would have fitted in beautifully with the distorted Nazi ideology that homosexuals were a "contragenic" group, to use Richard Plant's term, or "sexual vagrants," to use Heinrich Himmler's term, the "Grand Inquisitor" himself.

The Nazis' murder of homosexuals started earlier than that of the Jews. Ernst Roehm was a major Nazi leader, second only to Hitler as they rose to power in the 20s and early 30s. However, Roehm and his top cadre of "brownshirts" in this paramilitary group known as the SA were homosexuals. This was not a problem at the beginning for Hitler; only later did it prove an embarrassment and a threat. Ernst Roehm and other SA leaders were murdered without warning in a famous blood purge that began on June 30, 1934 and called the "Night of Long Knives." This purge was led by Himmler and other SS officers at the instigation of Hitler. The first Nazi pogrom against the Jews, on the other hand, was the Kristallnacht of November 9-10, 1938, and the actual industrial extermination of the Jews did not begin until the summer of 1941.

While hundreds of books and articles have been written on the Jewish genocide, the "gay genocide" has been either a taboo subject too delicate to touch upon or a topic too often obscured by other issues or simply omitted. Books on the subject include well-researched books put out by obscure publishers—for example, John Lauritsen and David Thorstad, *The Early Homosexual Rights Movement: 1864-1935* (New York: Times Change Press, 1974); Heinz Heger, *The Men with the Pink Triangle* (Boston: Alyson Publications, 1980); and works by the Gay Men's Press of London—and more widely circulated, flamboyantly written books with less regard for historical accuracy or good taste (but still fun to read) and published by large, well-known publishers—for example, Frank Rector, *The Nazi Extermination of Homosexuals* (New York: Stein & Day, 1981), Martin Sherman, *Bent* (based on the Heinz Heger book above), New York: Avon Books, a Bard Book, 1979); and Adriaan Venema, *The Persecution of Homosexual by the Nazis* (Los Angeles: Urania Manuscripts, 1979). There are, of course, the leather S & M Nazi books, pornography, and erotica that pass for literature, art, or even scholarship. (See, for example, movies like Luchino Visconti's *The Damned* and Antonini's *The Night Porter*.)

However, excellent books have appeared with Richard Plant, *The Pink Triangle: The Nazi War Against Homosexuals* (New York: Henry Holt, 1986) one of the most outstanding. It is clearly and eloquently written. Plant, a survivor of the Holocaust and a teacher at the New

School for Social Research in New York City, has written the best book on the subject, which stands with some of the best literature on the Holocaust. Many books needed to be translated from the German. Those begging for translation are Burkhard Jellonnek's *Homosexuelle unterm Hakenkreuz* (1990), Hans-George Stumke and Rudi Finkler's *Rosa Winkel, Rosa Listen* (1981), Claudia Schoppmann's *Nationalsozialistische Sexualpolitik and Weibliche Homosexualitat* (1991), and the works of Gunter Grau, a German sociologist from Berlin.

III.

Controversy surrounds every aspect of this genocide, even the label "genocide." Since gays could "pass" (unlike Jews or Gypsies), most survived the war. If they remained celibate or "in the closet," they could elude the Nazis and survive. Because they were difficult to detect, a considerable number were never rounded up. Thus, there are strong arguments (see Katz, 1995) not to call this a genocide.

On the other hand, there are strong opposing arguments: first, the stigmatization of homosexuals as "vermin," "plague," "cancerous ulcer," and "a tumor" is racist and genocidal. Under Himmler's direction, the ferocity of the attack gained momentum and sought to destroy or sterilize every homosexual the Nazis could find. By the United Nations definition, these acts of sterilization fall under the category of limiting births, thus genocide. It is not an easy decision but I adopt a non-genocide label, though it could fall under the rubric of *genocidal acts*.

Estimates of the number run from Lautmann's lowest conservative figures of 10,000 total interned to Jean Boisson's one million dead. Consoli's summary of estimates of the number of homosexual victims reflects the lack of precise data. He quotes sources that range from 5,000 gays killed under Hitler to 50,000 to 200,000 to 500,000. Stumke and Finkler show that for the years 1937-1939, about 95,000 homosexuals were arrested. Of those, only 33,000 (one-third) were even processed by the police; and out of them about 25,000 were sentenced by the courts. For the years 1941-1944, the most reliable estimate is about 12,000 homosexual men sentenced. Overall, we can reasonably estimate the number of males convicted of homosexuality from 1933-1944 at between 50,000 to 63,000, of which 4,000 were juveniles. (Also, recorded were the arrests of six lesbians, unusual since consensual sex between women was not against German law).

The number of homosexuals incarcerated in the Nazi concentration camps is also not known, much less the number who died there. Lautmann, whose figures are used by Plant and other writers, estimates that

> somewhere between 5,000 to 15,000 homosexuals perished behind the barbed-wire fences. These were victims who were labeled and processed as homosexuals. We will never know all the unknown homosexuals who died as Jews, Gypsies, Russians, Poles, or German/Austrian political prisoners. This figure of about 10,000 homosexuals is the one accepted by most German and American scholars as the highest death count.

Figures are thrown about wildly—for example in the play *Bent*—as if to say that the greater the numbers, the more tragic the event. Scholars such as Raul Hilberg, Steven Katz, and Yehudah Bauer, reject the category of genocide placed on homosexuals precisely because of problems with the numbers, the fact that the numbers are miniscule compared to six million Jews and half-million Gypsies, and because of lack of intent to commit this genocide.

Gay leaders and writers insist on the higher figures in order to legitimate their claim of special pleading. Why are 10,000 killed less tragic than one million? In the aftermath of the Holocaust, numbers themselves seem to lose their significance. In any case, the major Holocaust institution in the USA the US Holocaust Memorial Museum, recognizes the "gay genocide" and so do all of its research staff.

IV.

There are many other controversies that make this topic so fascinating, mixing as it does sex and politics, titillating erotica, and bloody violence. One question arises concerning the sexual politics of the Third Reich. Was Hitler homophobic? Were the Nazis homosexuals? Why did they kill gays if they in fact *were* gay? Or, were they gay or simply pragmatic and ruthless political leaders? It is historically clear that Rohm and the SA were decimated not *only* because they were gay but because they posed a military and political threat to Hitler.

According to Hans Peter Bleuel (*Sex and Society in Nazi Germany*, 1973, p. 100):

> ... Hitler had (Roehm) killed because he was an obstacle to his compromise with the Reichswehr, which he needed if he were to assume the Presidency after Hindenburg's imminent demise. Himmler and Goering staged the Roehm Putsch, as the bloodbath of 30 June became known, in order to destroy a powerful rival, eliminate numerous conservative opponents, and settle a long tally of old scores.

There were powerful conflicts within the Third Reich. After Hitler came to power, the Wehrmacht made him aware that the SA posed a threat to them, the regular army. In truth, Hitler no longer needed the SA. For external forces he had a professional military; for internal force, a disciplined police corps (the SS) that questioned none of his policies. Roehm and his cronies, their homosexual antics, and their politics of continuous national socialist revolution embarassed and threatened Hitler.

Furthermore, the palace intrigues of the SS under Heinrich Himmler and that of Hermann Goering to gain an upper hand proved successful with the "Night of the Long Knives," the Roehm Putsch of June 30, 1934. One ultra-reactionary publisher and long-time promoter of Hitler sent a letter complaining that Roehm was damaging the Nazi Party's reputation from every angle. The Fuhrer should prevail on him to resign quietly because Roehm was filling senior posts in the SA and SS according to his personal inclinations (homosexuality). "The fish stinks from the head downwards" the letter concluded.

The stench did not worry the Party leader. He needed his able mercenary commander (Roehm) and could not afford to imperil the efficiency of his smoothly functioning private army because of moral scruples. Even when he became Reich Chancellor, Hitler worried more about rival claims to authority on the part of his chief of staff, now Reich Minister Roehm, who was always sounding off about the "second evolution," than by the moral stench that emanated from him. A political strong-man in command of a 500,000-strong army which even the Reichswehr (Wehrmacht) had reason to fear, Roehm drafted an order of the day designed to show these "civilian swine" once and for all.

Hitler, ever the pragmatist, knew that the SA threatened the conservative circles of Franz von Papen, the Prussian aristocracy, the Wehrmacht, and military-industrial elite, all of whom were worried about this so-called "people's army." In such an atmosphere, Roehm and his homosexual lieutenants—SS-Gruppenfuhrer Edmund Heines and Gauleiter and Oberprasident Bruckner—all had to go in the interests of national security and "pure blood." One question that often arises is what was Hitler's attitude toward gays?

Did Hitler despise homosexuals? Was he ashamed of his own homosexual or asexual identity? These are areas of psycho-history that are beyond the scope of this essay. My own feelings are that Hitler was asexual in the traditional sense but had bizarre sexual requirements. He enjoyed women urinating and defecating on him. He had other fetishes perhaps with women's clothing. All these things were of course kept highly secret from the German people. They never knew the secret deviant perversions of their Fuehrer and his cohorts. See essay on Hitler in this book. But was he homophobic or simply politically pragmatic? Again Hans Peter Bleuel summarizes the issue best:

> Hitler's misgivings about homosexuality stemmed primarily from self-interest. His objection to it as a vice or symptom of effeminacy was only secondary. The main danger, as he saw it, was that it would infiltrate the political leadership and constitute itself a secret Order of the Third Sex. He was also concerned at the thought that population growth might be curbed by the heterosexual abstinence of those affected. It is noteworthy and indicative of his wholly amoral outlook that Hitler by no means regarded the homosexual proclivity as "genetically bad" by definition.

On the day Himmler arrested Roehm in the town of Wiesse, and even before the latter's murder, he issued Viktor Lutze, the new chief of staff, with a new order of the day containing twelve demands addressed to the SA:

> I expect all SA leaders to help to preserve and strengthen the SA in its capacity as a pure and cleanly institution. In particular I should like every mother to be able to allow her son to join the SA, Party, and Hitler Youth without fear that he may become morally corrupted in their ranks. I therefore require all SA commanders to take the utmost pains to ensure that offenses under Paragraph 175 are met by immediate expulsion of the culprit from the SA and Party. I want to see men as SA commanders, not ludicrous monkeys. (Quoted in Bleuel, p. 219)

With this pronouncement, homosexuals were finally declared open game. Roehm spent happy days and nights in his beloved Berlin, sampling the delights of the Kleist-Kasino, the Silhouette, and the Turkish baths. He also held boisterous banquets and orgies at his headquarters. "Chief of Staff Ernst Roehm requests the pleasure of the company of Brigadefueher Adolf Kob to a Punch Evening on Thursday, 17 May, at 9 p.m."

Six weeks later, Roehm was dead.

V.

A significant homosexual and sexual rights movement had existed in Germany since the 1890s, supported strongly by the Social Democratic and, later, Communist parties. Led by the renowned sexual reformer Dr. Magnus Hirschfeld, Director of the Berlin Institute of Sexology, this movement had worked for the abolition of Paragraph 175 of the German Criminal Code, a sodomy statute adopted in 1871 when the German Empire (the "Second Reich") was created under Bismarck. This movement was allied with a growing feminist movement in Germany and various left-wing causes.

Hirschfeld himself was a Jew, an anti-militarist, a pacifist, and socialist, and a homosexual. A petition drawn up by Hirschfeld's Scientific Humanitarian Committee was signed by thousands of German writers and intellectuals including Albert Einstein, Thomas Mann and Martin Buber. In the 1920s, during the Weimar Republic, prospects for reform looked excellent. However, in 1928, when letters were sent to German political parties asking for their position on reform, the Nazis' reply was as follows:

Munich, May 14, 1928

Community before Individual:

It is not necessary that you and I live, but it is necessary that the German people live. And they can live only if they can fight, for life means fighting. And they can fight only if they maintain their masculinity. They can only maintain their masculinity if they exercise discipline, especially in matters of love. . . Anyone who even thinks of homosexual love is our enemy. We reject anything which emasculates our people and makes them a plaything for our enemies, for we know that life is a fight, and it is madness to think that men will ever embrace fraternally. Natural history teaches us the opposite. Might makes right. And the stronger always win over the weak. Let's see to it that we once again become strong! . . .

In 1929, a Reichstag committee voted by a close margin of 15 to 13 to introduce a penal reform bill that would decriminalize private homosexual acts. The crisis provided by the 1929 stock market crash caused the bill to be shelved, however, just when successful reform appeared imminent.

The anti-homosexual nature of Nazism became evident in 1933, along with its anti-Semitism, when the Nazis vandalized and closed Hirschfeld's Institute. Hirschfeld himself watched the burning of his library on newsreels at a movie theater in France. He had left Germany in 1930 for a trip around the world; he never returned. Hirschfeld represented everything that the Nazis despised; his humanitarianism was the antithesis of everything for which they stood. He died in Nice, France, on May 14, 1935, at age 67.

VI.

The Nazi purge of homosexuals from their own ranks was only the beginning. On June 23, 1935, the first anniversary of the Roehm killings, the Nazis began a legal campaign against homosexuals by adding to paragraph 175 another law, 175a, which created ten new criminal offenses including kisses between men, embraces, even homosexual fantasies. Arrests jumped from 800 in 1933 to over 8,000 in 1937 and 1938 and then tapered off to just 2,000 in 1943 and 1944. More importantly, the Gestapo and the SS, under the notoriously anti-homosexual leadership of Heinrich Himmler, became involved in a stepped-up campaign to work gays to death in the camps. Himmler is quoted as follows:

> Just as we today have gone back to the ancient Germanic view of the question of marriage mixing different races, so too in our judgment of homosexuality—a symptom of degeneracy that could destroy our race— we must return to the guiding Nordic principle: extermination of degenerates.

Reich Legal Director Hans Frank commented as follows on the new penal code:

> Particular attention should be addressed to homosexuality, which is clearly expressive of a disposition opposed to the normal national community. Homosexual activity means the negation of the community as it must be constituted if the race is not to perish. That is why homosexual behavior, in particular, merits no mercy. (quoted from tk in Bleuel, p. 217)

The high flown language concealed a simple piece of arithmetic. In terms of population policy, homosexuals were considered "zeros." They negated the community by failing in their duty of racial preservation, in other words, by producing no children—and that, in a Third Reich hungry for population and obsessed with the birth rate, was an unpardonable crime. Yet, women were not part of the formula.

> The homosexually inclined male was stylized into the prototype of sexual abnormality. It is significant that the homosexually inclined female seldom figured in pronouncements by National Specialist guardians of morality. What mattered to them was man, the warrior and begetter of children. In the blinkered view of these reactionary sexual theorists, woman, being subordinate to man, could not decline her role as a preserver of the species. Being equipped for motherhood by nature, even a Lesbian could and must bear children at the behest of her spouse. Lesbianism presented no practical reproductive problems of any consequence, and these alone were what counted.

> The fanatical denigration of male homosexuals worked all the better because it was used to mobilize ingrained bourgeois hatred, not only of 'the others' but also of one's own kind. (Bleuel, p. 217).

VI.

The Nazi persecution of gays cut short two other phenomena: the homosexual-rights movement led by Dr. Hirschfeld and the sexual research movement, which was led largely by Jews. Thus, to be Jewish, sexually tolerant and liberal was to be *ipso facto* an enemy of Nazism. Sexual freedom, religious freedom, and intellectual freedom, including the freedom to pursue sexual research go hand in hand in a democratic society; conversely a fascist state has little room for these freedoms.

The museum in Washington, DC is torn between the "exclusionists" and the "universalists." Jewish "exclusionists" often seek to ignore the fate of the homosexuals. They argue that the Holocaust was unique to Jews. They do not wish to share historical memory with other victims. Others oppose sharing on the grounds that some of these minorities acted as informers, collaborators, and guards, or even murdered Jews—venting their frustrations and prejudice against them in anti-Semitism. For example, Yad Vashem in Israel has nothing on the homosexuals publicly.

"Universalists" on the other hand, agree to share the sacred memory of this devastating experience in which two-thirds of the Jews in Europe died and in which Jews so clearly predominated numerically with all the people who were murdered. They respectfully commemorate homosexuals as well as Gypsies, Jehovah's Witnesses, the disabled, POWs (mostly Russians and Poles), and anti-Nazi political prisoners from many nations, including Polish and Ukrainian citizens. The Holocaust *was* unique and the Jews were unique victims, but the other victims must also be honored and given a place of respect as well. The "universalists" seem to have won the day, at least for now.

(1996)

References

Porter, Jack Nusan (1998), *Sexual Politics in Nazi Germany*. Newton, MA: The Spencer Press.

Porter, Jack Nusan (1998), *The Sociology of Genocide*. Washington, DC: American Sociological Association.

See also references cited in essay.

Sources on Homosexuality and Nazism
Conference Proceedings, Institute Reports, Journals, Films

World League for Sexual Reform (Congress Proceedings): Berlin 1921. Copenhagen 1928; London 1929: and Vienna 1930; Founded in 1921.
International Congress for Sexual Reform Proceedings.
The Scientific-Humanitarian Committee (founded in 1897 by Magnus Hirschfeld and lasting for 35 years until 1932). It published a yearbook, *Jahrbuch fur Sexuelle Zwischenstufen* which appeared more or less regularly both as a yearly and a quarterly from 1909 to 1923. Also published were the *Quarterly Reports* of the Committee plus pamphlets and books; for example, a book about homosexuality called *What People Should Know About the Third Sex* (1903). An abridged version appeared in 1923 called *The Problem of Sexual Inversion*. A movie was also made on the subject but has never been found.
Institute of Sexology (1919); all its archives were destroyed by the Nazis.
Magnus Hirschfeld Foundation for Sexual Research (1918).
See also obituaries in the *New York Herald Tribune* and *New York Times* after his death, May 14, 1935. The "Hirschfeld Scrapbook," a collection of handbills, minutes of meetings, posters, and documents can be found at the Kinsey Institute for Research in Sex, Gender, and Reproduction, Indiana University, Bloomington, Indiana.
Several films should also be noted, some historical such as *Anders al die Andern* [Different from the Others], made during Weimar Germany and "starring" Dr. Hirschfeld, and modern documentaries such as *Pink Triangles: A Film About Prejudice Against Lesbians and Gay Men*, made by Cambridge Documentary Films of Massachusetts (P.O. Box 385, Cambridge, MA 02139) in the 1980's. Also available in videocassette with study guide.
Films inspired by Magnus Hirschfeld's work: *M*, by Fritz Lang, 1933.
Anders als die Andern [Different from the Others], 1919. Magnus Hirschfeld has a small role in this film.
Sexuelle Zwischenstufen [Sexual Intermediaries], UFA and the Institute for Sexual Science, Berlin, 1922.
Mann oder Weib [Man or Woman], 1923.
Gesetze der Liebe [The Laws of Love], Humboldt Films, 1924.
Das Recht auf Lieb [The Right of Love], Hegewald Film, 1924.

Geheimnisse einer Seele [Secrets of a Soul], by G. Pabst and H. Casparius [shown publicly], 1925.
Pandora's Box, by G. Pabst, Berlin, 1929.

Text of Paragraph 175

Text of Paragraph 175, with amendments as issued on January 28, 1935.

175:

1. A male who indulges in criminally indecent activities with another male or who allows himself to participate in such activities will be punished with jail.
2. If one of the participants is under the age of twenty-one, and if the crime has not been grave, the court may dispense with the jail sentence.

175(a): A jail sentence of up to ten years or, if mitigating circumstances can be established, a jail sentence of no less then three years will be imposed on

1. any male who by force or by threat of violence and danger to life and limb compels another man to indulge in criminally indecent activities, or allows himself to participate in such activities;
2. any male who forces another male to indulge with him in criminally indecent activities by using the subordinate position of the other man, whether it be at work or elsewhere, or who allows himself to participate in such activities;
3. any male who indulges professionally and for profit in criminally indecent activities with other males, or allows himself to be used for such activities or who offers himself for same.

175(b): Criminally indecent activities by males with animals are to be punished by jail; in addition, the court may deprive the subject of his civil rights.

Source: Richard Plant, *The Pink Triangle.* New York: Holt, 1986, p. 206.

MARKINGS OF CAMP INMATES IN THE CONCENTRATION CAMPS

Form and Color of Markings

	POLITICAL	HABITUAL CRIMINALS	EMIGRANTS	JEHOVAH'S WITNESSES	HOMO-SEXUALS	VAGRANTS
Basic Colors	▼	▼	▼	▼	▼	▼
Markings for Repeaters	▬ ▼	▬ ▼	▬ ▼	▬ ▼	▬ ▼	▬ ▼
Inmates of Penal Battalions	▼ ●	▼ ●	▼ ●	▼ ●	▼ ●	▼ ●
Markings for Jews	✡	✡	✡	✡	✡	✡
Special Markings	△ Race Defiler Male	△ Race Defiler Female	● Escape Suspect	2307 Number of Inmate	NUMBER OF INMATE [2307] REPEATER ▬ JEW-POLITICAL ▼ MEMBER OF PENAL BATTALION ● ESCAPE SUSPECT	
	▼ Pole	▼ Czech	▲ Members of Armed Forces	⬤ Special Inmate		

Chapter 9

Hitler: Sixteen Theories in Search of an Explanation

Introduction

The genesis of this essay began as a lecture in my course at the University of Massachusetts in Lowell on the Holocaust and comparative genocide. I was intrigued by an article by Ron Rosenbaum (1995) that appeared in *The New Yorker* on how difficult it was to explain the mind of Hitler and what had emerged were a series of "myths." Who was the real Hitler? What follows is an outlining of Rosenbaum's theses and a few at the end that I have added. The first eleven theories are from Rosenbaum; the last five are my own. I have also been very influenced by Professor Erich Goldhagen in the course on the Holocaust and the phenomenon of genocide that he taught at Harvard University in the fall of 1994. According to Prof. Goldhagen, the sources of the Holocaust lie in the private reaches of Hitler's mind, in the form of his idiosyncratic traits, his private neuroses, his collected wounds.

A number of historians, such as Hans Mommsen and David Irving, hold that Hitler alone is responsible for the Holocaust; in that it was the psychic pain and pathology of one man, and one man alone, who caused millions to die and countless others to suffer. One way to look at him would be through "Psychohistory," which is humorously, either the "history of psychos" or history based on psychoanalytic theory. Why psychoanalysis had a heyday with Hitler, most historians are speechless regarding Hitler. They find him hard to explain. Psychohistory itself is useful but we can never fully fathom Hitler's motives or for that matter any other cruel act. There will always remain something deeply unexplainable about Hitler.

The source of Hitler's hatred of the Jews was his own private psychosis. He was, as they say in Yiddish, "meshugeh"—"crazy" yet supremely intelligent and clever and manipulative. Even Hitler's own generals knew he was mad but were powerless to stop him. How indeed does one control a madman?

Rosenbaum (1995: 50) quotes from two of the most influential historians of the period: the late Hugh Trevor-Roper, known as Lord Dacre, maintains that "his character remains elusive"; and Lord Bullock, Alan Bullock, the Oxford historian and main rival to Trevor-Roper in postwar Hitler-explanatory theory, sums up his frustration after a lifetime of study: "The more I learn about Adolf Hitler, the harder I find it to explain."

And the French intellectual and film maker Claude Lanzmann concludes that "to understand Hitler is obscene," meaning that to understand is to forgive or to at least sympathize, and that is impossible.

1. The Genital Wound Theory

This is the story of the infamous billy-goat bite. Sometime in mid-1943, an obscure Army private names Eugen Wasner was arrested and faced a special court-martial and the guillotine. While the formal charge against Wasner was "maliciously slandering the Fuhrer," the actual crime for which he faced beheading was his embarrassing explanation of Hitler. Private Wasner's account was a variant of what Rosenbaum calls the genital-wound school of Hitler interpretation. It also ties in with the "one ball" or "maimed scrotum" theory that was reveled in song during the war and which alleged produced an asexual or sexually perverted individual. The story goes as follows:

As a youth, in order to impress his friends, Hitler decided to urinate into the mouth of a goat and the goat responded by taking a bite out of his penis or scrotum. Wasner told his buddies that "Adolf has been warped" ever since. Hitler was intent on destroying any aspect of his early life and Wasner was executed in 1943.

2. The Borderland Theory

Sir Isaiah Berlin in his book *Against the Current* advances a thought-provoking theory of charismatic political leadership which attributes the aggressive nationalism of such figures as Napoleon, Stalin and Hitler to their geographic origins—their birth in the outlying borders of the empire. Hitler was born in Braunau, an Austrian town just across the river from southern Germany. He, like many ardent Nazis were really Austrians, not Germans. This is the so-called "marginal man" theory in sociology that also explains such radical leaders as Stokeley Carmichael born in Trinidad, not the USA; Louis Farrakhan, also born in the Caribbean; and French 1960s radical Danny the Red, born in Germany, not France. Marginal men, outsiders, often make effective leaders.

3. The Genealogy Theory

Did Hitler somehow learn, during his childhood in Austria, a "terrible" family secret: that his father had actually been fathered by a Jew? Several postwar psychoanalytic Hitler explainers (among them Robert Waite, a Williams College emeritus professor of history have seized upon this recurrent rumor to suggest that Hitler's torment over the possibility that he was "tainted" or "poisoned" by Jewish blood, was the secret engine of his anti-semitism. Of course, Jewish identity comes from the mother or grandmother, not the grandfather, but it was enough of a rumor that Hitler in 1938 ordered the Gestapo to investigate his ancestry in an attempt to disprove such rumors, and subsequently Hitler ordered that the Austrian village where he grew up, Brunau, be evacuated, leveled, and converted to an artillery range. The fact that he even thought the rumor true could have been a factor in this destruction.

4. The Chemotherapy Theory

In 1907, Hitler, then eighteen, witnessed the agonizing death from cancer of his mother, who had been unsuccessfully treated by a Jewish doctor, Dr. Bloch, with the caustic chemical iodoform. Rudolph Binion, a professor of history at Brandeis, contends that Hitler's repressed anger at the Jewish doctor was the genesis of his hatred of Jews.

However, this theory does not ring true because Hitler loved Dr. Bloch and helped him emigrate to America before the war. Still, the psychoanalysts had a field day, contending that the death by gas of his mother would mean the death by gas of millions of Jews.

5. The Pornography Theory

Hitler's peculiar form of *sexualized* anti-semitism stemmed in part from his love of an illustrated semi-pornographic, anti-semitic publication called *Ostara*, which was edited by a self-styled Aryan mystic named Lanz von Liebenfels. The American writer John Toland and other writers argue that Hitler's variety of anti-semitism was in part derived from Lanz's obsession with tales of lustful Jews using sexual exploitation to defile blond blue-eyed Aryan maidens.

This obsession, they say, may have imprinted itself on the youthful Hitler's psyche and can be found echoed in passages of Mein Kampf redolent with sexual hysteria. "With satanic joy in his face," Hitler writes, "the black-haired Jewish youth lurks in wait for the unsuspecting girl whom he defiles with his blood."

6. The Hypnotherapy Theory

There were many thousands of anti-semites in Germany and Austria, but only one became Adolf Hitler. Why? In the late seventies, two writers—Binion and Toland—independently advanced a startling hypothesis about the origins of Hitler's murderous ambition.

In October 1918, Hitler, blinded by poison-gas on the western front during World War I, was admitted to a military hospital. In his blind, bedridden despair, he received a vision (or had an hallucination), heard a voice from on high, summoning him to great destiny—to save Germany.

He miraculously recovered from his blindness and vowed to avenge Germany's defeat. According to Binion, the voice that Hitler actually heard was not from on high but from a hypnotist, Dr. Edward Forster, the ranking psychiatrist at the hospital. Dr. Forster cured Hitler's blindness by using the then fashionable mesmeric techniques to put him in a trance and implant the belief that he was the savior of Germany. His spell worked only too well, transforming a previously obscure corporal into a world-stage monster of historic proportions.

7. The Serial-Killer Theory

This theory is too absurd even to mention. It is an example of what Rosenbaum (1995:55) calls the "psychobabble of serial-killer pseudoscience"; Hitler as the victim of a dysfunctional family. In short, this theory sees him as a misunderstood boy like Ted Bundy, John Wayne Gacy, and other such killers, a kind of workaholic Hannibal Lecter. If only he had had a positive self-image, he would have turned out all right.

8. The Abusive-Father Theory

At one time, this was a very popular theory but like the serial-killer theory, it too is absurd but it does echo other theories of familial turmoil that lie at the root of Hitler's obsession to kill all Jews. His obsession was focused on Jews—it was a war against Jews—not against women, not against homosexuals, not against male authority figures, but Jews.

Psychologists as different as Alice Miller and Erich Fromm have stressed his relationship to his parents. To Miller, Alois, his father, is the abusive monster; to Fromm, it is his mother Klara who is the real monster. Hitler allegedly had an incestuous relationship with his mother and hated his father: the "Norman Bates" syndrome (from the movie *Psycho*). Bad parenting, one could say, led to the Holocaust. Too simplistic, of course.

9. The Necrophilia Theory

Hitler's love of death and dead bodies, corpses, of mass killings, is the basis of this theory. His fixations, according to Fromm, on health; his hatred of poisons (syphilis and the Jews); his obsessive-compulsive cleanliness, all concealed a deeper, long-repressed desire to destroy not his father but his mother. In fact, one theory states that Hitler's deepest desire was to destroy all Germans (the Motherland) and not Jews (the Father-figure). But death and destruction, a *gotterdammerung*, was what really turned Hitler on, according to this theory.

10. The Coprophilia Theory

Closely tied to theories 1 and 9 is the coprophilia theory. Hitler could only reach orgasm through coprophilia and this was either the cause or the effect of his perverse hatred of the Jews: an enraged impotence. What is coprophilia? It is the love of feces or urine. According to this theory, Hitler never advanced beyond the stage in development where the child prizes his fecal matter. It is also tied to degradation ceremonies and strict toilet training.

Even Prof. Erich Goldhagen of Harvard University accepts this theory in that it explains several mysterious events in Hitler's life: his inability to have "normal" sex and the many women who committed suicide, perhaps in part, as a reaction to what Hitler asked of them: that is, to defecate or urinate on him in the shower. Coprophilia, according to Goldhagen, may have been a factor in the possible suicide of his niece Geli Raubal, the love of his life. She was engaged to him and either her attempts to go to the press about Hitler's secret or her shock at it—led either to suicide or murder. It is still a mystery exactly what happened to her: whether she killed herself or she was killed by order of Hitler.

11. The Syphilitic Theory

This theory, surprisingly promulgated from an odd source—the Austrian-Jewish Nazi hunter Simon Wiesenthal—is a quest to explain Hitler's psyche as a by-product of a bad case of syphilis contracted from a Jewish prostitute in Vienna. In some ways, this echoes, the lead paint or asbestos theories of the decline of the Roman Empire, that is, lead in their cooking pots and asbestos on their tables led to a slow decline in the mental capacity of Roman kings, the so-called "lead poisoning" theory.

In this case, Hitler's slow decline was due to the ravages of syphilis. In this theory, Hitler blames the Jews for his misery and deals with them accordingly.

However perverse these theories are, there are several more abstract, more macro-dynamic ones that I would like to propose at this time.

12. The Great Abstractions Theory

So far we have emphasized Hitler's uniqueness to the Shoah. In short, we have stressed Milton Himmelfarb's (1984)—"no Hitler, no Holocaust" thesis, one that I actually strongly believe in. However the "Great Abstractions" theory states that Christian anti-semitism, or Daniel Goldhagen's thesis of eliminationist German anti-semitism, was the cause of the Shoah; or Marxists say it was Modern Capitalism or European Racism or even Modernism itself that helped bring about the Holocaust.

If these larger forces would have produced a Hitler anyway, then Hitler's personal life becomes irrelevant. In short, great abstractions such as Marxism or racism leads to genocide.

And then there are other major factors, other great abstraction theories:

13. The "Fate" Theory

This theory posits that it was simply fate, luck, and good fortune, a fortuitous confluence of several historical and political elements that brought Hitler to power, and there is much truth to this. Hitler arose during the weak and vacillating Weimar Republic. The life of Germany had been disrupted by war, depression, and revolution. Irrationalism took over.

Hitler could never had arisen except for extraordinary good luck. He would have disappeared from the face of history as another obscure soldier or failed painter but for unforeseen phenomena that catapulted him to fame and power. He was also blessed with extraordinary skills that helped him take advantage of that luck.

First, he was a master orator, able to mesmerize his audiences and hypnotize his foes. He had great manipulative skills but was a poor organizer. He produced the great "vision," had few cabinet meetings, and let the technocrats run the country. He was not really interested in administration. He was a master tactician—insightful, shrewd, Machiavellian, brilliant, yet utterly irrational, bordering on madness and with respect to the Jews—a psychotic madness, according to Erich Goldhagen. This Janus-faced duality—the irrational mixed with shrewdness, marked him. He was a powerful charismatic leader who tied followers to him. SS men died with his name on their lips; women swooned in his presence; some committed suicide when the Fuhrer died.

14. The "War" Theory

War gave Hitler the ideal environment to rule the world and to carry out his genocidal designs. One can be more secretive about killing during wartime. Look at the examples of the Armenians and Cambodians. Bloodletting occurrs on a grand scale so that a few more million will not matter anyway. War is a great opportunity. Ninety percent of his time was devoted to war and the preparation for war.

Both Hannah Arendt and Lucy Dawidowicz felt that Hitler started World War II as a cover to kill Jews. He was obsessed with Jews from the beginning of his life to the very end in his bunker in Berlin. He was afraid the Jews even in death. He asked that he be cremated upon his death (by suicide) because he feared that the Jews would put him in a cage, torture and spit upon him, just as poet Ezra Pound, an American Nazi sympathizer, was put in a cage when captured.

That is why Hitler's body was burned and hidden in late April 1945. In essence, Hitler was not really the leader of Germany but its commander-in--chief. Most of his career was preparation for war and fighting a war. For this the German people will never forgive him—he caused 11 million of them to die for nothing.

15. The X Factor

I leave this to the end—the "black box" theory, the "X Factor," meaning that we will never have the answers to explain Hitler. But it is really not the answers, as a famous rabbi once said, but the questions that are important. It is the process, the trip itself, and not the final destination, that is crucial in our search.

16. My "Two-Step" Theory

It took both ideology and psychology; history and psychohistory; fate and luck. It took two-steps: the Great Abstractions of anti-semitism, racism, and anti-modernism was step one and then the personal, psychiatric, psycho-sexual motives fueled his drive—family, doctor, prostitute, pornography, sexual and physical abuse—all created a perverted individual who, combined with great and masterful political and oratorical skills, combined with luck, war, and fate—all combined to produce a deadly force in history, a force we are still dealing with.

(2000)

Sources

Berlin, Isaiah, *Against the Current: Essays in the History of Ideas*. Henry Hardy (ed), New York: Penguin Books, 1982.

Binion, Rudolf, *Hitler Among the Germans*. New York: Elsevier, 1976.

Bullock, Alan, *Hitler: A Study in Tyranny*. New York: Harper and Row, 1964. Originally published in 1952.

Dawidowicz, Lucy, *The War against the Jews: 1933-1945*. New York: Holt, Rinehart, and Winston, 1975.

Fromm, Erich, *The Anatomy of Human Destructiveness*. New York: Holt, Rinehart and Winston, 1973.

Goldhagen, Daniel Jonah, *Hitler's Willing Executioners*. New York: Knopf, 1996.

Himmelfarb, Milton, "No Hitler, No Holocaust," *Commentary*. Vol. 76, No. 3, 1984, pp. 37-43.

Irving, David, *Hitler's War*. New York: Avon Books, Rev. ed. 1990, originally published in 1977. Even though Irving has recently been discredited, this book has been quoted in the text and needs to be mentioned.

Langer, Walter C., *The Mind of Adolf Hitler*. New York: Basic Books, 1972.

Miller, Alice, *For Your Own Good*. New York: Farrar, Straus, & Giroux, 1983.

Porter, Jack Nusan with Steve Hoffman, *The Sociology of the Holocaust and Genocide*. Washington, DC: American Sociological Association, 1999.

Rosenbaum, Ron, "Explaining Hitler," *The New Yorker*. May 1, 1995, pp. 50-70.

——, *Explaining Hitler*. New York: HarperCollins, 1998.

Toland, John, *Adolf Hitler*. New York: Doubleday, 1976.

Trevor-Roper, H.R., *The Last Days of Hitler*. 3rd. edition, Chicago, IL: University of Chicago Press, 1992. Originally published in 1947.

Waite, Robert G. L., *The Psychopathic God: Adolf Hitler*. New York: Basic Books, 1977.

Chapter 10

Sexual Aberrations Among Nazi Leaders

Introduction

Too often, topics dealing with sex have been avoided in any discussion of the Holocaust or any other genocide for that matter. There were many reasons for this squeamishness. Why would one want to talk about homosexuality, for example, among the victims of the Armenians, Cambodians, Gypsies, Rwandans, or Jews? It would only demean them, it was felt. Alan Bullock, the British biographer of Hitler, said the same thing when asked in *The New Yorker* on why he didn't pursue more deeply Hitler's sexual aberrations, he responded that gentlemen scholars rarely raise such issues. (See Ron Rosenbaum, 1995).

Subtextually, underground so to speak, sexual aberration among Nazi leaders was well-known among American and British GIs during World War II, and Nazi leaders were the butt of many sexual jokes. For example, one of the most popular of ditties sung by soldiers on the front went as follows:

"Hitler, he had one big ball;
Goering had two but they were small;
Himmler had something similar;
but Goebbels had no balls at all."

If sexual analysis of the victims was felt to denigrate and dishonor them; sexual analysis of perpetrators has been rare, though more common today, for another reason—prurient interest. There are, for example, Neo-Nazi groups in Germany and America and elsewhere who not only have a historical interest in these subjects but glory in them and love to emphasize the sexual orgies and deviant aberrations of Nazi leadership. It is part and parcel of the mystique of Nazism—sex and violence. In this short entry, I wish to touch upon only a few issues:

Homosexuality and the Nazis

Homosexuality runs as a strange leitmotif throughout Nazi history. I have dealt with this issue in the previous entry and in many other of my publications (Porter, 1981, Porter, 1991, revised in 1995) and do not wish to become redundant on the subject. Here I simply want to briefly discuss the two camps of homosexual "research" and policy—one pro-homosexual and one, anti-homosexual. In other words, there is objective, humanistic research that deals with the subject matter in a fair, objective, non-prurient matter; and another, which deals with it a highly partisan, antigay manner, by linking homosexual rights movements with Nazism.

I also want to make a plea for more research on lesbians. There is an erroneous assumption that lesbians completely disappeared during the Third Reich. This is wrong. Lesbians were persecuted and went underground. (See Schoopman, 1995: 8-15). I would like to publicly thank scholars and friends such as James Steakley, Rudiger Lautmann, Gunter Grau, and Claudia Schoopman for their previous research in this area.

Secondly, I want to discuss the role of orgies in the Nazi leadership. Orgies are psychiatrically revealing. Not only are death and sex closely linked psychologically but sexual orgies proved to be a good means of stress reduction. Adolf Eichmann, for example, had few sexual inhibitions and conducted orgies late into the early morning, and would then arise to greet the next batch of victims consigned to their deaths.

And third, I add a brief discussion of transvestitism among both victims and perpetrators. In the case of victim, I utilize the story of Dr. Magnus Hirschfeld, Jewish sexologist, known as "Auntie Magnesia"; and among perpetrators, the case of Herman Goering. (See Porter, 1981)

My purpose in discussing such research is as an objective scholar, not prurient pornographer. Though I would not belie the point that such material is intrinsically titillating, I write about them with the utmost respect and care for the victims and even the perpetrators' families, but I am a scholar and I must go where the data lies and where the questions take me.

Masters & Slaves/Femmes vs. Leather Boys: Two Ways of Looking at Nazi Homosexuality

One rather bizarre theory has been put forward that the "gay question" (the so-called *homosexuellefrage*) was really a battle between effeminate gays and tough leather jacketed dykish gays. The "effeminate" gays were those German gays in the resistance, that is liberal, socialist, communist, progressive homosexuals, most of whom were rounded up and persecuted versus the more prominent fascist gays of the SA, the *Sturmabteilung*, led by Captain Ernst Rohm and his cohorts.

The "tough leather boys" of the SA won, only later to be decimated by Hitler and Himmler in the Night of Long Knives on June 15, 1934. What is of interest here is how Nazi Germany was able to tolerate certain kinds of gays and not others, and how Nazism, before 1934, was simply one form of homosexual domination over another. (See Kaplan, 1973)

This theory is of course totally absurd in some aspects, but it does highlight a controversial issue: were there "bad" gays as well as "good" gays during the Holocaust? This is an issue that even gay and lesbian groups have tried to avoid. Also, were there "bad" lesbians as well as "good" lesbians? "Bad" lesbians were the camp guards who, according to Harvard professor Erich Goldhagen, comprised the majority of the female prison and death camp guards; while the "good" lesbians were all those lesbians who had to go underground, even marry, in order to survive the Third Reich.

What we need is a much more inclusive history and sociology of homosexuals, those who were Nazis and those who were anti-Nazi; those who were innocent bystanders caught up in the antigay net of the Third Reich and those who were active perpetrators in persecuting homosexuals. Homosexuality is a sexual orientation; it does not bestow on the bearer any moral or spiritual authority or goodness. There can be "evil" homosexuals (who, in the end, were persecuted and killed, like Ernst Rohm) and "good" homosexuals who were innocent victims.

Sexual Orgies as a Means of Tension Relief

Recent discoveries have shown that Nazi leaders as high up as Adolf Eichmann were notorious in their use of sexual orgies as a means for tension release; that is, in order to do their evil work of massacring thousands of innocent people, sex served as just such a release. Comer Clarke in his 1960 book *Eichmann: The Man and his Crimes* (pp. 95-97) describes the following scenes:

> . . . the rather pedantic fusspot Captain Dannecker had a sideline which was also to interest S.S. Obersturmbannfuehrer Eichmann. He ran a string of risqué nightclubs in Paris. These nightclubs had belonged to Jews or other deported people, and Dannecker replaced them with cooperative French managers. But he was the boss and took the extremely lucrative profits. . . .
>
> Eichmann, already renowned for his off-duty licentiousness, enthusiastically made use of Dannecker's offerings. Whenever Eichmann came to Paris, Dannecker organized "Karl Nights," at which half a dozen of the most beautiful girls from the clubs would join Eichmann and his party at their table. It is a side to his character which is psychiatrically revealing and which will doubtless be studied in the future with the utmost interest.

Sadly, it has not attracted much attention from scholars but perhaps now it will.

Transvestitism Among Victims and Perpetrators

Transvestitism was common among some victims and perpetrators: I have already noted that the esteemed sexologist and anti-Nazi intellectual Dr. Magnus Hirschfeld was known as "Auntie Magnesia" for his transvestitism. (See Porter, 1981.) But also such noted Nazi leaders on the other side as Hermann Goering were alleged transvestites. Sexual orgies among SS men often included parading around in and wearing women's' clothes. This is not unusual—many macho subcultures, such as college and professional athletic players (note basketball star Dennis Rodman) engage in such sexual parodies.

For the SS there were few outlets for sexual tension. Homosexual behavior was severely punished; sexual relations with non-Aryan women was not only taboo but at times punishable by death or incarceration; and Aryan women were often scarce. Thus, transvestite parodies would be seen as harmless prankish outlets for release. Naturally, these parodies could not lead to actual homosexual sex, but then again, most transvestites are not homosexual anyway but heterosexuals who enjoy the allure and tension-release of wearing ladies undergarments.

Sex and Drug Usage Among Nazi Leaders

A variety of drugs were available to Nazi leaders. Such drugs were used for a variety of purposes:

a. Addictive drugs such as codeine and heroin for tension release.
b. Insomniac drugs from which to fall asleep
c. Amphetamines for weight reduction
d. Suicide drugs for terminating one's life. Toward the end of the Third Reich, drugs such as cyanide were easily available for entire families (e.g. Goebbels family) or individuals (e.g. Goering). See my essay on "Holocaust Suicides" in this volume.

Combinations of such drugs, plus alcohol, all facilitated sexual orgiastic parties. Wife-swapping, multiple partners, cross-dressing, even homosexual and lesbian lovemaking—all were part of the Nazi culture. Death and killing it seems, were for some, a great aphrodisiac.

Conclusions

These are a few of the many topics that have rarely been studied in Holocaust research. The time may be ripe to do so. With tact and sensitivity, valuable insights can be gained.

(2000)

Sources

Bleul, Hans Peter, *Sex and Society in Nazi Germany*, edited by Heinrich Fraenkel and translated from the German by J. Maxwell Brownjohn, Philadelphia and New York: J. B. Lippincott, 1973.

Clarke, Comer, *Eichmann: The Man and His Crimes*. New York: Ballantine Books, 1960.

Grau, Gunter (ed), *Hidden Holocaust? Gay and Lesbian Persecution in Germany 1933-45*. translated from the German by Patrick Camiller, London: Cassell, 1995.

Kaplan, J. "Homosexual Masters and Slaves in Nazi Germany," *Vector Magazine*. April 1973, pp. 23-32.

Mosse, George L., *Nationalism and Sexuality: Respectability and Abnormal Sexuality in Modern Europe*. New York: Howard Fertig, 1985.

Plant, Richard, *The Pink Triangle: The Nazi War Against Homosexuals*. New York: Henry Holt and Company, 1986.

Porter, Jack Nusan, "The Jewish Homosexual" in Porter's *The Jew as Outsider: Historical and Contemporary Essays. 1974-1980*. Lanham, MD and London: University Press of America, 1981, pp. 139-152. Despite the title of the essay, it is really the story of Dr. Magnus Hirschfeld, the German sexologist and opponent of Nazism.

———, *Sexual Politics in the Third Reich*. Newton, MA: The Spencer Press, 1991, revised 1995.

———, "Genocide of Homosexuals in the Nazi Era," see essay in this book and its bibliography.

Rosenbaum, Ron, "Explaining Hitler," *The New Yorker*. May 1, 1995, pp. 50-70. The essay was later expanded into a larger book of the same title published by Random House/Harper Perennial in 1998 but *The New Yorker* article is better and more concise in focusing in on answering the question: who was Hitler and what were his sexual aberrations?

Schoopman, Claudia, "The Position of Lesbian Women in the Nazi Period" in Gutter Grau, op. cit, 1995: pp. 8-15.

Chapter 11

Holocaust Suicides

In his essay on "Intellectual Craftsmanship," the late sociologist C. Wright Mills showed scholars how to use their files creatively. Everyone has files; the question is how to employ them, how to cross-index them. Take, for example, a file on Elie Wiesel, Martin Buber, Gershom Scholem, and the Lubavitcher Rebbe. Now take those same files and cross-index them to Hasidism, Zionism, or socialism. The results are provocative. What does the Lubavitcher Rebbe think of socialism or Zionism? How do Elie Wiesel and Martin Buber differ regarding Hasidism? The findings would make not only a good essay but a very interesting dissertation.

Now, let's cross-index another topic—suicide. Wiesel and suicide. Interesting. Buber and suicide. Perhaps. The Lubavitcher Rebbe and suicide. Maybe. The results may be ludicrous. But let's not give up. Let's expand the file system to include a few other items and see what happens. Holocaust and suicide, Holocaust writers and suicide, Holocaust survivors and suicide. Now, we have something, and it may even be worthwhile to ask what Wiesel, Buber, and the Lubavitcher Rebbe have to say about suicide, this most taboo of subjects, and in fact, they have much to say. Elie Wiesel has quietly taught a course at Boston University called The Literature of Memory: Suicide and/in Literature.

One of the founders of modern sociology, the French-Jewish anthropologist and sociologist Emile Durkheim, wrote a classic analysis called *Le Suicide* in 1897. In it he described several types of suicides and various correlations. This fundamental study showed that suicide is not just a deviant and isolated act but a key component in understanding how humans are integrated or not integrated into society. The higher the level of integration and group solidarity, the lower the rate of suicide. For Jewish people, it means a test of assimilation: the higher the rate of assimilation, the higher the rate of suicide. German and Austrian Jews had higher rates of suicide than Polish, Russian, or Hungarian Jews. Leaders higher than followers. Intellectuals and doctors higher than farmers and tailors. Men higher than women. The sickly higher than the healthy. The old higher than the young. Single and divorced higher than unmarried (especially for men—marriage is an inoculation against suicide). The deeply secular higher than the deeply religious. These findings are as true today as they were in Durkheim's time a century ago in France and Germany.

If this is so, then what explains the recent suicides, in the frame of five years, of prominent Holocaust writers and thinkers? Sociologically, let's examine the evidence and see if they prove Durkheim's theory correct, and by and large we will see that they do.

In these five years, 1987-92, the literary and academic worlds were shocked by the deaths of four world-renowned intellectuals, Jerzy Kosinski, Primo Levi, Terrence Des Pres, and Bruno Bettelheim, as well as the newspaper titan and Holocaust survivor Robert Maxwell. My research later uncovered others, some well-known, others less known— the Polish writer Tadeusz Borowski (1922-51), who died by filling his kitchen with gas when he was not yet thirty; the poet Paul Celan (1920-1970), who drowned in the Seine at age forty-nine; and the philosopher Jean Améry (1912-78), who died of self-inflicted wounds (Améry is an anagram for Hans Mayer, his original Austrian name, and that fits my theory too—a confused and convoluted identity); Arthur Koestler, Stefan Zweig, and Walter Benjamin could also be added. The three latter were refugees of the Holocaust. Benjamin died in 1940 on the Spanish-French border, a day away from freedom; Zweig and his wife committed a double suicide in Brazil in 1940; and Koestler and his wife also committed a double suicide but much later, after the war. Even Art Spiegelman's mother, Anya Spiegelman, committed suicide, a rare case of a woman. Primo Levi (1919-87) was a candidate for a possible Nobel Prize in literature when he died in Turin, falling off his balcony. Robert Maxwell fell off his boat in 1994. Bruno Bettelheim was a well-known psychologist and writer who committed suicide in 1990.

Altogether, we are talking about twelve well-known suicide cases in which the Holocaust, I believe—was a factor, and it is this hypothesis that I have to prove. I have not even mentioned other, less well known surviving victims who took their lives years *after* the Holocaust or Judenrat leaders who took their lives *during* the Holocaust or the many Germans and Austrians who killed themselves *before* the Holocaust.

All of them, except for Des Pres, an American-born lapsed Catholic and professor of English at Colgate University in upstate New York, were Holocaust survivors; all were engulfed in what the great Holocaust psychiatrist Leo Eitinger called the "survivors' disease." (Yet, one could arguably make a case that both Des Pres and Koestler, though not technically survivors, had become engulfed in, mesmerized by, and ultimately depressed by their study of the Holocaust, and so it should be seen as an important, though not the sole, factor in their respective suicides.)

Some might question whether Maxwell should be included since he is not a writer or intellectual, but if you look at Volume 10 of *Contemporary Authors you* will see him listed as a writer/editor of several books on economics and politics. Though he was more of an entrepreneur and publisher, I include him since I believe, first, that he committed suicide (though that is debatable, and many accidents are really disguised suicides; William Zellner, writing on "auto-suicide," found that over 12 percent of all automobile accidents were actually suicides, another example of how suicide is hidden behind other acts such as alcoholism, drug addiction, and car mishaps); and, second, he did so in a typical flamboyant style that supports my theory of "stigmatized identity," a theory that analyzes the use of multiple names, pseudonyms, anagrams, false identities, multiple personae, sexual deviance, and games of hide-and-seek. Several of these men (Kosinski, Maxwell, and Celan) lived with these trait.

I include non-Jews such as Des Pres and Borowski because by entering the hell of the Holocaust, they became in essence "honorary Jews" or "honorary Holocaust survivors" and suffered because of it. I should say that I respect these people, but I am simply an anthropologist, emerging from the dark jungles of the mind, reporting on what I see and asking sensitive questions.

They were all strong and forceful personalities who went out as they had lived—in full control of their faculties. They may have been depressed but I believe most knew exactly what they were doing. (There are some gray areas cases such as Primo Levi, who was being treated for severe clinical depression.) These were people who were usually in control during most of their lives, but the Holocaust and its burning memories became too much for them. That tied with such issues as aging, illness, and loss of control provides a classic reason for suicide. (Age and health are crucial independent variables in inducing people to commit suicide, but young people, in their teens and twenties, such as Borowski, are also prone to suicide.)

This is not a morbid subject for me. As a child of Holocaust survivors, I have lived with death my entire life. It is a fascinating subject. People need to talk more about death. Anything less is a form of denial, and these men were not deniers! They were more than simply Holocaust writers but some of the most interesting personalities of the twentieth century.

As a sociologist I was trained in graduate school to be sensitive to what Talcott Parsons called "pattern variables" and as a child of survivors, I ask what effect all this had on me and on my parents.

In graduate school, I learned not only about *Le Suicide* by Durkheim and *The Sociological Imagination* by C. Wright Mills taught me to see how personal anguish expressed by suicide could be a symptom of a larger, more complex societal pattern. One person unemployed is a private issue, but a million unemployed is a vast social and societal problem. One suicide could be dismissed as a single psychiatric aberration, but many (and that could mean only three or four in a high school, for example) would indeed show us that something wrong is going on, and we should look to society and not to a person's psychological "problems" for answers. These are Durkheimian "social facts," unexplainable by psychology alone. A sociologist and a social worker looks at suicide differently than a psychiatrist. The latter sees a case of depression; we see a sociological, societal, or historical pattern of great significance.

Granted, suicide is at once morbid, frightening, fascinating, troubling, perplexing and contradictory. Still, we must face it, head-on. It will teach us something. Among my sociology students, it is, next to sports and MTV, the most popular topic for discussion in class.

But let's return to the sociology of suicide. What are the pattern variables? I know that some literary critics hate this cold, mechanical manner of handling complex sociological data. They do not possess what Mills called the "sociological imagination," which helps us understand the nexus of biography and history and how personal problems can become emblematic of major societal and historical issues. But I will try to convince them in this essay. Let's use their imagination to diagram these pattern variables:

Holocaust Suicides 151

Independent Variables	Intervening Variables	Dependent Variables
Age	Aging	
Sex	Depression	
Social class	Immigrant status	
Occupation	Post-traumatic stress	Suicide
Race	Drugs/alcohol	
Religion	Survivor's guilt	
Education	Death of a Loved One	
	The "Meaninglessness" of Life	
	Illness, ill health	

Suicide is defined as an intentional, self-inflicted act that ends in death. At times, accidents, natural causes, and even murder are confused with suicide. The death of Robert Maxwell is a case in point: was his falling off his boat, the *Lady Ghislaine;* near the coast of Spain an accident? Some suggest he fell into the water due to a sudden lurch as he was peeing into the water; or that he had a heart attack that caused him to fall overboard; or that he was murdered by a disgruntled employee. Or was it really suicide? We may never know. The consequences that followed his death point to a possible suicide scandal. The same ambivalence was true of Primo Levi. Did he die as a result of premeditated suicide or by accident, falling off his stairwell? Was the death of Terrence Des Pres a risky, deviant act that went awry or was it suicide? Des Pres was a man who took many risks, intellectually as well as psychologically. I include him as a kind of "honorary survivor" who became engulfed in the danger of the Holocaust and fell under its spell.

What emerges, however, in this sociological search for patterns is fascinating: Koestler, Bettelheim, and Kosinski all killed themselves in the same way. All were members of the Hemlock Society. All did it by methods described by the society — each put his head in a plastic bag and submerged it in the water of his bathtub. All were aging, ailing, and depressed yet determined to die in their own way. Several were very assimilated, almost "hidden Jews," including Koestler, Kosinski, Bettelheim, Celan, and Maxwell throughout most or part of

Many had several "personalities" or personae: Maxwell, Jerzy Kosinski, and Jean Améry even had new names, Jean Améry was an Austrian named Hans Mayer; Maxwell was a Czech called Hoch; and Kosinski was a Jew originally named Lewinkopf; his mother's name was

Weinreich. His father was Moshe Lewinkopf, the son of Nusyn and Basia Lewinkopf. (Kosinski is a common Polish name similar to "Smith'; Paul Celan's original name was Ancel.)

What is certain was that Kosinski was constantly reinventing himself. In fact, it is hard to know at first that in his most important novel, *The Painted Bird,* the young boy is not even identified as "Jewish" but as a strange "gypsy" boy. Yet in fact the young boy is allegedly based on Kosinski's life. He supposedly hid as a non-Jew in the woods to escape being killed. Later, in America, he donned masks and walked around Manhattan in disguise. Both he and Robert Maxwell shared this obsession with disidentifications. In essence, both were geniuses as well as charlatans.

As a sociologist sensitive to patterns and as a child of survivors, I immediately asked myself—why? What effect does the Holocaust have on survivors? Were these simply "tired old men" who killed themselves when life became too painful, both physically and psychologically?

Who then is a survivor? I have a broad definition, perhaps too broad for some readers. I include refugees such as Walter Benjamin, Stefan Zweig, Bruno Bettelheim, and Arthur Koestler; young suicide victims who killed themselves soon after the war like Borowski; well-known suicides such as Jean Améry, Paul Celan, and Primo Levi; as well as unique and controversial cases such as Terrence Des Pres and Robert Maxwell.

This essay discusses differences between intellectuals and writers who have high suicide rates and ordinary survivors who have very low rates. It is important to emphasize that ordinary survivors rarely commit suicide. Rates of suicide for middle and working-class Jewish survivors are extremely low. What variables caused these so-called "intellectual suicides," or are there several explanations and several different types of suicides? Did their role as intellectual outsiders play a part in their suicide? Intellectuals, societal outsiders par excellent, are notorious for committing suicide because of the Durkheimian theory of anomie that I will discuss in a moment. What role does societal integration play? Assimilation into the general society, cut off from the primary group, being part of the *gemeinshaft* of Jewry turns out to be a very important variable, indeed.

Suicide occurred often as "choiceless choices," to use Lawrence Langer's term, in several stages, before, during, and after the Holocaust. Suicide before the Holocaust was most common among German and Austrian Jews from the rise of Nazism in 1933 on but especially after the Nuremberg laws were passed in 1935 ostracizing Jews and turning them into social lepers, to use Eric Goldhagen's phrase. Suicides escalated after *Kristallnacht* November 1938. It was said that one death in five was a suicide in Germany in the Jewish community in the 1930s.

These suicides are what Durkheim called *anomie* suicides. During that time of rapid, disruptive social and economic change, the rules for social integration were dismembered. The head of the family, usually a male, who ruled with an iron fist, was left with few guidelines—his entire world was turned upside down. Feeling cut off and alienated from his beloved German society, he might kill himself, often convincing his wife to do the same in a kind of modern-day suttee. This was very common among German and Austrian males of wealth and prestige. Polish and Russian Jews who had always been outsiders and who did not suffer such "relative deprivation," had much lower rates of suicide. Intellectual and upper-class Jews also were much more prone to suicide than working-class and religious Jews even if we hold ethnicity (German versus Polish identity) constant. Social groups who encourage highly individualistic moral decisions and who live highly autonomous lives whereby they felt they must control all aspects of their lives are prone to suicide when their world is shattered as in Nazi Germany.

The second period of suicide during the Holocaust occurred in the camps and ghettos. While anomic suicide was common, a new form, *egoistic* suicide, emerged. By contrast, egoistic suicide occurs when rules for social integration are clear enough but social integration is very low. According to Durkheim, a person who is excessively committed to personal beliefs and aims, rather than to those of the group will be inadequately socially integrated. Anyone with few social bonds, a person cut loose and alone is a prime candidate for egoistic suicide. Single, divorced, widowed, orphaned, and urban people, whose lack of contact with others often forces them to develop extreme self-reliance are good candidates for egoistic suicide. Homeless alcoholics and drug addicts are other examples of egoistic suicide candidates. Survivors who were able to maintain some family ties or who had a sister or brother, father or mother, or even a friend and substitute sister or brother in the camps had a better chance to survive and were less likely to kill themselves.

A third type of suicide according to Durkheim, was *fatalistic suicide*. He spends very little time on this type in his book, but it too was common during the Holocaust. It is a suicide that says I have very little to live for, my death is imminent, therefore I will kill myself by throwing myself onto the electrified fence or by attempting to scale the ghetto wall, knowing full well that I will be shot by a guard. Other historical examples would be black slaves on ships bound for the American plantations who threw themselves into the sea. Fatalistic means fate, not fatal. It means you are going to die anyway, why delay the agony. Naturally, anomic and egoistic influences contribute to this suicide type.

A fourth type of Durkheimian suicide was also common during the Holocaust; in fact, it is common in wartime in general and it is what he called *altruistic* suicide. This occurs when a person's sense of responsibility to the group is so great that it overwhelms the individual's sense of self and the person sacrifices his or her life for the sake of that group, either to save the group directly or to act as a public symbol of defiance. Naturally, overtones of the other types of suicides can color this type as well. We must remember that these are Weberian *ideal types*. Life is always more complicated than our theories can possibly explain.

The suicide of Adam Czerniakow (1888-1942), chairman of the Warsaw Judenrat, is a good example of altruistic suicide. Initially, he cooperated in the deportations but committed suicide upon finding out that deportation meant death.

Arthur Zyglboim, the Bund's representative to the Polish government in exile, also committed suicide. His remains were brought from London in 1961 to be buried in Writers' Row in New Mount Carmel Cemetery located between Brooklyn and Queens. His ashes are under a stone set off by shrubs at the end of a row. His gravestone, a hexagonal monument, topped by a carved flame, quotes his 1943 suicide note: "I cannot remain silent, I cannot go on living, when the remnants of the Jewish people whom I represent are being annihilated. My life belongs to the Jewish people in Poland and, therefore, I give it to them."

Durkheim calls these suicides "altruistic" because they are emblematic of a person who so loves his people or nation that he is ready to lay down his life for them. These suicides are a sign of protest, though some might see it as a sign of despair. Perhaps they are both. Buddhist monks during the Vietnam War who set themselves on fire are a similar type. Kamikaze pilots who crashed into American destroyers during World War II in the Pacific are another, though very different, example.

Men and women in the partisans, in the army and navy, and in other military arenas also have the opportunity to engage in altruistic suicide. The soldier who throws himself on a grenade to save his buddies is an example of the partisan who, though wounded, holds off the enemy so that the platoon can escape. My father, a partisan commander, told me stories of such bravery: one of the most powerful examples of altruism etched in his mind was the story of five young boys chosen from the Soviet army and asked to become human land mines. Buried in the road, wrapped in grenades, they would count off the first five tanks and then rip open their wooden "caskets" and plunge the grenades deep into the bellies of the German tanks as they made their way toward Leningrad. Each one was given the Hero of the Soviet Union medal in a ceremony before the mission.

But it is suicide *after the Holocaust* that is the focus of this essay. Let us look at a few of these cases more closely. We will begin with Jerzy Kosinski.

Byron L. Sherwin, in a "Friend's Reminiscence" (June 1991), wrote the following:

> Jerzy Kosinski was my friend. His death is a loss that cannot be recovered. . . . There was no one like Jerzy. He was, in his own words, "his own event." Jerzy's life embraced countless contradictions, but few ambivalences. He always knew who and where he was. Jerzy was an abused child, and the scars from that abuse continuously festered throughout his life. . . . Hide-and-seek was, for him, not a childhood game, but a strategy for sheer physical survival. . . . He could enter any room and hide somewhere. Neither adults nor children could ever find him when he wished to remain hidden. Though a public figure, a celebrity, he never stopped hiding. It became for him a strategy for spiritual survival, a way of evading those who wished to harm him. Jerzy's personal motto, derived from Descartes, was *larvatus prodco*—"I go forth disguised." He was a socialite in hiding, a paranoid with real enemies.

Professor Antony Polonsky of Brandeis University, a British historian and expert on Polish historiography, knew both men and told me that Kosinski was, like Robert Maxwell, always trying on new identities, always playing a kind of hide-and-seek with reality, even with the truth.

Both Maxwell and Kosinski tried to hide their true identities and had several personae. Kosinski wrote under the name Joseph Novak early in his career, and in his last book, *The Hermit of 69th Street,* describes a writer named Norbert Kosky ("Kosinski without the sin") who is unjustly accused of telling tales and at the end of the book is drowned by thugs.

According to John Taylor, writing in *New York Magazine* (July 15, 1991): "When that book was perceived as a critical and commercial failure, according to [one] theory of his suicide, Kosinski believed his ability to continue writing and publishing was threatened." Actually, his novels were critical and commercial failures (except for *Being There*) long before 1991. His talent had precipitously declined after *The Painted Bird* appeared. Taylor, in his masterful essay, describes Kosinski's tortured last few months and his sudden death, a death that left his many friends angry.

It was *a Village Voice* article in 1982, however, that was the most devastating, and from which he never fully recovered. It suggested that his first two books, non-fiction accounts of life in the Soviet Union, were somehow sponsored by the CIA; that his celebrated first novel, *The Painted Bird,* had been written in Polish and then translated with no credit given to the translator; and finally, that assistants, again never given full credit, helped write his later books. Zbigniew Brzezinski, a friend and fellow Polish exile, said that the allegations contributed to his death.

There were also allegations as well that he lived the war years comfortably in a Polish dacha and that his well-connected parents were always aware of his whereabouts. Kosinski often led people to believe that the life of the main character of the Gypsy-Jew boy in *The Painted Bird* closely paralleled his own experiences. At other times, however, Kosinski conceded that some of the episodes were either invented or based on the experiences of other children. Even more astounding, he once told Elie Wiesel that he was not even Jewish.

There is much more to say about his confused identity, his merging of truth and illusion, but the point I am trying to make is that identity problems coupled with other factors, such as deteriorating health, may have triggered his suicide, and, furthermore, the similarities of his suicide with other Holocaustal suicides are, to say the least, uncanny.

Robert Maxwell, an editor and publishing titan on several continents, was also a "bluffer." He was born Hoch Shmulevich from an Orthodox Hungarian and Czech background (the British, always infatuated with lovable rogues, often referred to him as the "Bouncing Czech"); later he earned a medal of honor in the British army and became Captain Ian Robert Maxwell. He liked to be called Captain Bob. Like Kosinski, he married a non-Jewish woman of some means, and his children were raised as non-Jews. Also like Kosinski, Maxwell, late in life, "returned" to Judaism and to a love of Israel and the Jewish people (though that was often hidden from the general public and from his public persona). Maxwell organized the first European Conference on the Holocaust at Oxford University and supported, through Macmillan Publishing Company, several journals and books dealing with the Holocaust and genocide. Kosinski, too, immersed himself in Jewish texts toward the end of his life, forming a close relationship with Spertus College of Jewish Studies in Chicago and its vice-president for academic affairs, Rabbi Byron L. Sherwin. Unlike Maxwell, however, Kosinski was disturbed by the "Holocaust-centered mentality" that dominated American Jewish life, manifested in the construction of multimillion-dollar museums and monuments to commemorate the Holocaust. Instead he advocated building Jewish "identity centers," akin to Jewish community centers, which would advocate a deeper awareness of the "Jewish presence" in history, art, and science. As always, his views were seen as controversial and a bit strange by the Jewish community. Many were surprised, upon his death, that he was even Jewish, so identified was he with Polish culture.

Kosinski was, like Maxwell, always trying on new identities. He was a strange bird, a "black bird" that imitates others, a rara avis, a linguist, photographer, sociologist, raconteur, a hyper-depressed and creative individual, often out of step with the world and with the Jewish community. Many of his works are psycho-biographical. See, for example, his novel *Steps*. To continue this discussion of "identity confusion," let us look at several other survivors.

Both Celan and Améry had anagrammatic names. Celan's original name was Paul Ancel or Antschel, and he was born in Czernowitz in the Bukovina region of Romania in 1920. From his surname he formed the anagram "Celan" in 1947. That identity, according to Lawrence Langer's *Art from the Ashes* (1995:598), had complex geographical and cultural origins. Even more confusing was the fact that in spite of his long years of self-imposed exile in France, German remained Celan's mother tongue. He was born in Romania, wrote in German, but is thought of (from his name) as a French poet. He died in Paris, drowned in the Seine in April 1970. Jean Améry, like Celan, had Germanic-French identity problems. He was born Hans Mayer in Vienna in 1912. His father was Jewish, his mother Catholic. In 1937 he married a Jewish woman, and in 1938, after the German annexation of Austria, he fled with her to Belgium. During the war he was tortured in several Gestapo prisons in Belgium and Holland.

Langer, in *Art from the Ashes (p.120),* has a short but pithy analysis of why Améry, like Celan and Primo Levi, took his life; disillusionment and disenchantment with the world. Rejected by the world's seeming indifference, disillusioned and depressed, coupled with illness, both psychic and physical, these survivors saw suicide not as a cowardly act but a courageous one. They felt that no one was listening, that no one cared any more. As Langer poignantly says: "We are left trying to decide whether his [Améry's] suicide was a victory or a defeat."

Perhaps no man planned and brooded about his death as much as Bruno Bettelheim. He was a world-famous psychoanalyst and child psychologist and, what was less known, had spent ten months and eleven days in Buchenwald and Dachau. He was a refugee rather than a survivor, having come to America before the war started. He was later director of the University of Chicago's Sonia Shankman Orthogenic School for emotionally disturbed children, especially violent, self-destructive autistic children, and the author of many books, including *The Informed Heart* and *Love is Not Enough*.

He committed suicide on March 13, 1990. In an interview with David James Fisher, published posthumously in the sociological journal *Society* (April 1991: 60-69), Fisher asked: "Tell me your particular thoughts about old age," and the old curmudgeon replied: "Don't reach it! What I have experienced is a deterioration of physical strength and energy which I find very hard to take. It is depressing. . . . My children no longer need me. I feel that I have done my life's work, and I am fairly satisfied with it. But I feel a weakness that makes it very difficult, if not impossible, for me to go on." What he feared is what everyone his age (mid-eighties) fears—to be completely incapacitated and dependent on others and to live like that for many years in a nursing home at great personal cost and family anguish.

Bettelheim had several significant personal changes in his life, perhaps too many too soon—the recent death of his wife, a move to Los Angeles after many years living in Chicago, and then a move to Washington, D.C., a minor stroke that left him with difficulties in swallowing, and anxieties about an incapacitating illness. He could no longer write; he had lost his wife, Trude, and had become alienated from his children.

"What I wish for," he says in the Fisher interview, "is a fast and easy death. That's easy to wish for." But Bettelheim feared something more than a painful death, and that was a life devoid of meaning. As he is quoted in Nina Sutton's biography: "So, intricately, so inextricably interwoven are death and life's meaning so that when life seems to have lost all meaning, suicide seems the inescapable consequence . . . very few suicides are due to the wish to end insufferable pain. . . . More frequently suicides are the consequences of an unalterable conviction that the person's life has completely and irremediably lost all meaning" (pp. 512-I3, originally in his collection *Surviving and Other Essays* [New York: Knopf; 1979], p. 4).

The next topic in Bettelheim's interview with Fisher is his impression of Los Angeles as compared to Chicago, which is instructive, and the interview comes back to cognate issues that bear on his state of mind— survival guilt, self-destructiveness, the concentration camp expereince, Dachau, Buchenwald, and Primo Levi. Ironically, these two survivors knew each other, and Bettelheim admired Levi's work. Bettelheim framed his camp experiences as "the death drive" *(thantos)* and noted that it could easily lead to self-destruction.

We are now coming closer to an explanation of Holocaustal suicide. Bettelheim echoes Jean Améry's encounter with torture in the camps. According to Langer *(Art from the Ashes,* 1995;120), torture was ineradicably burned into Améry. "The lingering sensation of having been reduced to nothing more than a creature of helpless flesh—an experience shared by countless inmates of the death camps. This coupled with a source of permanent humiliation to many who endured it," Langer writes in *"Arts from the Ashes."*

Furthermore, while Améry's self-inflicted death remains a mystery to Langer, he admits that Améry's health was impaired by the harsh physical conditions of the camps. This, coupled with what Améry calls the "shame of destruction," led to self-immolation and suicide.

Améry drifted toward this act of death; Bettelheim, however, consciously analyzed his condition and deliberately went about killing himself according to instructions from the Hemlock Society. But each of them killed themselves, as did so many of the others, because of a perceived meaningless of life and felt impression that the world no longer cared.

As a rule, suicide increases with knowledge and learning. Learning does not determine progress. It is innocent. Nevertheless, the more knowledge one has, the more learning, the more education, the greater the likelihood one will commit suicide. Man kills himself more often, however, because of the loss of contact with his religious community; it is secular learning that results in a drift away from community. Learning Torah within the religious community in some way strengthens a person;

learning outside the context of a community disintegrates a person, and when secular knowledge has no answers people may turn to suicide as an alternative to meaninglessness. Religion, in short, has a prophylactic effect on suicides, and Judaism in particular has a positive influence. Suicide rates are low for most Jews, but they tend to be high among highly assimilated intellectuals and professors, especially those cut off from the Jewish community.

The irony in all this is that suicide is not the normal option for most Holocaust survivors, and this is true not only for Jews but for other minority groups such as blacks or Gypsies. True, blacks jumped overboard from slave ships on their way to America, but once on the plantation, the solidarity of the black family, especially the mother, kept an integrity that mollified the possibility of suicide. The reasoning: why give the white man a victory, why do the job for him? The same, by and large, is true for Jewish victims of pogroms, ghettos, and, later, the death camps. We are finding out, however, that as blacks and other minorities enter the middle class and adopt "white" patterns, suicide rates increase.

I have found many things in my study, but one of the most important is that being Jewish is healthy, being religious is healthy, being part of a religious community is healthy; and having a religious mother is healthy.

It is the isolated, alienated intellectual who is in deep trouble unless he aligns himself with a community or primary group. (Steve Katz has pointed out to me that this was also true in that Gulag-intellectuals committed suicide more often than Russians.) I do not judge these intellectuals. I will only say that they might have coped better with their existential condition had they believed in God more and been more integrated into their religious community. But then again, had they done so, they would not have become the critics of society that they were. That is why Elie Wiesel did not commit suicide, and that is why so many of his fellow survivor writer/intellectuals, his peers, did.

In short, being Jewish, religiously Jewish, is good for you.

(1998)

Sources

Améry, Jean (Hans Mayer), *At The Mind's Limits: Contemplations by a Survivor on Auschwitz and Its Realities,* Trans. By Sidney Rosenfeld and Stella Rosenfeld, Afterword by Sidney Rosenfeld, Foreword by Alexander Gillie (New York: Schocken 1986). See also Alvin Rosenfeld, "Jean Améry as Witness," in *Holocaust Remembrance: The Shapes of Memory,* ed. Geoffrey H. Hartman (Oxford: Blackwell, 1994), pp. 59-69, 275,76.

Bettelheim, Bruno, *The Informed Heart,* (New York: Avon Books, 1971). Also see David James Fisher, "Bruno Bettelheim: Last Thoughts on Therapy," Society, April 1991, pp. 60-69. There is also a new biography on Bettelheim, by Nina Sutton, *Bettelheim: A Life and a Legacy,* (New York: Basic Books, 1996).

Borowski, Tadeusz, *This Way to the Gas, Ladies and Gentlemen.* Selected and trans. Barbara Vedder, Introduction by Jan Kott, Introduction trans. Michael Kandel (New York: Penguin Books, 1976). See also a short biographical note on Borowski (as well as several other writers mentioned in this essay) in Lawrence L. Langer, ed., *Art from the Ashes: A Holocaust Anthology* (New York: Oxford University Press, 1995), pp. 342-56.

Celan, Paul, *Poems of Paul Celan,* trans. Michael Hamburger (New York: Persea Books, 1988). See his poems "Night Ray" and "Death Fugue" in Carolyn Forche, ed., *Against Forgetting: Twentieth Century Poetry of Witness* (New York: Norton, 1993), pp. 379-82. There is a book by Paul Felstiner, on Celan but it is a literary analysis, not a sociological or historical account *[Paul Celan; Poet, Survivor, Jew* (New Haven: Yale Univ. Press, 1995)].

Des Pres, Terrence, *The Survivor: An Anatomy of Life in the Death Camps,* (Oxford: Oxford University Press, 1976).

Eitinger, Leo, "Identification, Treatment, and Care of the Aging Holocaust Survivor," in *The First National Conference on Identification, Treatment, and Care of the Aging Holocaust Survivor: Selected Proceedings,* ed. R.E. Kenigsberg and C.M. Lieblich (North Miami, Fla.: Southeast Florida Center on Aging, Florida International University, 1990) pp. 5-21, is an excellent and sensitive discussion of survivors and suicide, many of them writers mentioned in this essay. Eitinger is a world-renowned psychiatrist and researcher on Holocaust survivors. He discusses the suicides of such aging intellectuals as Kosinski, Jean Améry, and Primo Levi. One question that begs an answer is what were (are) the strengths of Elie Wiesel that precluded him from committing suicide. The answer follows my Durkheimian theory. First, he had a strong support system of sisters and friends after the war, and second, at base he is really an Orthodox Jew, a Hasid. Being religious is a healing mechanism that makes it difficult to commit suicide because it anchors one into a community, integrates one into a supportive system of coreligionists, and forces on to rely on God, not on oneself alone. Also, suicide is a sin, a great taboo to Orthodox Jews. Thus Elie Weisel's life supports my theory that being a religious person is good for both body and soul. It is not only "good" to be a traditional and committed Jew. It is also very healthy.

Kosinski, Jerzy. See his many books with numerous editions, though several of them are out of print *The Painted Bird (1965), Being There* (1971), *Steps* (1968), *Cockpit* (1975), *Pin Ball (1982), Blind Date (1977), Passion Play* (1979), plus the movies *Reds* and *Being There.* See also his last book, *The Hermit of 69th Street* (1991), and his collection of essays, *Passing By* (1992). His non-fiction scholarship and criticism in a previous persona include *American Sociology* (1958); *The Future is Ours, Comrade* (written under the pseudonym of Joseph Novak, (1960), *No Third Path* (also as Joseph Novak, *1962).* Notes of the *Author on "The Painted Bird"* (1965) and *The Art of the Self: Essays as propos "Steps"* (1968). See also Byron Sherwin, "The Pained [sic] Bird: A Friend's Reminiscence of Jerzy Kosinski," unpublished paper (Chicago: Spertus College of Judaica, June 1991). For an excellent essay in the wake of his death, see John Taylor, "The Haunted Bird: The Death and Life of Jerzy Kosinski," *New York Magazine, July 15, 1991,* pp. 24-37. also see the fine biography by James Park Sloan, *Jerzy Kosinski: A Biography* (New York: Dutton, 1996).

Langer, Lawrence L., *Art from the Ashes: A Holocaust Anthology* (New York: Oxford University Press, 1995). I have found this book useful for thumbnail sketches of Celan, Levi, Améry, Borowski, and others. See also him many other books, including *Admitting the Holocaust* (New York: Oxford University Press, *1995),* and *The Holocaust and the Literary Imagination* (New Haven: Yale University Press, 1974); as well as *Holocaust Testimonies* (New Haven: Yale Univ. Press, 1991), *Versions of Survival* (Albany, NY: State Univ.

of New York Press, *1982),* and *The Age of Atrocity* (Boston: Beacon Press, *1978).*
Levi, Primo, *The Drowned and the Saved* (New York: Random House, 1989), esp. P. 127. His many other works include *Survival in Auschwitz* (London: Collier Books, 1969) and *The Periodic Table* (New York: Schocken Books, 1984). His poems can also be found in Forche, ed., *Against Forgetting, pp. 373-76.* See also Eitinger, ("Identification," pp. 10-12; and Langer, *Art from the Ashes, pp.* 106-18.
Maxwell, Robert. See the biography by Tom Bower, *Maxwell, The Outsider* (New York: Viking Books, *1992).* Several new biographies on Maxwell have appeared, including one by his widow, Elizabeth Maxwell, *A Mind of my Own* (New York: Harper Collins, 1994).
Porter, Jack Nusan. See *The Jew as Outsider* (Lanham, MD: University Press of American, *1982),* which will be reprinted soon, and "Is There a Survivor's Syndrome? Psychological and Socio-Polictical Implications," *Journal of Psychology and Judaism* (Fall-Winter, 1981), and "On Therapy, Research, and Other Dangerous Phenomena," *Shoah (1979).* Both essays as well as others on cognate issues can be found in Jack Nusan Porter, Confronting History and Holocaust: Collected Essays, *1972-1982* (Lanham, MD: University Press of America, *1983),* pp. *79-82* and 83-105. See as well "The Affirmation of Life After the Holocaust: The Contributions of Bettelheim, Lifton, and Frankl," in *Confronting History and Holocaust,* pp. 122-129. See also Jack Nusan Porter, "Social-Psychological Aspects of the Holocaust," in *Encountering the Holocaust,* ed., Byron Sherwin and Susan Ament (Chicago: Impact Press, 1979), pp. 189-221.
Sociological Sources: See Emile Durkheim, *Suicide* (1897; reprint, New York: Free Press, 1951), and such sociology textbook discussions as John J. Mactonis, *Sociology,* 5th ed. (Englewood Cliffs: Prentice-Hall, 1995), pp. 4-6, 117-120; William Levin, *Sociological Ideas,* 4th ed. (Belmont Calif.: Wadsworth, 1994), pp. 396-402. For "autogenocides," see William Zellner, Vehicular Suicide: In Search of Incidence" (M.A. thesis, Western Illinois University, 1978, quoted in McGraw-Hill, 1992), pp. 54-55. See also Diana Kendall, *Sociology in Our Times* Belmont, Calif.: Wadsworth, 1996), p. 74. See Donna Barnes's work on black suicides, Sociology Department, Northeastern University, Boston, Mass. 1996.
Holocaust reference sources: See Abraham J. Edelheit and Hershel Edelheit, *History of the Holocaust* (Boulder: Westview Press, 1994),

pp. 264-65. On Arthur Zyglboim, see Naomi Seidman "Letter from a Cemetery," *Forward* (New York City), September 20, 1996, p. 1 and 3, for a fascinating article on a "secular cemetery" of European writers and intellectuals buried in New York city. For quotes of American survivors and their views of suicide, all too short though tantalizing, see William Helmreich, *Against All Odds* (New York: Simon and Schuster, 1992).

Interesting connections between the suicides of Walter Benjamin in 1940 and an earlier suicide attempt by Arthur Koestler and then a successful one in London in the 1980s, see Martin Jay, *The Dialectical Imagination: A History of the Frankfurt School and the Institute of Social Research, 1923-1950* (Boston: Little, Brown, 1973), pp. 198 and 336 (nn. 112-124). See also U.S. Holocaust Memorial Museum, *Fifty Years Ago: In the Depth of Darkness* (Washington, D.C.: 1992), p. 236 (Bruno Bettelheim), p. 244 (Tadeusz Borowski); p. 246 (Primo Levi, Jerzy Kosinski, Jakov Lind); and p. 248 (Art Spiegelman).

Part IV

Social and Psychological Issues

Chapter 12

Toward a Sociology of Evil: Why Men Kill

In this short essay, I will try to explain what van der Dennen's calls the "terrifyingly normal" roots of evil. Naturally, I cannot answer this question in so short a space; the best minds in the world have tried to answer the question of why men kill. This essay is also an entry point for a dialogue with my colleague Prof. James Waller (2002) of Whitworth College who lays out the nature of extraordinary evil in even more detail.

We are scientists, not theologians, and we must approach this issue with scientific rigor. In short, let us develop a sociology of evil as a scientific field. Too often, the field has been left to preachers and novelists to define evil. This perspective goes back to Elie Wiesel in his "effability theory"; that is, he feels that the Holocaust is so "ineffable," so incapable of being expressed in words, so indescribable, that humans will always fail in their attempt; in fact, Wiesel feels that it is almost "taboo" to even try to describe the evil that occurred during the Holocaust.

We must reject Prof. Weisel's thesis or else we would have to "close shop" as social scientists. Ordinary men carried out the Holocaust and other genocides, not aliens from another planet, and thus, ordinary men and women can understand and even predict such behavior.

A second point: I use the word "men" purposely in the title. I feel that it is *men* who have done most of the killing on earth and men who continue to do so. Not that women are incapable of killing but that *sociologically*, most women do not get the opportunity to do so in large "genocidal" terms; perhaps individually, they commit *homicides*; however, they rarely direct massive *genocides*. I also feel that men have more of an inclination, being the aggressor, to kill than women, by and large.

The Genetic Basis: The "Bad Seed" Theory

This is the "evil gene" theory, the "bad seed" that Patty McCormack's character played in a movie of the same name, where she kills a young boy just because he acted in a certain way. Yes, there may be a genetic component within us that is triggered under certain social conditions; that is, like a cancer or infection, it lies just below the surface, ready to be triggered by certain environments. It may be provocative to say so but just as there is a "bad seed" so too one day, there may be an antidote as well. Where one could get close enough to a genocidal leader and slip the antidote in the food not to kill him but to change that part of the brain that is the killing center. It sounds like science fiction but it may not be far off in reality. The problem will not be in the neuro-medical breakthrough to find such an "anti-genocidal" drug but in its delivery system.

Just as Freud predicted a biological basis for neurosis with medication to treat mental illness (a reality today), so too, one day there will be a pill that a future Hitler or Pol Pot could take to stop their genocide.

It is also possible that men have this "killing gene" more so than woman so there is a gender as well as neurological and biological basis for evil.

The Theological or Metaphysical Theory

One could see evil as the work of the "devil," as a part of a Manichaean world of the good kingdom of God, associated with the forces of light, and an evil kingdom of Satan, associated with darkness. Awareness of light causes greed, hate, and envy in the darkness, and provokes an attack of darkness against the sons and daughters of light. This is the mythological background to basic Manichaean philosophy. In essence, one could see the Nazis as the forces of darkness who came to destroy the forces of good.

Christianity adapted some of the teachings of the founder of the Manichaean religion, Mani (A.D. 216-277). In Christian mythology, Lucifer, the fallen angel, was once a favorite servant of God but became rebellious out of pride. He rose up against the Lord, deserted from heaven, taking one-third of the angels with him to hell. ("Better to reign in hell than serve in heaven," Milton wrote). From Hell, Lucifer conspires to spread evil throughout the world.

Greek philosophy sought a different explanation. Socrates, for example, held the intellectualist stance that no one would willingly stray from *agathon*, the good, except out of ignorance. His disciple, Plato, by contrast came to view good and evil (*kakon*) not as value judgments but more as hypothetical realities (or forms), objects potentially willed by the soul. Evil was thought to be removable from the soul by purgation (*katharsis*), somewhat analogous to sweating out a bodily disease.

Aristotle in turn developed the Pythagorean notion of evil as imbalance by treating evil as excess in his *Nichomachean Ethics*; however, he also treated it as the indeterminate, inexplicable "other" (*apeiron*).

The view of evil as ambivalent power, and not simply as the opposite of good, reverberates in many people's minds on how to explain misfortune. If our world were in "good" order, good things would happen to good people and bad things would happen to bad people. However, in reality, good things often happen to bad people and bad things to good people. This poses a problem to people who believe that the world is ruled by a good God. It has often led to the "death of God" theology or that God is "on vacation" during evil times. In other words, God is either absent or totally ineffectual, leaving the world to Satan and Lucifer. Many theologians have wrestled with this implication, and there are no easy answers.

The Psychoanalytic (id-ego-superego conflict) or Psychological (projection) Theory

The psychoanalytic perspective sees man as outwardly normal and sane (and good) yet inwardly seething with neurotic conflicts, leading to anger, pain, torture, and evil acts. It was this Victorian world that Sigmund Freud laid bare. World War I in essence proved him correct: namely that man was basically conflicted and that given the right circumstances was capable of extraordinary evil. Freud was surprised neither by the slaughter of World War I nor the rise of Nazism leading to World War II (sadly or happily he died in 1939, right before the war began).

Freud developed a theory of the mind that has come to dominate modern thought. His notions of the unconscious, of a mind divided against itself, where the id (instinctive drives) battles the superego (morality, conscience) with the ego as an often embattled and losing referee, have helped shape modern consciousness. According to Freud, repressed sexuality was also identified as a cause of evil.

People kill because they are in conflict, because they have insufficient defenses against their id, their evil instincts. This internal conflict is inevitable. Aggression, the death instinct turned outward, was a normal outcome of such conflict, and Freud remained pessimistic about reason and conscience winning this battle.

When an individual, group, or society is in inner crisis, the temptation to blame external forces or others for this evil is frequently utilized. Evil is projected onto an unwanted object, which serves as a scapegoat. If this scapegoat has traditionally been the "other," so much the better and the easier to kill. This is projection theory, blaming the other for one's misfortunes, and then killing the "other" in order to gain peace of mind, wealth, power, and control.

Social-Psychological Theories of Evil

Social psychologists such as Stanley Milgram (1975), Philip Zimbardo (1978), Edwin Staub (1989), Herbert Kelman, and Solomon Asch subscribe to the thesis that peer-pressure or authority-driven pressure induces evil. In the famous Milgram experiments at Yale University in the early 60s, "teachers" were told by the experimenter (dressed appropriately in a white coat akin to a doctor) to use electric shocks on "students" who failed a word test. Over 70 percent of the "teachers" shocked their "victims" to the maximum, all the while being assured that the experimenter would take total responsibility for any "repercussions" such as injury or even death to the "student-victim." A classic and controversial experiment, and one that cannot be replicated today.

Zimbardo, a social psychologist at Stanford University one quiet summer, asked for volunteers among students, some to play guards, some to play prisoners, in a mock prison in the basement of an office building. Zimbardo had to stop the experiment after a few days because the "guards" got so involved in their roles they started abusing the "prisoners." Zimbardo was shocked at how plastic human personality was in a group setting. Monsters could be created in just a few days.

Staub (1989) found that ordinary psychological processes and normal, common human motivation are the primary sources of evil. Frequently, a perpetrator's own insecurity and suffering cause him to harm others. However, this view is not uncontested. Baumeister (1996) came to the conclusion that violent people tended to have highly favorable opinions of themselves and were in fact conceited, arrogant, and often consumed with thoughts of their own superiority. This runs contrary to the well-entrenched view that low self-esteem is a major cause of violence.

However, Staub (1989) regards evil in groups as similar but not identical to evil in individuals. Moral constraints are less powerful in groups than in individuals as there is a diffusion of responsibility in groups. Members often relinquish authority and guidance to the group and to a strong leader. They abandon responsibility to the group and develop a commitment that enables them to sacrifice even their lives for it (Campbell, 1965).

Naturally, in real life, people with a conscience, altruistic personalities who would risk their lives to stop evil and save at-risk victims, would be killed off quickly, leaving behind a dispirited population overwhelmed by an authoritarian cadre. The social-psychological literature on group pressure is vast and hotly contested. Real life is vastly more complex. We are neither cowards nor heroes—but something very human in between. (For a discussion of these issues and other interpretations of evil, see the Dutch political scientist from the University of Groningen, J.M.G. van der Dennen (1999/2000).

The Goldhagen-Browning Controversy

The controversy between Daniel Goldhagen (1996) and Christopher Browning (1992) is a real-life adaptation of such social-psychological theories and reflects the difference between ideological theories of evil (anti-semitism, racism) as espoused by Goldhagen and peer-pressure theories as a espoused by Browning. In short, do people—in this case, did the ordinary German kill because they hated Jews or because they were pressured by the Nazi Party, by one's peers, and by one's officers. As Waller (2002:36-39) in his book, points out: "Goldhagen contends that an extraordinary German culture, infused with a rabid, eliminationist anti-semitism, predisposed its citizens to the commission of this extraordinary evil." Browning (1992:189), however, concludes his book with these words: "Within virtually every social collective, the peer group exerts tremendous pressures on behavior and sets moral norms. If the men of Reserve Police Battalion 101 could become killers under such circumstances, what group of men cannot?"

As I've shown in other of my essays in this book, I espouse a "two-step solution"—anti-semitism began the process and then peer-pressure and a totalitarian state re-enforced the killings.

Conclusions

The view that most violence is performed by a small minority of truly evil people is mistaken. Especially in a group context of a nation at war, mass violence tends not to be committed by extraordinary villains but by rather normal people like you and me (See van der Dennen, 1999/2000: 20).

This position goes back nearly four decades to Hannah Arendt's classic book *Eichmann in Jerusalem: A Report on the Banality of Evil* (1964/1994). Arendt concluded that "the trouble with Eichmann was precisely that so many were like him, and that the many were neither perverted nor sadistic, that they were, and still are, terribly and terrifyingly normal."

These chilling words resound even today. Whether we speak of serial killers such as Jeffrey Dahmer and Ed Gein or mass murderers such as Adolf Eichmann and Franz Stangel, they are "terrifyingly normal" to the outward eye.

Group membership, such as being a member of the National Socialists, provided people like Eichmann with ideological, material, and emotional support and justification for their deeds while the diffusion of responsibility in the large organization pacified conscience. Other ways to reduce scruples was to devalue the victims, to place them, as sociologist Helen Fein says, "outside the moral universe of human responsibility."

They are thus labeled as subhuman, a danger to society, standing in the way of a better future. Blaming the victim for past and present troubles also serves to dehumanize them.

Individuals who kill do not see themselves as part of a collective. They see themselves above morality, above God. Nazis who killed, on the other-hand, saw themselves as part of a group and the group helped them to kill ever more efficiently and in greater numbers.

In looking at these theories, we come to the awful truth that evil is not a mystery at all; it is "terrifyingly normal," but the real question is: Why don't people who kill value life? Why is life so valueless to them?

(2001)

Sources

Arendt, Hannah, *Eichmann in Jerusalem: A Report on the Banality of Evil*. New York: Viking, 1994. Originally published in 1964.

Baumeister, R.F., *Evil: Inside Human Cruelty and Violence*. New York: Freeman, 1996.

Browning, Christopher R., *Ordinary Men: Reserve Police Battalion 101 and the Final Solution in Poland*. New York: Harper Perennial, 1992

Campbell, Donald T., "Ethnocentric and Other Altruistic Motives" in Donald Levine (ed), *Nebraska Symposium on Motivation*. Lincoln, NE: University of Nebraska Press, 1965.

Goldhagen, Daniel Jonah, *Hitler's Willing Executioners: Ordinary Germans and the Holocaust*. New York: Alfred Knopf, 1996.

Milgram, Stanley, *Obedience to Authority*. New York: Harper and Row, 1975.

Staub, Erwin, *The Roots of Evil: The Psychological and Cultural Origins of Genocide and Other Forms of Group Violence*. New York: Cambridge University Press, 1989.

Van Der Dennen, J. M. G. "Interpretations of Evil: The Terrifyingly Normal Roots of Evil" in *PIOOM Newsletter and Progress Report* (Leiden university, the Netherlands). Vol. 9, No. 1, Winter 1999/ 2000, pp. 17-20.

Waller, James, *Becoming Evil: How Ordinary People Commit Genocide and Mass Killing*, New York: Oxford University Press, 2002.

Zimbardo, Philip G., "The Psychology of Evil: On the Perversion of Human Potential" in L. Krames, P. Pliner and T. Alloway (eds), *Aggression, Dominance, and Individual Spacing*. New York: Plenum Press, 1978, pp. 155-169.

Chapter 13

The Goldhagen Controversy: A Response and a Solution

Daniel Goldhagen's book *Hitler's Willing Executioners: Ordinary Germans and the Holocaust* of 1996 has become the most controversial book on the subject since Hannah Arendt's *Eichmann in Jerusalem* came out in 1963. It has become a bestseller both here and in Germany yet every single major Holocaust scholar has condemned it as deeply flawed. How could this have happened? The story tells us a great deal about a field that is in deep disarray.

How do you sell a controversial dissertation? Get a young Harvard professor, a fresh new face, a powerful and influential publisher, and create a media circus. A major book company gets caught up by Harvard's reputation and by scholars who are not Holocaust scholars; Stanley Hoffman, Peter Hall, and Sidney Verba, Danny Goldhagen's dissertation committee, none of them are experts on the Holocaust; fine political scientists and Europeanists, yes, but not one of them a Holocaust scholar; and they are as embarrassed and upset as anyone by this controversy. Harvard hates both popularity and controversy, and the contentious debate over his book may have also harmed Goldhagen's chances to have become Harvard's first holder of a Holocaust chair, the Helen Zelaznic Chair in Holocaust and Cognate Studies endowed by Kenneth Lipper, a philanthropist and former New York deputy mayor, who named the chair in honor of a family member who was killed in the Holocaust. The one person who could have helped Danny Goldhagen—his father—a Holocaust scholar, albeit rarely published—should have written this book but this being a dissertation, even at Harvard, a father cannot write a son's dissertation. However together, and heavily edited and shortened, this might have a been a great book. In any case, to publish a dissertation with a premier publisher like Knopf is extremely rare. Knopf became entranced by the Harvard name and by their own media hype.

Goldhagen thanks his Dad on page 604 for "keen insights" but his father, at least from remarks in his own classroom, in a Holocaust course in which I sat in at Harvard says geometrically the opposite, that it was *careerism as well as anti-Semitism* that propelled these "willing killers," especially among the Einzatzgruppen and SS guards.

I got from his father a much more textured, multi-layered approach to the issue and it is doubly strange in that even his own father does not hold to Goldhagen's extreme view. There are multi-causal, not monocausal, reasons for the Holocaust. The older Goldhagen understood that the Holocaust cannot be reduced to one single factor, important as it was. Anti-Semitism was a factor but not the sole factor and, in some cases, perhaps not even a factor at all.

Bureaucracy, obedience to orders, peer pressure, careerism, protecting one's pension, all those good sociological, social psychological, and organizational theories that scholars from Raul Hilberg to Robert Lifton to Stanley Milgram to Helen Fein have presented over the years were simply brushed aside by a boyish-looking junior professor from Harvard!

Anti-Semitism is, of course, crucial to understanding Nazi racism and we should thank Goldhagen for re-emphasizing this point, but sorry, he doesn't go far enough. Germans were not zealous anti-Semites as much as Goldhagen thinks nor was the zealotry caused by anti-Semitism. The "socialized need" to do a complete and exacting job (*punctlichkeit*), a trait, it seems, endemic to Germans, and to destroy all traces of the evil Jews perpetrated, made them zealots.

Goldhagen's treatment of German anti-Semitism in his early chapters is however quite enlightening and has been overlooked by critics.

It is *chutzpadic* on his part to say thirty years after Hannah Arendt that scholars have done little in this field and have "overlooked" anti-Semitism. This is nonsense and perhaps insulting. That explains why scholars such as Yehuda Bauer, Raul Hilberg, and Hans Mommsen are so incensed about the book. Some of it is due to envy, that's true, but more likely it is the reaction of an older father to an insolent child. Goldhagen is the insolent and boyishly charming child who won't listen to his elders.

The Goldhagen Controversy: A Response and a Solution

No book since Hanna Arendt's *Eichmann in Jerusalem* has generated such controversy: but while Arendt was a self-hating Jew who wrote a book critical of Jews, Danny has written a book critical of Germans and loved by Jews. It is also ironic that many of these same scholars (Hilberg, Mommsen, Bauer) were just as critical of Arendt's book as of Danny's dissertation.

My theory: a two-step approach: Anti-Semitism was the animus that launched the Holocaust but then bureaucracy, obedience to orders, careerism, peer pressure, and all the myriad sociological, organizational, and psychological motivators mentioned above took over. What Erich Goldhagen calls the "foot in the door" theory explains the perpetrators' actions: that once the killing started it took on a momentum of its own. This is "Porter's Two-Step Theory" and combines both Arendt and (Daniel) Goldhagen. Anti-Semitism was of course a crucial element but not the only element: the Holocaust showed that you could kill Jews without being an anti-Semite!

Furthermore, my theory takes into account the one book and scholar that Goldhagen relegates to footnotes in his book. Never once does he mention in the context of his book the contribution of Christopher Browning's classic volume, *Ordinary Men: Reserve Police Battalion 101 and the Final Solution in Poland* (1992). He relegates him simply to obscure footnotes.

This is not only disingenuous but scandalous. First, because Goldhagen came across Browning personally in Germany while working in the same archives of the police battalions and knew of his work. Second, the book's title "ordinary Germans" was chosen to directly contradict Brownings "ordinary men": and third, most crucially, Browning comes to exactly the opposite conclusions to Goldhagen after studying the judicial interrogations of these 125 men. *Ordinary Men* clearly shows that Reserve Battalion 101 was comprised of ordinary (some would say decent and honorable) men turned into hardened killers.

Why did most men in this battalion become killers, while only a minority of perhaps 10 percent—and certainly no more than 20 percent—did not? Browning offers a number of explanations: wartime brutalization, racism, Segmentation and routinization of the task, the suddenness of the orders, not wanting to be seen as cowards by their peers, peer pressure, careerism, obedience to orders, deference to authority, ideological indoctrination (anti-Semitism), conformity, and perhaps I would add a distinctive German trait—the ability to finish the job, any job, no matter how heinous. Maybe that's racist to say but Germans are like that. They are told what to do and they do it. If they had been told to plant a sloppy kiss on every Jew, they would have done that as well. In that sense, it's not that we are all "Nazis" but that many Germans knew how to obey orders better than other people and thus they became "good Nazis." There are a small portion of any nation, even our own, that can become "good Nazis," that is people who will commit mass murder. Racism and anti-Semitism comprise only one aspect of the motivation.

Collective guilt. Did all Germans support the Final Solution? Again, no. More should have rebelled, it's true; more should have stood up especially amongst such major institutions as the church and the army but no, I don't believe in collective guilt, then or now. I simply don't, and I think most Holocaust scholars concur with me. Germans lived in a totalitarian police state, where even Hitlerjugend informed on their parents. It was very difficult to resist. Most Germans were against the genocide of the Jews even if they supported Hitler in other areas.

I also don't believe that "eliminationist" anti-Semitism is inbred into the German soul, though even Raul Hilberg does write about Luther and compares Luther's writings to later Nazi creeds. Jews flourished in Germany before the rise of Nazism: ten percent of all doctors and lawyers were Jews, nearly all the department stores in Germany were Jewish owned. In fact if a poll would have been taken of the German people in the 1930s to (a) exile the Jews; (b) kill all the Jews; or (c) turn them into second-class citizens by a process of marginalization, the vast majority of Germans would have chosen answer (c).

Furthermore, many other people also held "eliminationist" views, such as the Austrians, Poles, Ukrainians, Lithuanians, Roumanians, and Hungarians. Why pick only on the Germans? Also, a difference needs to be made in each occupied country between ordinary people and Nazis or Nazi-aligned groups and especially between Germans and Nazis; not all Germans were Nazis, an obvious point that needs to be stressed. Daniel Goldhagen says that 100,000 Germans took part directly in the Holocaust "death machine"; that is an abominably high figure but still only a fraction of one percent of Germany's 60 million people. To paint the concept of "eliminationist" anti-Semitism onto the Germans is as racist as what the Nazis did to the Jews.

Goldhagen's book has raised such a storm that we need a forum for the world's most eminent scholars to present their views in a civil manner and to have Daniel Goldhagen and his father respond if they wish.

The Goldhagen Controversy: A Response and a Solution

People should of course read the book *first* before they jump on the bandwagon of criticism. Many critics simply have *not* read the book or have relied on hearsay and gossip. This also echoes what happened in the 1960s to Hannah Arendt and her book.

There are many useful features to Goldhagen's book, and it is important that he has re-directed our attention to anti-Semitism, a factor too many scholars did indeed take for granted, but that still does not diminish the fact that the book is deeply flawed and could have been corrected at the dissertation stage. Only at Harvard it seems could this have occurred.

It shows us how little the public knows of the Holocaust and how easy it is for newcomers in the field to promulgate their theories. I have never seen a book highlight the *gap* between the scholarly and intellectual world as this one has. Here is a study that has been nominated for every major book prize by panels of intellectuals who know little of the Holocaust except what they have seen in *Schindler's List* or *Night and Fog*. Come to think of it: perhaps *that* is the scandal and not Goldhagen's thesis.

(1997)

Chapter 14

Is There a Survivor's Syndrome? Psychological and Socio-Political Implications

An analysis of the children of survivors and their parents through the use of sociological observation and examination of the literature is presented, showing that there exists a psychological survivor's syndrome among the victims of the Holocaust. Also, the basis for a socio-political syndrome is indicated. As for the children of survivors, most of whom are now between 20-35 years of age, there is not enough data to say for sure, but it is highly unlikely that a pathological syndrome exists, though a mild secondary guilt syndrome may appear in some cases. More research with larger samples is necessary. As for a socio-political syndrome, superficial observation yields that a large number of children of survivors are committed to making sense out of the Holocaust and this can lead to a wide variety of creative political and religious actions. Also presented are some observations on the third generation of survivors, the offspring of the children of the original survivors.

* * * * *

The purpose of this paper is to present a survey of the highlights of the socio-psychological literature concerning the aftereffects of the Holocaust upon survivors and their children, and to answer the question whether there exists a "survivor's syndrome" among both survivors and their children. Furthermore, this paper will introduce a new concept, the *socio-political syndrome* among survivors and their offspring. In short, it will try to answer the question whether one can generalize about a socio-political syndrome as well as a psychological syndrome among these two groups.

Literature in this area divides into two parts, each overlapping the other; psycho-analytical case studies written by psychologists and psychiatrists and personal memoirs or journalistic accounts written by survivors themselves or by sympathetic writers. Though a significant body of literature exists, most of it is based on small clinical samples. There is a great deal of work to be done not only by psychologists but by sociologists and political scientists in order to expand our knowledge of survivors. Researchers in the past too often emphasized severe pathology not only of the first generation but the second generation of survivors as well. This paper questions whether a "pathological" approach is sufficient. It proposes that social psychological and sociological studies be developed in order to examine those survivors and their children who function normally and who are not beset by severe psychological problems. In other words, the socio-political aspects of these groups must also be examined in order to round out the picture of the Holocaust survivors.

Disaster Studies: An Overview

Generally, studies of the Holocaust victims fall under the broad category of disaster research. These studies contain several labels—"trauma research," "stress or seige studies," "collective behavior," "catastrophe studies," and "disaster research." There are four major approaches which scientists take (Grossen, Welchsler, and Greenblatt, 1969).

General Systems Theory

General Systems Theory is concerned with the structure and process of systems of social phenomena. The concepts of adaptation to stress, equilibrium maintenance in reaction to such stress, information-processing, inputs, and outputs are all used in this approach. General systems theory is useful in precisely defining and manipulating social variables within a given system, especially through the use of computers and statistical models. It is an important tool in research and should be used more widely in this field but I find the approach too mechanical and consequently will not use it in this discussion.

Collective Behavior Theory

Collective Behavior Theory is another popular approach to disaster studies. Collective behavior is actually a generic term for various social phenomena; crowds, riots, revolts, propaganda, public opinion, mass migration, and natural and man-made disasters. Such an approach emphasizes group morale, leadership, cohesiveness, collective defense, rumor control, and other manifestations of group behavior. This theoretical approach is also a useful tool but will not be stressed in this article.

Socio-Political Theory

Socio-Political Theory emphasizes the sociological, religious, cultural, political, and economic adaptations of survivors and victims to disaster. This approach will be widely used in the discussion of a possible "socio-political syndrome" among survivors and their children. This approach places the survivor in his/her normal socio-economic setting after the Holocaust and stresses the *positive* rather than the pathological adaptations of the victims.

Psycho-analytical Theory

Psycho-analytical Theory puts its major emphasis on individual reactions to stressful situations. The vocabulary of this approach concentrates on such concepts as trauma, emotional reaction, threat, defense, anxiety, guilt, and internal conflict. It is both a therapeutic and analytical approach; that is, it is both therapy and theory. Bruno Bettelheim, Viktor Frankl, Elie Cohen, Robert J. Lifton, William Niederland, Judith Kestenberg, H.Z. Winnik, Vivian Rakoff and John Sigal are the most widely-read figures in this field. This approach will be used in this paper in describing the "psychological syndrome" of survivors and their children.

One danger is to rely solely upon one approach. Each perspective gives only one view of the subject. It is necessary to utilize as many approaches as possible in order to obtain a complete picture. For example, the weakness of much of the Holocaust research is that it is rarely comparative. Concentration camp research is actually a subcategory of research on such total institutions as military prisons, POW camps, and civilian prisons. If Jews in such camps were compared to soldiers in POW camps, a more balanced and less defensive perspective could emerge. If the Jewish reaction to ghettoization and persecution were compared to reactions of civilians to such diverse phenomena as nuclear attack, natural disasters, air-raids, and collective panic, then research would show that the Jews reacted similarly to other groups (Grosser, Welchsler, and Greenblatt, 1964). If Jewish survivors could be compared to Armenian or Gypsy survivors, again a more balanced picture could be drawn. In short, the appearance of guilt and other psychological reactions are as normal for survivors of the Holocaust as they are for survivors of nuclear attack, natural disasters, war combat, or intense life-depriving accidents such as plane or car crashes.

What is a Survivor?

Before the outbreak of World War II, there were about 8.8 million Jews living in Europe. Approximately 5.8-6.2 million Jews were killed in the Holocaust. Of the three million who remained, it has been estimated that between 400,000-500,000 survived the war years in labor camps, in the partisans, hiding in caves, in the forests or the countryside. No more than 75,000 outlived the concentration camps (Epstein, 1977). Thus, there are about a half million or three million survivors depending on one's definition. I will adhere to the half-million figure: that is, *a survivor is someone who has survived an immediate and traumatic life-threatening experience*. Otherwise, one could say that all Jews everywhere were survivors because it was the Nazi aim to exterminate all of them. But this, while true in a metaphorical sense, would only confuse the issue.

We could say that there are about one-half million children of survivors in the world, the majority of them between 25-35 years old. Their parents range in age from 55 to 75, assuming they were between 20-40 years old when the war ended in 1945. The largest number of survivors went to live in Israel, with many coming to the United States and Canada, and with other large pockets of survivors in South America, England, France, and the Soviet Union. Many of these survivors and their children live in distinct communities set apart not only from the non-Jewish, but also from the already established Jewish community.

The label of survivor will be used for anyone who experienced life-threatening traumas and who left Europe in the 1930s—mostly German and Austrian Jews, as well as those who went through the DP camp experience and left in the late 1940s and early 1950s for Israel, Canada, the Americas, or other countries. The children of survivors are defined as those who are the offspring of survivors, whether or not these children experienced the Nazi trauma first-hand or not. That is, it includes those born in Europe during the war, those born in DP camps after the war, and those born in the "new" country long after the war.

This paper will outline the psychological symptoms of survivors and the socio-political coping behaviors of first-generation survivors. It will then explore the psychological and then the socio-political coping behavior of the children of survivors. Some feel that the Nazi trauma is re-experienced in the lives of the children and even the grandchildren of survivors. Is this true only for those who were death camp survivors or for all types of survivors? What is the magnitude, severity, and duration of these effects? How are these effects passed on to future generations? It may not be possible to answer all these questions in this paper, but they will be raised so that others can find an answer.

Clinical Symptomology of Holocaust Survivors

Psychiatrists have attempted to explain whether or not there exists an entity called the "survivor syndrome" and if so, what are its manifestations. One of the world's foremost authorities on psychic trauma, . William G. Niederland, has outlined some of the primary and secondary characteristics of adults on whom repeated traumata has been inflicted (in Krystal & Niederland, 1971).

> Personality changes in the survivor of such experiences are related to quantitative factors. Massive traumatic experiences of this kind have devastating effects on the total ego organization. Most survivors suffer from chronic or recurrent depressive reactions often accompanied by states of anxiety, phobic fears, nightmares, somatic equivalents, and brooding ruminations about the past and lost-love objects.
>
> The sequelae of massive and repeated traumatization are:
>
> 1. Anxiety, usually associated with phobic or hypochondriacal fears, alone or in combination.
> 2. Disturbances of cognition and memory.
> 3. Chronic depressive reactions characterized by guilt, seclusion, and isolation.

4. Psychosomatic symptoms or disorders.
5. Psychosis-like psychotic manifestations.
6. Life-long sense of heightened vulnerability to and increased awareness of dangerous situations.
7. Disturbances of sense identity, body-image, and self-image.
8. Permanent personality changes. (pp. 1-9)

Let us examine in more detail what Niederland calls the sequelae or aftereffects of traumatization.

Anxiety

This is the most common complaint and is associated with fear of renewed persecution. Victims manifest deep disturbances, phobias, anxiety dreams, and rerun nightmares. Chronic insomnia occurs due to these recurrent nightmares and anxieties.

Disturbances of Cognition and Memory

Amnesia, especially upon waking up from nightmares, is the most prevalent disturbance here. Lost or bewildered states and a sense of disorientation from the present are also found.

Chronic Depressive Reactions

These reactions, from masochistic character changes to psychotic depression, cover a wide range. In their severity, the reactions are correlated to the intensity of survivor guilt based on the loss of loved ones.

Tendency to Isolation, Withdrawal, and Brooding

Survivors are marked by unstable or difficult relationships and problems with intimacy. These psychological states manifest themselves in other social settings and victims often withdraw from political and community involvement.

Alterations of Personal Identity

These include impairment of body image and self-image and manifest themselves in frequent complaints of "I am a different person," "I am a weaker, more abhorrent person," or in some cases, "I am not a person." At its most extreme, the image of the *musselman* or living corpse appearance which some victims exhibit is an example of this alteration. Robert Lifton makes similar statements about Hiroshima survivors who exhibit a kind of psychic numbing, a closing-off of feelings, manifested by a macabre, shadowy, shuffling, and ghost-like impression. The all-encompassing psychological scar on the total personality is often a defense against death anxiety and death guilt. In milder forms it appears as sluggish despair consisting of diminished vitality, easy fatigability, "weakness," "exhaustion" of the nervous system, and "inadequate functioning of an organ system of the body." One must, however, be careful with facile comparisons between a sudden event like nuclear attack as in Hiroshima and long-term trauma as in concentration camp life.

Psychosomatic Conditions

Such conditions are quite common and form the basis for many German restitution claims. They can exhibit themselves immediately after liberation for the trauma or many years later. Research is needed to find out if there is a "ticking-clock" syndrome—illnesses induced by the Nazi experience 20, 30, or 40 years after the event. These conditions include diseases related to chronic states of tension or anger; gastrointestinal conditions, peptic ulcers, and related symptoms; cardiovascular disturbances such as angina pectoris, heart disease, etc.; cancer; and the typical survivor triad of headaches, persistent nightmares, and chronic depression accompanied by various psychosomatic complaints.

Psychotic and Psychotic-like States

These occur in the most extreme cases of survivor traumata. Regressive and primitive methods of dealing with aggression can result in schizophrenic-like symptoms such as hallucinations, fantasy-building, states of depersonalization, hypochondriatic symptoms, or paranoid manifestations, all having a very specific history and determination.

Conclusion

Research in the field definitely shows that Holocaust survivors do manifest a psychological survivor syndrome with at minimum, the survivor triad mentioned above, and at maximum, the more pathological problems stated above. It should be emphasized however that most survivors have adapted quite well to their traumatic experience and live fairly normal lives. Psychologists tend to generalize from small clinical samples and emphasize only the pathological. They should take a cue from Abraham Maslow and begin to balance the picture with case studies of the strengths and self-affirmations of Holocaust survivors. They too often dwell only on the negative. Research on the *positive* aspects of "survivorship" should be encouraged.

Coping Behavior of Survivors: Social and Political Adaptations

The study now moves away from psychological studies into the realm of sociology. Research on the sociology of Holocaust survivors and their children is almost non-existent. While there is some literature on the socio-political acculturation of immigrant groups to America, the following section is a first step towards a description of socio-political adaptation of specifically post-World War II Holocaust survivors. What follows is a brief series of observations and hypotheses that require more quantitative verification. The observations are generalized from the survivor community of Milwaukee, Wisconsin, where I lived from 1948-1968, and I discuss an Ashkenazic, Eastern European milieu. Other survivor communities, such as those composed of Sephardic or Austro-German Holocaust survivors, would differ in some respects from this sample in the areas of education, religiosity, assimilation, and other factors.

Jewish survivors of the Holocaust are also new immigrants to their host country, whether that be Israel, the USA, Canada, England, or Argentina. The burden of adapting to a new life style, language, and culture is added to the already heavy burden of the Holocaust trauma. The kind of adjustment they make to their new homeland depends on many variables. Among these are family situation, maturity, age, level of education, job opportunities, religious background, support of relatives and social agencies, and support from within the community of survivors.

Despite all the difficulties, most survivors have adjusted quite well. Financially, they are fairly secure; some have even become quite wealthy in the short time they have been in America. Doing fairly well does not mean that in terms of occupational status and prestige, survivors have moved far up the social ladder, but they have done better than expected given generally low levels of education and training. Many of the Russian and Polish Jews of Milwaukee went into marginal trades; tailors, caterers, scrap metal, or used auto parts dealers, mom and pop grocery stores, and garment industry jobs. A few became Hebrew teachers, cantors, sextons, and rabbis. Engineers, doctors, dentists, and professors are virtually non-existent in this community. German and Austrian Jews, on the other hand, because of their education and training were more likely to be engaged in law, medicine, or other professions.

Like most American immigrants, survivors desired for their children the utmost in schooling, and for the most part they succeeded. Within a single generation, their children very nearly caught up occupationally and educationally with their host-country contemporaries. A great many survivor-children married non-survivor children and with their advanced training and education, they entered into professions such as teaching, social work, law, accounting, or business. A few joined their parents in the family business, a fact that their parents viewed as a step-down in prestige even though these same children are much better off financially than if they had gone into, for example, teaching.

Most parents expected their children to surpass them in education and occupational mobility, and though this caused some tension between generations, it was an accepted fact. Many survivor-parents sacrificed their lives for the sake of their children's careers. This kind of sacrifice is not new in American Jewish history. It occurred at the turn of the century during the great waves of immigration from Europe, and Jewish parents have been sacrificing ever since. It will be interesting to see whether the second generation of children will sacrifice for their children.

Survivor-parents of the Milwaukee Jewish community number about 1,000 out of a total of 24,000 Jews, and they tend to cluster around six synagogues, four of them Orthodox, on the northwest side of the city. Their children and even a growing number of the parents have moved to the east or northeast part of town, a more affluent section, yet they retain their ties to the "old" Jewish neighborhood. While some parents may be non-observant, or even anti-observant, most continue to live in the religious community and observe traditions out of respect for the memory of their parents or because they truly believe in their Orthodox life style. They know no other. The relationship to their rabbis—two of the shuls are led by Hasidic *rebbes*, is the same one they maintained in their *shetlack* and cities in Eastern Europe. As one rabbi told me: "I didn't leave Rovno; I brought it with me here and built an American Rovno in Milwaukee."

Politically, survivors tend to be somewhat passive and conservative. They keep a low profile, rarely becoming involved in city, state or national politics. They try to avoid controversy, political or otherwise. Given their previous experiences, this conservatism is understandable. But another reason may simply be that they see themselves, even after thirty years in the country, as greenhorns. They are often ashamed of how they speak English, or how they act or dress. They feel that they are too ignorant of the political process to become involved, or that they will look foolish. Some are deeply suspicious and even mortally afraid of authority figures, whether policemen, politicians, or petty bureaucrats. Their children do not suffer from this fear.

Some survivors try to assimilate into the general Jewish community, and a tiny few into the general Christian population, but the vast majority seem most comfortable with their own kind. They feel that not only non-Jews but even other Jews do not really understand them or their past traumas. They react to their Americanized children in the same way. At times, neither the survivor nor the kin understands the other. Sometimes, the kin are ashamed of the survivor, and even feel the survivor is guilty for having survived.

In two areas, however, survivors are politically involved and their involvement comes with such force and devotion, that it sometimes shocks non-survivor Jews. These areas are the fate of Israel and the plight of Soviet Jewry. Survivors are very active in various fund-raising activities for these two causes, either within their synagogues or through survivor organizations such as the New American Club. These clubs should be studied more intensively. They form the nucleus of social activity for many survivors with their dances, raffles, and fund-raising events. These clubs are an opportunity for survivors to relax, speak Yiddish, and enjoy oneself in the company of a closeknit community of survivors. In fact, it is only at these clubs and at family events (weddings, bar mitzvot, a *bris*-circumcision) that I have seen survivors relax and temporarily forget their past traumas.

Their ties with Israel are extremely close, not only spiritually, but socially. Many survivors have relatives in Israel and there is much contact between them. Israel is crucial to survivors psychologically as one of the few havens for Jews anywhere in the world. A disproportionate number of them support militant pro-Israeli groups such as the Jewish Defense League or the Revisionist Zionists, though many are ambivalent about the violence associated with these two groups. Many survivors also join and support the Pioneer Women, Farband, and other Labor Zionist groups and, if Orthodox, they will support the Mizrachi (Religious) Zionist organizations.

Survivors, like other Jews, have been staunch Democratic Party supporters from the time of President Truman. While there was some slippage toward the Republicans and to Richard Nixon in 1972, this was because Senator George McGovern, Nixon's opponent, was thought to have been soft in his support of Israel. In the future, too, it seems that survivors will support those candidates that are firm in their defense of Israel regardless of the candidate's other positions.

Conclusions

There is much more that one could say about the sociology and politics of survivors. We can conclude that these survivors tend to live in tightly-knit survivor communities which consist of others who speak the same language, carry on the same customs of the Old Country, of the *shtetl* or the urban ghetto of Europe. They live a richly traditional but quiet life apart from other Jews in the community, and they donate much of their limited energies to their *shul*, their rabbi, Israeli causes, and the lives of their children and grandchildren. They work very hard, sometimes too hard, perhaps in order to try and forget the past. They are politically active and quite concerned, even paranoid, about anti-Semitism and about Israel.

There is a socio-political "syndrome" that one can generalize. Survivors do share many common sociological features. Quotes around the word "syndrome" are used because the common dictionary meaning of the word is that of a complex or a group of traits that are abnormal and/or undesirable. The meaning of the term "syndrome" has been changed to include in this case a group of traits that are positive and normal; in other words, syndrome is used to mean any group of shared traits or features. In this sense, survivors do share a socio-political syndrome as well as a psychological one, and future studies must be social-psychological in the sense they begin to understand the survivor and the children *within* the context of, and not in isolation from, the community.

Coping Behavior of Survivor-Children: Psychological Adaptations

Who precisely is a child of survivors? Judith Kestenberg, an American psychiatrist who has done extensive research in this area, defines the child of survivors as "one who was born after the Holocaust or has not been himself subjected to persecution or maltreatment" (1972, p. 323). Though this definition is fine for now, a more complex one may be needed to also convey the impact of escape, migration, and childhood development in a family of survivors as well as the direct persecution by the Nazis. The subsequent post-war experience in DP camps can also lead to psychological conflicts. Kestenberg's definition is adequate even though it spreads over a large net of survivor-children, yet it technically leaves out those who *have* been subjected to persecution or maltreatment. I suppose these children could then be considered both survivors *and* children of survivors. In any case, Kestenberg's definition will prove adequate for this discussion.

In the past few years, there has been an increased interest in the children of survivors by psychologists and by the children themselves. One should really call them young adults rather than children because most of them are now between 20 and 35 years old and are at an age where they are forming groups of survivors' children in order to discuss the implications of their self-identity. A few years ago there was not a great deal of data on the subject except for several symposia and scattered articles, all of them emphasizing the psycho-analytical impact. However, the children of survivors themselves have begun to write about their experiences and have initiated research on the topic. Much of the earlier psychiatric literature is sketchy and has small clinical samples. Also, the non-psychiatric writings are impressionistic. However, new research should soon reveal if a psychological syndrome exists among the offspring of survivors and what its parameters are. It seems, however, that with some pathological exceptions, there appears to be a mild syndrome in the making; nothing that should alarm people, but enough of a syndrome to study and evaluate.

Kestenberg herself believed (in 1972) that there was no specific syndrome among children of survivors but she was cautious about closing the book on the subject. A rather bizarre and exceptional case had forced her to keep the question open:

Some years ago I analyzed a young adolescent who behaved in a bizarre way, starving himself, hiding in woods and treating me . . . as a hostile persecutor. Soon after I connected his psychotic-like behavior with the real experiences of his parents' relatives in Europe, his symptoms abated but his analysis had to be prematurely terminated, chiefly because of his parental resistance. Haunted by the image of this patient, who came to me emaciated and hollow-eyed like a Musselman in a concentration camp, I looked at children of survivors in Israel and thought I could recognize in some faces a far away look, reminiscent of the stare of survivors of persecution. (1972, pp. 311-312)

A conclusion reached by Kestenberg was that psychiatrists themselves resisted unearthing the frightening impact of Nazi persecution on these young people. This fear appears to have abated in the past few years as more therapists are becoming aware of the need of these children to talk about their experiences.

A large number of survivors' children have sought psychiatric treatment for general problems but few therapists discuss the Holocaust as an important aspect of the child's socialization. process, even though it often is an important factor.

Therapy can be of great help not only in relieving the stress of emotional conflicts but more importantly in accelerating communication between parents and child. As one child comments:

My parents never told me anything about the war. . . . It was like sex. You didn't talk about it in my house. . . . The house was like a tomb. Sometimes we went on picnics together. But underneath something was missing. (Mostysser, 1975, pp. 4-5)

What was missing was emotional contact between the generations and a deeper, cathartic sharing of the parent's fate and its effect on them as well as upon their children. Too often parents were too ashamed or afraid to discuss the subject with their offspring. They did not wish to burden their children with their sufferings and their stories. Yet the child could sense the parents' suffering while not understanding its root in the other. At times children would blame themselves for their parents' suffering and a complex web of sadness, guilt, and helplessness would develop. Happily, more and more parents are talking to their children today. The NBC Holocaust TV special helped and the children themselves are older and more mature, more capable of initiating discussion of this formerly taboo subject. As one son of survivors recently told me: "After the NBC special, now everyone knows what I mean when I say that my parents went through the Holocaust. Everyone can share the burden a little bit, a burden that I have carried alone for over 30 years."

Eva Fogelman, a New York psychologist and a daughter of survivors, has been quoted as saying:

> I saw that psychiatrists were beginning to extend the Survivor Syndrome to us, that severe pathology was being attributed to the second generation just as it had been to our parents. . . . I began to feel that this was all wrong. Sure we were effected. But not to the pointed where we're not functioning normally or where we have more psychological problems than the normal population. (Epstein, 1977, p. 14)

Ms. Fogelman and her colleague Bella Savran began to run "awareness groups" for children of survivors in the spring of 1976, similar to women's consciousness-raising groups, or better yet, like rap-groups for Vietnam veterans. I would agree with Fogelman and Savran (1979) that a pathological secondary syndrome does not appear to exist, but a milder guilt syndrome may be a possibility. Robert Lifton calls this syndrome the "death imprint." Children may feel ashamed of their parent's victimization. This shame in turn can often lead to a series of conflicts within the child, between parent and child, and between the child and the outside world.

Steven Greenblatt (1978), in a study of ten children of Nazi concentration camp survivors, half of whom were engaged in some form of psychotherapy, with the other half having no such treatment, found that the clinical group expressed a great deal more emotional turmoil, were more frequently exposed to Holocaust material than the non-clinical group, and had stronger feelings of inherited attitudes, most notably more survival guilt feelings due to unresolved grief reaction, inadequate coping mechanisms, and subsequent crises proneness. One could question both the size and the reliability/validity of the sample, but it is one of a growing number of studies that is finding some kind of secondary syndrome at work.

Often the parents are so preoccupied with the unending mourning process and the problems of starting a new life in a strange country that they are unable to relate to their children's needs or respond with the necessary flexibility. The children's demands become overwhelming and are seen by parents as draining their already limited emotional resources. The parents then attack their children for not listening and for not understanding them. Often it is difficult to tell who is the child and who is the adult in these cases. Because they are unable to cope with the continuous anxious responses of their parents to their behavior, the children may either go out of control or respond by withdrawal into fantasy at best, or into an affectless state at worse (Sigal, 1971, pp. 58-59).

What are the effects on the survivor's children, if their parents raised them with few controls and with over-permissiveness, since because they had suffered so much, they could not tolerate their children being deprived in any way? If one has lost everything in the Holocaust, a parent may take no chances in making this "special" survivor-child unhappy. It fits the typical Yiddishah Mamma, but the survivor-parent may greatly exaggerate the usual overprotectiveness of the Jewish mother. There can appear some minor forms of sado-masochism as well, with their roots in an ambivalence toward parents. They both love and are disgusted by their parents for many reasons: (a) for not being "American" or "modern" enough, and thus being ashamed of their parents; (b) seeing their parents as weak and passive before the Nazis, and thus coming into conflict with the usual image of a strong, powerful parent; (c) blaming their parents for their suffering and misery, thus setting up a round of guilt and anger and then more guilt.

Another component of a syndrome, if a syndrome does in fact exist, is the child's behavior toward authority figures, including parents, and subsequent feelings of guilt which anger and aggression toward these figures provoke. The child who has violent urges of aggression is confronted with a paradox, and either consciously or unconsciously says: "How can I attack someone who has already suffered so much?" Parents and child then turn on each other, each escalating the other's feelings of guilt. Each blames the other for their mutual sense of deprivation and frustration. A lack of communication, a blurred sense of identity, and a potential for depression can result from the dynamics of this game of guilt (Sigal, 1971, p.59).

All of this still leaves open the question of whether there is a psychological syndrome among the children of survivors. Nevertheless, any syndrome theory will have to take into account the following variables:

Age

There is some impressionable data that the first child born after the war may suffer more intensely from secondary guilt syndrome than other siblings and that all the conflicts mentioned earlier may affect him or her more than later children. The first-born child is a special child to the parents, with much promise and responsibility. It represents the rebirth of the family and the resurrection of earlier children killed by the Nazis. While the first-born may carry extra burdens, it may also be far more ambitious, successful, and creative precisely because it has been imbued with the special hopes and needs of the parents. The child may have messianic ambitions. Children born subsequently may suffer less than the first-born, but may also achieve less.

Time of Birth

An important variable may be when and where the child was born; whether in the death camps, in the forest, the ghetto, the DP (displaced person) camp after the war, or later, in the host country.

Post-Holocaust Experiences

These experiences are often overlooked in analysis but can prove crucial. The shock of the European liberation, the displacement from previous homes, the escape from Communist countries, the trip to the host country, the formation of new families or of families re-uniting, and adjustment to the hardships of the new country are all crucial components in any syndrome theory. The post-Holocaust phase is rarely mentioned in the literature yet can be as traumatic to survivors and their children as was the actual war-time experience.

Time of Departure

Did the survivors leave before or after the war? Many German and Austrian Jews were able to leave Germany in the mid to late 1930's. Was their trauma different from the Russian or Polish Jews who managed to survive the war?

Emotional Stability of Parents

All persons suffered severe personal trauma during the war. The level of emotional maturity before and during the war is important in understanding to what extent the Holocaust affected parents and their children. The intactness of the family is also important. If there was a loss of a spouse, survivors tended to remarry as soon as possible after the war. These dyadic relationships were very strong even if romance or deep love was missing; often these were marriages of convenience. All these factors can affect the children.

Reaction to New Stress

Adaptation after persecution is of course the key element to understanding the impact of Holocaust experiences on the children. The need to succeed and the need to work to help forget the past can lead to a tendency for over-achievement and over-involvement whether in school, business, or politics, among the children of survivors. This will be discussed in the next section.

Participation in Wars of Liberation

Active participation in either the regular army, the World War II resistance movements, or the Israeli wars seems to have had a beneficial effect on both survivors and their children. The channeling of feelings of powerlessness and worthlessness against a common enemy, whether Nazis or Arabs, was beneficial for mental health. The ability to take revenge was also satisfying, though never totally, since no amount of revenge could replace the loss experienced. If a parent could not fight, then vigorous support for Israel and/or for militant Jewish groups such as the JDL would suffice vicariously. Whether the parent resisted or simply hid in a cave during the war may have an important impact on the children of survivors in the sense that a socio-political response could develop as a result, i.e., joining the JDL or some leftist radical group as a form of continuity in resisting anti-Semitism and racism.

Conclusions

Quite likely a minor secondary guilt syndrome among the children of survivors will be found but it is too early, given the data, to say for sure.

Even so, it will be mild compared to the parents. If left to the psychiatrists, they will frighten us with predictions of a severe, pathological second-generation survivor's syndrome. I do not believe that a pathology exists, and if there is a syndrome, it will be benign. A balance of the psychiatric side of the coin with sociological analyses is necessary. Such analyses will present the positive and creative side of being a child of survivors and balance the negative. Furthermore, larger samples, at least 50-100 offspring of survivors, are needed in order to generalize about all children of survivors. Without these large samples, an incomplete picture of the situation will emerge.

Coping Behavior of Survivor Children: Social and Political Adaptations

Several writers (Robert J. Lifton, Viktor Frankl, Michael Barkun) have noticed that the Holocaust, whether of Hiroshima or of Auschwitz, has imposed a sense of confusion and unspeakable horror. While some have been psychically numbed, to use Lifton's phrase, others have attempted to remake' the world. Being a survivor can lead either to silence or to chivalry. The children of survivors have discovered that they must make some sense out of the Holocaust, to give this awesome and meaningless mass death some meaning. Their responses have often been creative.

According to Helen Epstein (1977, p.14), children of survivors are quite diverse. They range in age from late teens to middle-thirties and include housewives, students, teachers, business people, artists, social workers, doctors and others. They are single, married, divorced, homosexual, and heterosexual. They include strictly Orthodox and anti-religious Jews. Their political affiliations are radical, liberal, conservative, Zionist, anti-Zionist, or apolitical. They live in the cities or in the country. Some say that their parents' experience has affected them only slightly while others say that it has determined their choice of profession, friends, and spouses.

Yet despite their diversity, Epstein maintains that there is a sense of affinity among children of survivors, or as one put it: "There is a tacit understanding between us;" "A completeness without conversation," as another said. It is this affinity that has brought children of survivors together into groups with names like "One Generation After."

Is there a socio-political "syndrome" among the children, of survivors? Are there distinct socio-political responses to the Holocaust, if not from all children, then from large segments of them? If there is a syndrome of some kind, and it is too early to say as of new because of lack of research, then it will consist of two major components, each component containing two parts: (1) Particularistic (or Jewish involvement) (a) Religious, (b) Political, and, (2) Universalistic (or beyond the Jewish realm) (a) Religious, (b) Political.

Let us first examine some examples of the particularly Jewish ways of confronting the Holocaust. A good number of survivor-children are involved in some form of Jewish commitment. This commitment is based on the idea that young Jews feel they must not give Hitler a posthumous "victory;" that is, they must not assimilate and disappear as Jews, thus giving Hitler his ultimate triumph—the annihilation of the Jewish people. These young Jews become survivalists, and in defiance of anti-Semitic abuse, they emerge as "new" Jews, fighting-proud Jews. Religiously, this can lead to Orthodox or Hasidic life styles; politically to a variety of expressions ranging from a tough chauvinistic stance like the Jewish Defense League or the right-wing Revisionist Zionist position of youth groups like Betar, to a tough socialist, leftist position.

It can include being Jewish activists; being involved in the rights of Soviet Jews; editing Jewish magazines; organizing religious communal groups; and other similar pursuits. Israel becomes important as the visible continuity of Jewish survival. These interests are of course effected by similar parental political activity and by Jewish education in Hebrew schools, but can also emerge from other sources; the direct immersion in Holocaust literature, a visit to Israel and its Holocaust centers (Yad Vashem or Kibbutz Yad Mordechai, for example), or a particular writer or teacher, such as Elie Weisel or Emil Fackenheim. In the past ten years, whenever Israel was threatened, the nightmare of another Holocaust re-appeared and this too has led to increased political activity on the part of Holocaust survivors and their children.

In the universalistic setting beyond the Jewish realm, young Jews would see in the Holocaust a motif for present-day political concerns— nuclear Holocaust, the Vietnam war, racism, air and water pollution, and violence. Jewish universalists have found a Jewish setting for their activities too narrow and confining. Therefore, they would go beyond Judaism to embrace other elements. Religiously, this could include a millennial religious movement or cult in which they could work not only for the salvation of the Jews but for all people. It would be interesting to find out how many children of survivors have joined such cults. In all likelihood the number is small because such a non-Jewish cult would be a negation of their Jewish identity which the Holocaust etched so sharply, yet some young Jews would opt for this alternative despite the anguished reaction of parents and friends.

More likely, Holocaust survivor-children will be involved in universal *political* movements, either radical groups such as socialist or Marxist sects or liberal groups working in the area of human rights, ecology, nuclear energy, and race relations. The image of the Holocaust is powerful and while not the only factor, it is an important one in understanding why and how some children react to their parents' experience by joining radical or liberal political movements.

Is There a Survivor Syndrome? A Conclusion of Sorts

What can be said in summary? First, with regard to the presence of a psychological survivor syndrome among first generation parents of the Holocaust, the evidence for its existence is overwhelming. The works of Winnik, Krystal, Neiderland and others, plus the compendium of literature on the subject of Krystal and Niederland, (1971) confirms this conclusion. It should be emphasized that most survivors have adapted to their trauma quite well, and more stress should be placed on the positive side of this adaptation. Furthermore, more research is needed on the social psychology and the sociology of survivors and of survivor communities in the world. Too often, psychiatrists have emphasized the pathological and they have done so using clinical samples that are too small and unrepresentative of the range of adaptations and coping mechanisms that survivors utilize.

As for a socio-political syndrome, the evidence shows that there does appear to be a constellation of adaptive mechanisms at work—conservatism, traditionalism, political paranoia, concern for Israel, but more research is needed to confirm the range of this syndrome politically, sociologically, and religiously.

As for the children of survivors, there exist some problems with generalizations. Some scholars feel that it is too early to report about the exact specificity of a psychological syndrome or its absence (Kestenberg,

1972). A good deal of research is being undertaken now and some reliable answers should be available soon. There is a basis for a secondary guilt syndrome emerging in the children of survivors; a second-generation syndrome may emerge. It will likely be mild in its psycho-pathological aspects, but there will be some exceptions, as Kestenberg herself discovered. One should not exaggerate the severity of such a syndrome; most children of survivors are the normal everyday neurotics that one finds among any highly educated group.

Regarding a socio-political syndrome among the children of survivors, again there may well be not just one syndrome or constellation of responses, but several kinds, either religious or political and either universal or particular. The offspring of Holocaust survivors have to mold some kind of response and find some form of meaning to their experience, and this can lead to a fascinating and diverse set of reactions. Naturally, the Holocaust is not the only independent variable affecting one's social, political, or religious life. Other variables such as one's secular and religious education, childhood relationships with parents, political and cultural socialization, the politics of one's parents, and related factors, aside from the Holocaust, are clearly crucial. What is certain is that a small but significant number of the children of survivors have a fascination for revolutionary, radical, or millennial movements and this fact in itself is a significant observation worthy of future research.

The cycle continues. The second generation is getting married and having children. Some of these children are already in their early teens. Most of the third generation survivors' (grand) children are young. It is still too early to predict about a syndrome on their part. There should be no psychological syndrome of any consequences unless the parents have serious psychological problems directly related to *their* parents' Holocaust experience. But as for a socio-political syndrome, it would not be surprising if particular traditions related to the Holocaust are passed on to future generations. Just as the Daughters of the American Revolution continue to adhere to a tradition many generations later, so too there may well be socio-political and religious responses specifically developed by the offspring of survivors, trailing far into the future.

Funding for this research came from the Wein Foundation of Chicago under the direction of Dr. Byron Sherwin of Spertus College. This article is a greatly expanded version of a paper which appeared in the anthology, *Encountering the Holocaust*, edited by Byron Sherwin and

Susan Ament (Impact Press/Hebrew Publishing Co., 1979). Reprint permission from Byron Sherwin (Ed.). An earlier version of this paper was read at the Second International Victimology Conference, held at Northeastern University in Boston, in September 1976. Thanks to Dr. Robert Ravven and the staff of the Countway Medical Library of Harvard University for their support and assistance.

(1979, 1981)

References

Epstein, H. The heirs of the holocaust. *The New York Times Magazine.* June 19, 1977, 12-15; 74-77.

Fogelman, E. and Savran, B. Therapeutic groups for children of holocaust survivors. *International Journal of Group Psychotherapy.* 1979, 29(2), 211-236.

Greenblatt, S. The influence of survival guilt in chronic family crises. *Journal of Psychology and Judaism.* 1978, 2(2), 19-28.

Grosser, G., Welchsler, H., and Greenblatt, M. (Eds.). *The threat of impending disaster: Contributions to the psychology of distress.* Cambridge, Mass., MIT Press, 1964.

Kestenberg, J. "Psychoanalytic contributions to the problem of children of survivors from Nazi persecutions." *Israel Annals of Psychiatry and Related Disciples.* 1972, 10(4), 311-325.

Krystal, H. and Niederland, W. (Eds.). *Psychic Traumatization.* Boston: Little, Brown, 1971.

Mostysser, T. "Children of survivors: Growing up in America with a holocaust heritage." *Martyrdom and Resistance.* 1975, 1(6), 4-5.

Sigal, J. "Second-generation effects of massive psychic trauma." In H. Krystal and Wm. Niederland (Eds.), *Psychic Traumatization.* Boston: Little, Brown, 1971.

Chapter 15

On Therapy, Research and Other Dangerous Phenomena

With the recent upsurge of interest in the Holocaust because of the NBC-TV special, there has also been an increase in the number of Holocaust survivor's groups, therapy groups, discussion groups, and research on such groups especially as it relates to the children of survivors. Psychologists have found a rare species of animal that they have overlooked—the children of survivors—and they are going after them vigorously. They will question them, tag them, give them all kinds of erudite clinical labels, and publish the results in the most prestigious psychiatric journals. Beware! They might not have the slightest idea of where they tread. (How could they? It's such a new field!) Worse they may even cause psychological damage and suffering if they are callous, ill-trained, or unprofessional.

I would like to discuss two of these areas—psychological research on the children of survivors and so-called therapy groups for these same children. (Children is a misnomer; nearly all of these "children" are by now over 18, and most are in their mid-20's to late 30's).

* * * * *

Most of the research on survivors and their children is from a psychological point of view, and little of it is done from the much broader perspective of sociology, politics, or religion. This is not to deny that there is much research on the psychological problems of survivors and their children that is valuable, but it is only valuable on a case-by-case approach. Psychiatrists have agreed that there is a survivor's syndrome, a collection of problems (anxiety, nightmares, depression, psycho-somatic ailments, etc.) that survivors tend to have. I would be very surprised if they didn't have them after what they had gone through. I agree that such a syndrome exists, but now psychiatrists are beginning to talk of a syndrome among the children of survivors, of terrible afflictions and maladies that are to befall them. They can tentatively call it a syndrome, but they have not the slightest bit of evidence to prove it. There are two powerful biases in much of the psychiatric literature on survivors and their children:

It is automatically biased toward pathology, which always seems to stress the negative aspects of any "syndrome." What about the *positive* side of being a Holocaust victim? What about the strengths, both psychological and otherwise, that survivors and their children have? And finally, what about most of the survivors who are psychologically stable, even healthy? One never sees this perspective in the literature.

It is biased methodologically. All of the studies I have read have extremely small samples—six patients here, 17 survivors there, 22 somewhere else. Any statistician can tell you that one cannot generalize about all survivors or their children from such small samples. The only way to make generalizations is to have a sample of at least 100 survivors, 100 children of survivors, and an equal number of a control group, such as American-born Jews. Such research, if it contained psychological tests as well as sociological questionnaires, would easily cost $20,000 or more. Until such a large sample is undertaken, there can be few generalizations about survivors that will have any validity.

Yes, we do need research. We need psychological case studies. They are useful, but we need more sociology, political science, and anthropology graduate students and their teachers engaged in studies such as the sociology of "New American" clubs, the differences between the ways that Israel deals with survivors and the Holocaust when compared to Diaspora countries, the meaning that the Holocaust has for Jewish children, and a host of other studies. I believe we have had enough psychiatric studies, and I am tired of being a guinea pig for yet another psychoanalyst.

* * * * *

In line with the rise of children of survivor's groups, such as One Generation After in Boston and The Generation After in New York, has come therapy groups for the children. I have been in such therapy groups, and my experience has been mixed. First, on the positive side, the people who led them were sincere and dedicated. I would not wish to deprecate them and their efforts. (They are usually children of survivors themselves.) Everyone in the field is well-intentioned—but they can still do harm! Secondly, there is nothing wrong with discussion groups, "rap" groups, and similar get-togethers of children of survivors. These can be both educational and healthy. To meet people who have had similar experiences or similar parents or similar interests can be refreshing.

Some of these so-called therapy groups can never decide exactly what they are. First of all, some of the therapists are ill-trained and professionally immature. The Holocaust is a complex trauma and needs a highly experienced and mature therapist. Secondly, these ad hoc groups contain people who do not need therapy or have already had intensive therapy. People of diverse psychological backgrounds and needs are thrown together and the result can be confusing at best and harmful at worst. Third, many therapists have not carefully formulated the goals for such groups. If sensitive matter is raised and someone in the group is deeply agitated by it, there is little follow-up or referral to another therapist or to the same therapist. Finally, some people are let into such "therapy" groups only to discover that they are being used as research subjects for someone's practicum or master's thesis.

I could go on with other abuses but enough said. As in nearly every other aspect of this society, the survivor-consumer must heed the advice of *caveat emptor*. It is good that the helping professions have been made aware of survivors and their children, but like the sensitivity-encounter movement of the late 60s, these new survivor therapies also have their share of incompetents.

The response to this editorial was immediate but surprisingly not on the subject of therapy groups and their lack of professionalism. Most people seemed to agree with me. Where I did receive heavy criticism was from scholars in the field (such as Professor Leo Eitinger of Oslo and Haifa) who questioned that the sample size of survivors and their children were small and inadequate in number. Professor Eitinger gave examples (in *Shoah*, Vol. 2, No. 1, Spring-Summer, 1980 issue) of research that contained samples of 1,000, 6,000, and nearly 20,000. I stand corrected on the survivors but I will continue to maintain that the samples of the children of survivors are still small. We definitely need a large, comparative, cross-sectional sample of them. Another point that

Professor Eitinger made which is salient is that the early post-World War II studies stressed the pathological in order to counteract the prevailing view that the Jewish trauma was minimal, that mental illness was endogenous and innate, and that restitution was not necessary for the victims. It was through the fine work of Professor Eitinger and his colleagues that so may Jews and non-Jews were able to receive *Weidergutmachung*. I learned a great deal from the response to the article, and a more balanced view of psychiatry emerged on my part. In fact, ironically, I belong to a study group on the children of survivors at the Boston Psychoanalytic Society!

(1979)

Chapter 16

The Affirmation of Life After the Holocaust: The Contributions of Bettelheim, Lifton, and Frankl

Too often what emerges after studying or reading about the Holocaust is a debased image of man and woman. However, in examining the works of certain psychologists, what we find is just the opposite: the affirmation of life. The goal of this short essay is to present a brief synopsis of the major contributions of three psychotherapists regarding the lessons to be learned from the Holocaust.

These three men are perhaps the three best known figures in this field (aside from Erich Fromm): Viennese psychiatrist. Viktor E. Frankl (author of *Man's Search for Meaning: An Introduction to Logotherapy*); University of Chicago psychiatrist Bruno Bettelheim (author of *The Informed Heart: Autonomy in a Mass Age*); and Yale psychiatrist Robert Jay Lifton lauthor of *Death in Life: Survivors of Hiroshima*; *History and Human Survival*, and with Eric Olsen, *Living and Dying*).[1]

These three men have confronted the "unthinkable" while forcing their readers to confront the evil in men. All three have not only confronted but transcended it with a psychologically and politically healthier vision of the future.

Bettelheim and Frankl are both European Jews who not only survived World War II but personally experienced the concentration. camps themselves. Lifton, a much younger man and an American Jew, derived his lessons not from the Nazi Holocaust alone, but from intense interviews with survivors of the first A-bomb blast in Hiroshima. Of the three, only Frankl has developed the most comprehensive theory *and* method—existential therapy or logotherapy. Logotherapy emerged in Frankl's mind as he was struggling to survive in a death camp where his father, mother, brother, and wife had died. With every possession gone, every value destroyed, everyone close to him dead, cold, hungry or brutalized, how could he not merely survive but continue to find meaning in life?[2]

He survived the camps with the same techniques that he later used in therapy with patients. He found meaning in life through several ways—by conjuring up happy images of his wife and family, by interviewing camp inmates and gathering material for his future book, and by controlling his thoughts in an institution that hoped to control not only bodies but minds.

Bettelheim did the same though his camp conditions were much more comfortable than Frankl's. Both survived because they strove for "autonomy in a mass age." In a world that had gone beyond the wildest fantasies of Orwell's *1984* and Aldous Huxley's *Brave New World*, they and Lifton hope to teach others what integrity and hope mean in a world that either pleasurably or painfully takes away freedoms and infiltrates minds with both trivia and perversions.

While Freud stressed frustration in our sexual life, Frankl stressed frustration in our *will-to-meaning*. To Frankl, our neuroses are existential in nature; they are caused by an estrangement from life and an inability to find a full and satisfying meaning in life. For Frankl, love and suffering are solution. As he put it, "the crowning experience of all . . . is the wonderful feeling that, after all (man) has suffered, there is nothing he need fear anymore—except his God."[3] For Frankl, the final destination of psychological health is a closeness to man and a reverence for God. More than either Lifton and Bettelheim, Frankl's ideas are a very *religious* psychiatric experience.

Bettelheim shares Frankl's ultimate vision of inner-directed autonomy in the face of over-powering technology and dehumanized bureaucracy, but his theory of survival lacks an inner coherence and is, in many ways, more vague. His experiences at Dachau and Buchenwald led him to two conclusions.[4]

This first conclusion is that psychoanalysis was by no means the most effective way to change personality. Being placed in a particular type of environment could produce much more radical changes and in a much shorter time. The environment could produce much more radical changes and in a much shorter time. The environment can be a negative or positive one. A concentration camp or prison can produce pathological behavior; a warm and happy setting can reduce psychopathology. In a sense, Bettelheim presaged Abraham Maslow, who also talked about growth-inducing environments. What Maslow called self-actualization, joy, and creativity can be stimulated by such environments while neuroses will develop within settings where the individual was not living up to his/her potential and where the surroundings were not conducive to growth. Bettelheim, later at the University of Chicago, would apply this insight to his school for emotionally disturbed children, the Sonia Shankman Orthogenic School.

Bettelheim's second conclusion posited the inadequacy of psychoanalytical theory; that it was unable to fully explain what had happened to him and other prisoners. It gave little guidance for understanding what is meant by the "good" life or the "good" person. Psychoanalysis had its limitations: within the appropriate frame of reference, it is clarified much but applied to phenomena outside its province, it was not only inadequate but distorted meaning as well.

Rather than reject psychotherapy entirely, Bettelheim attempted to build an environment of love for his children, an environment where the "heart would be informed with reason" (hence the title of his book) while reason would be invaded by a daring heart. It is this symbiotic symmetry which should be the goal of humanity.

Bettelheim furthermore felt that the oppressive state of Hitler's Germany was a *passing* phenomenon. In fact he saw it as a challenge and a temporary setback to people's ingenuity. He hoped that this challenge would force people to reach a "higher integration and a deeper consciousness of freedom." His final statement is one of hope, but not false hope. The struggle for mastering the new conditions set by the atomic age will tax all our mental and moral powers if we do not want a "brave new world but an age of reason and humanity."5

Robert Jay Lifton continued the work of Frankl and Bettelheim, lifting their vision to higher and higher planes. Unlike his elderly mentors, Lifton did not personally experience the Holocaust; in fact, his theoretical perspective is informed not by the destruction of the Jews in Europe but by two other phenomena: the Japanese survivors of the atomic bomb dropped on Hiroshima and Nagasaki and the returning veterans of the Vietnam War. His writings almost beg inclusion of the Jewish survivors of genocide. While he is aware of the role they play in his theory and while he uses examples of their plight, I am surprised at how few references there are to Jewish concerns in his work. In any case, this does not weaken his case. It only leaves it open to others (including the present writer) to apply his paradigm to the Jewish condition. Lifton has elevated the concept of survivor to include all of us. He has elevated the discussion of death and destruction to monumental psycho-historical heights, and in the process has made it possible for those who are not direct survivors or who have, not directly experienced the Holocaust to gain access to the meaning of meaningless death. All of his books have led up to the one book, upon which I shall rely to present to the reader his most important contributions: *Living and Dying*, written in collaboration with Eric Olson.[6]

Lifton's fourth mode of immortality is achieved through continuity with nature, again an ancient form of religious communion. Lifton quotes the Hebrew Bible: "From dust you come and to dust you shall return," and comes away with a striking reflection that this represents a Biblical injunction against pride as well as an expression of confidence that the earth itself does not die. Mankind has always looked to nature for spiritual refreshment and revitalization of the spirit.

Lifton's final mode of immortality is what he calls experiential transcendence. This mode differs from the others in that it depends solely on a psychological state. This state is one of rapture, ecstasy, of being "at one with oneself and with the universe." It can also be a state where one "dies and is reborn." This mode can be found in the search for a theological rebirth, but there are other means: music, song, dance, battle, athletics, sexual love, childbirth, and intense comradeship. This experience can occur in relation to the four other modes (biological, creative, theological, natural) or by itself. Over the centuries, humans have used heightened states of consciousness to reach this form of immortality: fasting, drugs, liquor, or combinations of these.

In many societies and religions, including Judaism, experiential transcendence is encouraged through fiestas, carnivals, holidays, and celebrations which help people to break free from the restraint of routine and to sing, dance, drink, laugh, and love in a spirit of excess. The Hippie movement of the middle-to-late sixties was a movement of spiritual transcendence, and even though it was later over-run by hustlers, violent criminals, rip-off artists, and hard drugs, it nevertheless was a movement spawned by the threat of destruction and meaningless. In a recent issue commemorating the 10th anniversary of Haight-Ashbury, the San Francisco center for "hippies," the writer noted the following:

It seemed like a nation gone mad, at war with Asian peasants, with its own black citizens in urban ghettos, and with its own white children. And lurking in the background of any war, for the past 30 years, has been the specter of atomic war and total annihilation. Technology itself was more suspect than for any preceding generation. Along with undreamed of wealth and power, it had created undreamed of potential for evil, and the potential for good was being used in only the drabbest and most cautious ways. Technology had proved a blind alley. The Haight was pressure cooker of new thought, of a new search for new was to deal with the dangers of modern society.[7]

Lifton understands this generation well, and would easily understand the young children of Jewish survivors who took part in this anti-death movement of the 1960's and who continue to say a collective "no" but in more quiet ways today. In conclusion, Lifton's greatest contribution to these issues is his description of the impact of such "death imagery" on our society, and his hope in the ability to affirm life in the face of death. *L'chaim* ("to life") may seem to be just another cliche in Jewish life, but in the works of Frankl, Bettelheim, and Lifton, and to all the survivors of all the "Holocausts" from Hiroshima to Auschwitz to Vietnam, it is the single most important affirmation in the world today.

(1980)

Notes

1. See in particular the chapter called "The Survivor" in Lifton's *Death in Life: Survivors of Hiroshima* and Robert J. Lifton and Eric Olson, *Living and Dying*.
2. Frankl. Preface to *Man's Search for Meaning*, p. viii.
3. Ibid., p. 148.
4. Bettelheim. *The Informed Heart*, pp. 18-19.
5. Ibid., p. 300.
6. Lifton and Olsen. *Living and Dying*, pp. 60-74.
7. Charles Perry, "From Eternity to Here: What a Long Strange Trip its Been," *Rolling Stone*, Feb. 26, 1976 (Issue No. 207), p. 52.

My thanks to Harvard University's Frances Countway Library of Medicine and its staff for opening up their vast resources to me, and to Dr. Robert Ravven of Boston for his encouragement and support. Funding for this research came from a grant by the Wein Foundation of Chicago under the direction of Dr. Byron Sherwin of Spertus College. A much larger version of this paper appeared in an anthology edited by Dr. Sherwin: *Encountering the Holocaust: An Interdisciplinary Survey*, Chicago: Impact Press, 1979; distributed by Hebrew Publishing Company of New York City.

Part V

The Future

Chapter 17

Holocaust Controversies

This essay aims to describe several areas of conflict and controversy in the field of Holocaust studies. The following controversies are examined: the intentionalist vs. functionalist theses; the uniqueness vs. comparability theses; the mystification thesis; the anti-Semitism vs. racism theses; Holocaust-centered vs. genocide-centered scholars; the definitional abuse thesis; Holocaust denial vs. genocide denial; the resistance controversy; and the Goldhagen controversy. In conclusion, the question is posed whether there are really two fields of study—Holocaust studies and genocide studies—or one; some controversies have widened the gap and could divide the discipline. Nonetheless, with hopeful caution, I conclude that these controversies can and will be mediated, for they are quite bridgeable; and that in teaching the Holocaust at the college or high-school level, one can blend the two fields into one course.

The Controversies

A. Intentionalist vs. Functionalist Theses

Was there an intent from the very beginning to destroy the Jews, or was the process of destruction of the Jews more complex and evolutionary? Did the lethal process of the Final Solution emerge from the beginning of Nazi thinking, or did the Final Solution really begin only after the invasion of Russia in June 1941? The intentionalist thesis is that there was a clear-cut intent to destroy the Jews from the beginning of Hitler's thinking and the rise of the Nazi party. The functionalist thesis is that although vicious anti-Semitism and persecution of the Jews were the hallmarks of Nazism, and images of getting rid of the Jews were evoked from early on, the plan and actuality of the Final Solution emerged only as an unfolding sequence, with each earlier stage as it was unopposed by the world leading to the next. The term "intentionalist" is also used in section B below in respect of arguments for the uniqueness of the Holocaust, especially by Steven Katz *The Holocaust in Historical Context, Vol. 1.* New York: Oxford University Press, 1994] when he states that "the Holocaust is phenomenologically unique by virtue of the fact that never before has a state set out, as a matter of intentional principle and actualized policy, to annihilate physically every man, woman, and child belonging to a specific people" (p. 28).

B. Uniqueness vs. Comparability Theses

Is the Holocaust so unique that there is no other case of full-blown genocide? This is the controversial Katz hypothesis. Many scholars hope to develop a common agreement on what was genocide, to the effect that the homosexuals, the Gypsies, the Armenians, the Cambodians, the Indians and many others were all victims of genocide, but Katz attempts to demolish any such consensus. He is implacable in his demands that the Holocaust was unique. Many other scholars, like Michael Berenbaum, adopt a more benign position that the Holocaust was the most prominent and in a sense the most evil genocide in the twentieth century, but that there were many other victims of the Holocaust besides the Jews, some victims of genocide (Jews and Gypsies), some victims of non-genocidal persecution (homosexuals, the disabled, political opponents, Jehovah's Witnesses); and that, following more or less the United Nations definition, there were many other genocides in the twentieth century such as the Armenian Genocide; and that other persecuted groups should be (and are to an extent) represented in the US Holocaust Memorial Museum. For Berenbaum, there is no problem doing full honor to the Jewish memory and the singularity of the Jewish experience and paying full respect to the totality of the Nazis' victims.

Indeed, this issue comes up as a "very practical issue" in decisions about what to include and what to exclude in a museum on the Holocaust. Edward Linenthal's book on the creation of the US Holocaust Memorial Museum *[Preserving Memory: The Struggle to Create America's Holocaust Museum.* New York: Viking Press, 1996] illuminates this controversy well. Ironically, while the Wiesenthal Museum of Tolerance in Los Angeles begins with a very universalistic, inclusivistic message that group hatred and intolerance led to the Holocaust, it rejects that message at the end of the tour by focusing on a particularistic "Never Again" theme. Conversely, while the US Holocaust Memorial Museum in Washington, DC focuses on the particularism of the Jews, it has a greater universalistic impact than the ostensibly universal Los Angeles Museum of Tolerance. The US Holocaust Memorial Museum works on many levels because it honors and commemorates the Jews who died as well as recognizing the other victims—political prisoners, homosexuals, lesbians, Jehovah's Witnesses, and the disabled. Although the museum is, in fact, devoted to the Holocaust, it contains a universal message and educates on many levels. It is a profound experience that succeeds in applying the meaning of the Holocaust to other acts of genocide and oppression. The Los Angeles Museum of Tolerance seems less successful and Yad Vashem in Jerusalem does not really attempt a universal message. As Michael Lerner, editor of Tikkun, so eloquently puts it: "'Never Again' does not mean never again to Jews; it means 'Never Again' to any group, any race, any culture." Elie Wiesel echoes this same sentiment when he says that the particularist message of the Holocaust is the most universalistic.

C. The Mystification Thesis

Tied closely with the "uniqueness controversy" is the idea that the Holocaust is so ineffable, so evil, that it is beyond comprehension. It is an evil that it is beyond evil. This is the thesis of Emil Fackenheim, that there is no language to describe the Holocaust. It is beyond words. This is the Elie Wiesel thesis. However, most scholars have taken the position that ordinary men and women committed these cruel acts, and ordinary men and women can study them. Perhaps the Holocaust is beyond our moral understanding. One many be upset, angered, shocked, or deeply moved by the answers we find, but human beings committed these acts and not aliens from another planet. Hitler and his comrades were not insane or irrational. They were—sociologically speaking—perverted deviants, spiteful, hateful little men, but they were not insane. They knew exactly what they were doing, like serial killers. This is itself a chilling thought, more chilling than insanity, this bifurcation of the mind to killer and saint.

D. Anti-Semitism vs. Racism Theses

Best-selling Harvard University author Daniel Jonah Goldhagen [see *The Goldhagen Controversy,* below] has argued that anti-Semitism was the sole cause of the Holocaust. Years ago, Helen Fein argued in her award-winning book *[Accounting for Genocide: National Responses and Jewish Victimization during the Holocaust.* New York: Free Press, 1979] that extermination of the Jews in different European countries correlated with the long-standing tradition and prevailing political levels of anti-Semitism of the different countries. Anti-Semitism was part of racism—and also forms of white supremacy, patriarchal, sexist and even homophobic attitudes all together gave an ideological basis for the Holocaust. The Jew was the epitome of evil but there were many other targets—Bolsheviks, modernists, radicals, socialists, Communists, free thinkers, the effete, the weak, the meek, and the lame. Aryanism was the religion of the Nazi Supermen (though Nietzsche might not have sided with them and could have gone into the ovens along with the Jews because he was a radical and innovative thinker). If one concentrates only on anti-Semitism, then the Holocaust becomes a Jewish interest and a uniquely Jewish event. However, if one sees anti-Semitism as part of racism, one sees a broader, more universalistic and more accurate picture. At the same time, anti-Semitism is, of course, crucial to understanding the Holocaust.

E. Holocaust-Centered vs. Genocide-Centered Scholars

This is a subset of section B. We need to find the golden mean between people who are not sensitive to the special persecution of Jews during the Holocaust and who make statements like, "The Ukrainians or the Poles suffered just as much as the Jews"; and the "special pleading" of the Jews that says that Jews suffered more than any other persecuted and murdered people ever in history. Many Jews tend to be Holocaust-centered particularists and to use the Holocaust as a special badge.

Holocaust-centered scholars too often ignore the genocides of other peoples. Genocide-centered scholars, on the other hand, are at times insensitive to the uniqueness of the Holocaust. Helen Fein (1990) has pointed out that sociologists especially have the greatest difficulty handling unique events such as Hiroshima, the Vietnam War, or the Holocaust because sociology is best with stable, recurring, non-provocative, normative events.

F. The Definitional Abuse Thesis

Do we exclude the mass murders of certain groups from being defined as genocide if they do not pass our definitional test? Or do we label every case of mass murder genocide just in case? Does the label help save lives, meaning does labeling something a genocide help the United Nations and other agencies move into action and intervene?

Not all killings or mass murders need be considered genocides. What makes genocide unique? There are scholars who argue that there must be intention, whether carried out or not, whether successful or not: an intention to kill every man, woman and child of that particular group. According to this point of view, if that intention is not there, it is not genocide. The extreme of this point of view leads to a position such as that of Katz who said that the Holocaust is the only real genocide because it was the only state-sponsored genocide that had as its intent the destruction of an entire group. In all other genocidal killings of witches, women, Gypsies, homosexuals, even Armenians and Cambodians, or Rwandans and Bosnians, there was never any intent to kill every single man, woman and child of the targeted population.

I do not accept Katz's tortured arguments. His definition of genocide is idiosyncratic and is not accepted by most scholars in genocide studies. Most scholars accept some variation of the UN definition. But what is and what is not genocide? Is intent important? Is completion crucial? Who is excluded and why? What's in a name, in the ideological semantics of Armageddon—decimation, democide, extermination, genocide, Holocaust with a small "h" or a "capital H," mass murder, anti-genocide, politicide, nuclear omnicide?

G. Holocaust Denial vs. Genocide Denial

Holocaust denial is a serious problem, but genocide denial is even more complicated. To deny the Holocaust or to say that a major aspect of it, such as crematoria, is a fabrication is clearly to lie. But to claim that a case of mass murder is not genocide is not to deny the event, or even its seriousness, but to assign the event a lesser significance. Such "genocide denial" can be as offensive to Armenians, Gypsies and homosexuals as outright Holocaust denial is to Jews.

H. The Resistance Controversy

Genocide scholarship was a field in turmoil from the outset, long before a discipline of genocide studies began to emerge. For immediately after the Holocaust, there developed the controversies of the "sheep to slaughter" thesis—did Jews resist enough?; and the Judenrat controversy—did Jews collaborate in their own deaths?; and the Arendt-Enchmann controversy about the "banality of evil" thesis—were the Nazis lunatics or bureaucrats or both? Now, years later, there seems to have emerged a quieting consensus that the Jews were not so much "sheep" as trapped in circumstances none of us can judge; that they did not so much collaborate with the Nazis as they were drawn under desperate conditions to mistaken efforts to save Jews by undue cooperation with their mad oppressors; and that much of the killing was indeed by ordinary people serving the bureaucratic machinery. But the passions and partial truths of the contrary theses are not, and perhaps cannot ever be, extinguished.

I. The Goldhagen Controversy

Daniel Goldhagen's *Hitler's Willing Executioners is* arguably the most controversial book since Hannah Arendt's *Eichmann in Jerusalem*. It was an extraordinary phenomenon. His argument was threefold: one, that the Holocaust was monocausal, that is, only anti-Semitism caused the Holocaust, not following orders, not peer pressure, not careerism, but ordinary Germans harboring "eliminationalist anti-Semitism" who carried out the Holocaust. Second, these ordinary Germans willingly participated in the killing, not banal bureaucrats simply following orders as Arendt wrote. Third, anti-Semitism is deeply rooted in the German culture. Germany itself has a racist character going back to Martin Luther. The Holocaust could only have taken place in Germany. No other country had the technological power, ideological will and bureaucratic style to carry out such an awesome undertaking.

A "two-step solution" seems much more accurate. Goldhagen is half right. Anti-Semitism, deeply rooted in German culture since the Middle Ages, was the animus that began the Holocaust; and then peer pressure, obedience to orders, careerism, fear, police state threats and punishments, and other social and psychological mechanisms came into play. One needs both elements, anti-Semitism and the social psychological, to understand so complex a phenomenon as the Shoah.

J. The Future of Holocaust and Genocide Studies: Two Fields or One?

What is the future of these two fields? Can they be bridged? I believe they can, for we are one field and we need to heal these divisions.

Conclusion

All historical events are unique to some degree. All are comparative. Instead of fighting over what is and what is not genocide, we should do much more research into the Holocaust and other genocides through diligent work in archives and personal interviews and solid analyses of issues.

(1999)

Chapter 18

Impaired Memories/Distorted History

Introduction

Along with Holocaust denial are more subtle yet no less troublesome examples of impaired memoirs that distort history and can lead to denial. At best, they confuse historical accounts; at worst, they support Holocaust deniers who can raise the issue of distortion in these cases and thereby, by extension, deny or distort more important issues such as the presence of gas chambers in the death camps or of Jews as victims of genocide. Some of these distortions are well-meaning, some are inadvertent and unintentional, and some, like the Benjamin Wilkomirski book, *Fragments: Memories of a Wartime Childhood* (New York: Schocken Books, 1995), are outright shocking forgeries that fooled such eminent figures as Larry Langer and Raul Hilberg—in fact, all of us—and all cause serious problems with the historical record and with our integrity as a serious discipline. I hope to give a few examples and to present a theory to explain these forgeries at this time in history.

The Donald Watt and Helen Demidenko Case

Darren O'Brien, an Australian Holocaust scholar, wrote an excellent exposé of a book by Donald Watt about an Australian soldier who allegedly said that he was *a Sonderkommando* in Auschwitz ("The Perils of Testimony," *Internet Genocide Centre Newsletter,* vol. 3, no. 3, March-April 1997: 4-9). Watt was a gentle, well-intentioned follow who wrote the book to confront Holocaust deniers in Australia as well as to educate the Australian public.

The Donald Watt case is a perfect example of a problem in what sociologists call the "sociology of knowledge" or better, "the sociology (and psychology) of memory distortion"; that is, what is "knowledge" and how do we know whether certain kinds of knowledge are true or not.

Sociologists are always looking for patterns and pattern variables and one detects one in making here: namely, the growing number of strange and wonky memoirs and Holocaustal oddities that are appearing at this time in history; and while they are not as dangerous and outrageous as outright Holocaust deniers, they do cause extensive damage in that precious energy is wasted refuting or correcting these impaired memoirs.

The Donald Watt book, *Stoker: The Story of an Australian Who Survived Auschwitz-Birkenau* (Sydney, Australia, 1995), also echoes the case of Helen Demidenko and her book *The Hand that Signed the Paper* (see the *Genocide Centre Newsletter, Vol. 2, No. 3,* 1996). This was an account of the Holocaust in the Ukraine, allegedly written by the daughter of a Ukrainian immigrant and won the prestigious Australian/Vogel Award and the Miles Franklin Award (equivalent to the Booker Prize in England and the Pulitzer in America) as well as the National Book Award, and the judges have never recanted nor apologized for their error.

In some ways, this echoes the Daniel Goldhagen book, a deeply flawed volume, that was nevertheless nominated for the PEN Award in the USA, the National Book Critics Award and several other major prizes but luckily did not win any of them, though it did achieve a great deal of notoriety and finalist status and it did win a major German award. It too shows the gap between the intellectual "writing" world and the academic scholarly world. Interestingly, according to Raul Hilberg, in a speech at Yale University in the spring of 1999, both Goldhagen and Wilkomirski had the same editor at Random House.

In August 1994 it was revealed that Helen Demidenko was actually Helen Darville, the daughter of English immigrants who had in fact no Ukrainian background. Thus, in the span of a few years, Australia was rocked not by one but two major literary scandals. It seems that this phenomenon was worldwide, happening in America, England, Israel, and elsewhere and will no doubt continue into the foreseeable future. (I would like to thank Australian genocide scholar Paul Bartrop for his input on this section.)

The John Sack Case

Next, we have the case of non-survivors writing books that are problematic but in a different and more dangerous sense. For example the book by journalist John Sack on "Jewish revenge" after the war. This is more serious. These are adult journalists or "scholars" and have no excuse to distort the truth or simply make things up. A child survivor I can forgive, but not an adult writer who should check his or her facts and know better. Sack's book has been severely condemned and criticized by such eminent scholars as Professor Antony Polonsky of Brandeis University in Waltham, Massachusetts. Polonsky says the book is nonsense.

In essence, Sack, a former special correspondent for CBS News and its bureau chief in Spain, writes in *An Eye for an Eye: The Untold Story of Jewish Revenge Against Germans in 1945* (New York: Basic Books/Harper Collins, 1993) that many editors found it "disturbing," "shocking," but "well-written" and still rejected it.

Sack writes that the Soviet Union set up a special Office of State Security and deliberately recruited Jewish survivors of the Holocaust to carry out a policy of "de-Nazification," meaning torture and starvation. The Office allegedly entered German homes and rounded up German men, women, and children—99% of them noncombatant, innocent civilians—and took them to cellars, prisons, and 1,255 concentration camps where inmates subsisted on starvation rations, where typhus ran rampant, and where torture was commonplace. In this brief period, between 60,000 and 80,000 Germans died in the Office's custody.

This is utter nonsense and even smacks of red-baiting, doubly shocking that a major publisher Harper Collins published it. There were trials of collaborators and hangings in the Soviet Union, some as early as 1943, for example in Krasnador. There were harsh punishments for any SS captured; and there were individual acts of torture and revenge. But to talk about some kind of organized "Jewish revenge," to put the blame on Jews being used by the Soviet or Polish Communists to kill Germans is red-baiting of the worst kind, and that is why eminent scholars such as Antony Polonsky have criticized this book. The writing style alone shows that this is a passionate book with a message that only a Hollywood screenwriter or pulp-fiction hack might scribble. It is not scholarship except for some poignant interviews with certain individuals.

The entire issue of "Jewish revenge" is a sensitive and difficult question to answer. We will never know the full story. My father was a

Soviet Partisan leader in the Kruk-Maks Group in Volynia, Western Ukraine under Ukrainian Commander Nikolai Konishschuk (nom de guerre "Kruk") and Polish Commander Joseph Sobiesek ("Maks"). After the war, my father came to the USA along with several partisan friends. One of them, let's call him Jacob, told me an astounding story of his killing a Ukrainian collaborator in the United States. After Jacob died, his widow told me that it was a pack of lies. He never killed anyone. Who knows for sure?

All I know is that my father and his fellow Soviet Partisan friends did indeed kill a few collaborators immediately after the fighting stopped, perhaps some Germans also unluckily got caught, but "institutionalized revenge," no. I was told of none of that. Jews wanted to get out of Poland and the former Soviet Union as quickly as possible, heading for Israel, Canada, America, or Australia. They were in no mood for the dangerous task of "revenge." Sack's book is nonsense and even anti-semitic and of course red-baiting, but it is illustrative of the kind of work that can hoodwink even the best of book editors and publishers.

The Wolf Girl of the Polish Forests

Getting back to childhood memoirs, a recent book has come out in Boston about a young girl who from 1941-1946, starting at age seven and ending at age twelve, allegedly roamed through Belgium, Germany, Poland, and the former Soviet Union, seeking her parents, whom the Nazis had arrested, all the while with help from her canine friends.

It is the strange case of Mishka DeFonseca (not to be confused with Isabel Fonseca's excellent book on the gypsies called *Bury Me Standing: The Gypsies and Their Journey* (New York: Vintage Books, 1995). De Fonseca alleges that all sorts of animals helped her, especially two wolves named Ita and Rita. The book is called *Misha: A Memoir of the Holocaust* (Boston: Mt. Ivy Press, 1997).

Here too caution is recommended, just as caution was recommended in Jerzy Kosinski's life as described in his *The Painted Bird*. Here too a young child, either gypsy or Jewish, roams the Polish forests living off the land, encountering a frightful array of Polish peasants who help him survive but in the process nearly kill him. Kosinski got into a great deal of trouble over his own memory lapses. In truth, Kosinski lived a life totally unlike the young hero in *The Painted Bird*. Instead, he and his parents (his name was then Lewinkopf) lived in an attic, under a slanted room in a fine home on the outskirts of Sandomierz, Poland.[1] He did not suffer unduly during the war compared to other survivors.

I thought of Kosinski's lies (he was about the same age too) when I read the DeFonseca book. But then Kosinski was not the only Holocaust writer/thinker/survivor to distort, camouflage, and fool the world. Note the cases of Robert Maxwell and Bruno Bettelheim. (It's also ironic that all three committed or are alleged to have committed suicide. In Maxwell's case, it may have been an accidental death, but we will never know for sure.)[2]

It is not that the DeFonseca book is without merit. There is much we can learn about children "raised" by wolves, gazelles, or other animals. Such literature is quite old, going back 200 years to the "wild boy of Aveyron" in France.[3]

While the entire context of these questions raised are broad and complex, Jean-Claude Armen (1974: 103-104) distinguishes three basic categories of wild children, and there are more:

1. Those brought up by animals; their "imprinting" varies according to the age at which the child has assumed an animal existence; these children can be subdivided into herbivorous (the gazelle boy of Mauritania for "educated" by the environment). The slightest failure of practical intelligence, interest, attention, and adaptability to the environment can result only in rapid elimination. This category includes the famous "Savage of Aveyron," whose sense of smell, sight, and hearing had been trained to a high degree for survival even in severe winters.
2. Children who have been placed in isolation and are not "wild" in the strict sense of the word. Owing to the extreme weakness of the "stimuli" received, their inventive imagination has not developed. The result is almost invariably the "backward" child, whom only the psychiatrist is competent to observe. These are cases of children or adults hidden and abused, isolated from human contact for many years.
3. The "wolf girl" of Poland is a new type. Not "wild" in the sense that she was raised by wolves. Not with the ability to bound and leap and survive like the "gazelle boy." But a new form: simply a young girl who gets lost in the woods

and is befriended, and perhaps protected to some degree, by wild wolves, who take care of her until help comes. In this sense, the wolves are akin to family pets and see in the young girl neither fear nor danger.

As late as 1946, a wild child was discovered in Syria, with some gazelles, a boy apparently twelve to thirteen years old whose galloping leaps enabled him to move as quickly as his animals. (See pp. 98-99 in Jean-Claude Armen's book *Gazelle Boy,* 1974.) He was eventually captured and his Achilles heel cut, hobbling him, making him unable to escape.

But DeFonseca was not a wild child. She has human language, human intelligence, and normal body outline. How she survived in the woods at age seven is a mystery. It's possible, but highly improbable, without human help. Perhaps she repressed the worst aspects; perhaps she conflated events and her relationship with animals. Perhaps she is simply mad. We may never know unless we get facts (places, transport times, train destinations, dates, towns), documentation that can be proved historically or by witness verification. Otherwise, it remains a nice story for Hollywood to film.

Theories, Theories, Theories

Childhood distortion of memory is one theory. My second theory is perhaps more apropos to non-Jewish soldiers and older survivors rather than children, and that is that the aging process among survivors can lead to dementia, memory loss, and memory distortion. It can also lead to a "hero's complex" where actual events are magnified and exaggerated. This can be due to a need for recognition, a desire to leave the world with a special and unique tale, even a sympathetic alliance with the victims.

There are other reasons, some laudatory, such as being a bulwark against Holocaust deniers. For if a soldier in the Australian, New Zealand, British, or American army, such as the Watt case, was at Auschwitz, then you see, the Holocaust had to be true. Why even a GI was there, goes the logic. Darren O'Brien intimates that in his article. I also sense that Donald Watt was well-intentioned as are most of the people that I discuss in this article. They are not purposeful Holocaust deniers or distorters yet they are harmful because they present a false depiction of history and it is that which can fall into the hands of sophisticated Holocaust deniers. Something else however is going on here that I am trying to grapple with. I call these issues—a "post-modernist" approach to Holocaust studies.

A third explanation, a subset of the first one, is that as first-hand adult survivors die off, we will see more weirdness, more fraud. Part of this is due to my fourth theory—the impact of millennium craziness (the Heaven's Gate Syndrome, for example). These, however, are easy to dismiss; much harder are survivor memoirs, since demographically, as more survivors die, we will next have the memoirs of older, then younger, teenagers, then young children, then childsurvivors, babies, and then the children of survivors, older ones like myself, who remember nothing of the war but a few things from the DP camps (yet that too could all be conflated and distorted) and so on and so forth to children of survivors, born long after the war in Australia or America, who remember nothing but might conflate and distort their parents' memories as photographs and pass them off as/"truth." I mistrust these children of Holocaust survivor's memoirs as "history." Again, as,'iiterature, that's something else, but as history they are biased and extremely problematic except as anecdotal material. (For example, they could tell us what the DP camp looked like from a child's point of view and that is important, but a child will be unable to tell us anything about the political or social movements in the camps or obviously in the world beyond the DP camps.)

Why Now?

Why are we seeing increased numbers of these problematic accounts as we approach the millennium? I have several theories, some demographic, some psychological. My first theory is that as we move away from the Holocaust we encounter a time where most of the adults have died and the only survivors alive today were children during the Holocaust (the youngest survivors today are in their mid-60s). Therefore, their memories are that of a child, not an adult, and thus they conflate and distort events as a child might. However, such children's accounts can be quite poignant.

This point hit home during a training I had by the Righteous Person Foundation (the socalled "Steven Speilberg" Foundation) to train us to interview survivors. They told us to put ourselves in the place of the survivor; thus, if the survivor was a ten-year old girl, don't ask her what she thought of "National Socialism," but what party shoes or party dress she wore, what games she played, etc. (For a moving account of such children, see Laurel Holliday, *Children in the Holocaust and World War II: Their Secret Diaries* (New York and London: Washington Square Press, Pocket Books, 1995).

The point was also reiterated to me on TV during a recent documentary on the Eichmann Trial. I noted that not only was Eichmann relatively young (probably in his fifties in 1961) but the famous witnesses, who were only teenagers in the camps or ghettos, fifteen years later were still under 30 years of age or at worst in their early 30s. Thirty-five years later, many have died and witnesses are quite elderly, even senile. Could this time difference have had an impact, for example, on the Demjanjuk trial, with its very different final verdict than Eichmann?

Children accounts are eloquent and moving, but they have obvious limitations and must be used cautiously as "history." Not as literature. They can serve a purpose as literature, but as "history" they may be biased. The most famous example is *The Diary of Anne Frank* and the Laurel Holliday collection of children's diaries.

As my colleague and mentor Professor Antony Polonsky says so eloquently: "Only in America is memory and history considered to be the same, and we know painfully how untrue that is: memories are flawed, and history needs to be verified by documents."

Conclusions

In conclusion, we see that demographic, sociological and psychological theories can include childhood distortions and limitations, adult aging dementia, a need for fame and recognition, or outright fraud. These will not decrease but increase in the future as we move away, time-wise, from the Holocaust. As survivors age and die, we will not have the adult survivors themselves around to correct us. Thus, the Steven Spielberg Foundation Project, the Fortunoff Archives at Yale University, and others need to quickly interview survivors, even though we are often twenty years too late, and they need to accelerate those interviews. Time is running out. We need their voices on tape now.

But it will not stop the fraud and distortion. For this, we need to raise not only a generation of professionally trained graduate students and scholars, but a skeptical and educated public. I fear, as a child of survivors, that we will see such distortions continue long afer even the second generation is gone. It will remain a major problem into the future. We must remain ever vigilant of Holocaust denial and distortion.

(1998)

Notes

1. For proof of this, with actual photos of Kosinski's lovely home and comfortable quarters, see James Park Sloan, *Jerzy Kosinski: A Biography* (New York: A Dutton Book, Penguin Books, 1996); see the photos following page 250 and pp. 18-27.

2. See my essay "Holocaust Suicides" in this book on the life and deaths of Primo Levi, Jerzy Kosinski, Robert Maxwell, Bruno Bettelheim, Terence Des Pres, and other writers and survivors.

3. See for example, Lucien Malson, *Wolf Children and the Problem of Human Nature* (New York and London: Monthly Review Press, 1972). It also contains on pp. 89-179 the complete text of "The Wild Boy of Aveyron" by Jean-Marc Garpard Itard. For a young Arab boy raised by gazelles in sub-Saharan Morocco, see the very moving and informative account by Jean-Claude Armen, *Gazelle Boy* (New York: Universe Books, 1974).

Chapter 19

Toward a Sociology and History of Peace

Introduction

This ambitious essay welds two separate issues that are extremely important for Europe and the world today: how can we identify peaceful societies throughout history? and how can we apply principles of nonviolent social change in order to bring about peaceful change? Furthermore, what are the attributes of a peaceful society? What are the socio-political dynamics that create such peaceful epochs? I have also tried to bring the attention of Western readers the contribution of sociologist Matthew Melko of the United States (Wright State University in Dayton, Ohio) and the work of the Martin Luther King, Jr. Center for Nonviolent Social Change in Atlanta, Georgia.

Six specific steps are described in creating such nonviolent change. The B'nai B'rith Anti-Defamation League's program "A World of Difference" is also mentioned as another similar program for social change, as are organized trips to Israel by right-wing youth. Such programs are already being implemented in Germany, Northern Ireland and Israel in order to reduce intergroup hatred and violence. Underlying all this is my concern that Holocaust Studies *internationally* must turn to the study of *peace and nonviolent social change* if the field is to remain a vibrant and relevant one in the future. *A history and sociology of peace* is simply the opposite side of the coin to Holocaust Studies and could become a driving and creative force within the field in the next few years as we confront post-Holocaust genocides in Bosnia, Chad, Burundi, and other parts of the globe as well in such hot spots as Somalia, Haiti, Northern Ireland, and the former Soviet Union.

How can we avoid war and genocide through peaceful change? Man has been grappling with this question for eons. The concepts of peaceful societies, pathways to nonviolent change, and a sociology of peace are all the flipside of what we know as Holocaust and genocide studies. In fact, I predict that if we are to persevere as a vibrant and relevant field, we in Holocaust studies must turn our attention to the analysis and creation of peaceful societies through nonviolent social change. In this essay, I describe a few of these directions.

I must first acknowledge the contribution and dedication to "peace studies" of such luminaries as Elie Wiesel, Martin Luther King, Jr., Gandhi, Nelson Mandela, Israel Chamy, Chanan Rapaport, Leo Kuper, Gene Sharp, Helen Fein, Luis Kutner, Matthew Melko, Elise and Kenneth Boulding, Barbara Half, Herbert Kelman, Louis Kreisberg, John Burton, Roger Fisher and William Ury, Paul Wehr, and others. (See also my two books, *Conflict and Conflict Resolution: A Historical Bibliography* [New York and London: Garland Publishing, 1982] and *Conflict and Conflict Resolution: A Sociological Introduction* with Ruth Taplin of London [Lanham, MD, and London: University Press of America, 1987] for more on the sociology and mediation of conflict.) These men and women laid the foundation for "peace studies."

In this essay, I would like to discuss two of these contributors: Professor Matthew Melko, an often overlooked theorist on peaceful societies and the researchers at the Martin Luther King, Jr. Center for Nonviolent Social Change. Our future task must be to test Melko's and King's work and see if they in fact work. We can learn from what worked in the past during peaceful epochs in order to reduce the level of violence in the world today. The nonviolent approach of Martin Luther King, Jr., Gandhi, and Nelson Mandela is the way to achieve these goals and reduce violent deaths and genocidal destruction, at least in theory.

Peace in the Western World: The Contribution of Matthew Melko

Professor Melko (1973, 1981, 1984, 1985) is the pre-eminent scholar in the field of what constitutes peaceful societies. In one of his articles (1985: 48), he proudly and, I might add, happily announces that "peace is far more common than war." He then goes on to describe the history of peace from ancient to medieval to modern times.

Modern western history, beginning with the 15th century, has been punctuated by three great crises: the Thirty Years War, the Napoleonic Wars, and the 20th Century World Wars. Around these periods of crisis and violence were longer periods of ten to fifteen decades of peace, all but one of which have come to be known as an "Age": the Reformation, the Baroque, and the Victorian. Since these ages, like Chinese emperors, get their names only in retrospect, the fourth age (ours) does not yet have a name but, according to Melko (1985: 50-51), our "age" (should we call it the "nuclear age" or the "computer age"?) began around 1945-1950 and figures to run about 100-150 years or to 2050 to 2100 A.D. (see Figure 1).

One reason why we do not see our age as peaceful is that Melko only considers 100 years or more *without* wars or local conflict (like in the Middle East or the Falkland Islands) as a "peaceful age." We are not a peaceful nation nor a peaceful planet at this stage in our history.

Pre-conditions of Peaceful Societies: The Ancient World
(From Melko & Weigel, 1981: 183-187)

Melko and Weigel (1981: 8) feel we must study ancient societies in order to sort out what is universal about peace from what is unique to modern civilization. If conditions occurred in ancient times as well as in modern, we might be able to generalize that these are *universal* themes.

The ancient world is roughly defined as existing in time from the origins of civilization along the Tigris and Euphrates as well as the Nile rivers until the demise of the Roman Empire, during the 400s A.D. Geographically, it surrounded the Mediterranean, extending to the western borders of India, south into Africa, north toward the Baltic, and east to the Atlantic—a huge chunk of the world.

Centuries of peace do seem to have occurred in the ancient world. Great political areas larger than most contemporary states were able to maintain peace, as were very small states that would seem not to have the population to defend against sustained attack.

What were some of the pre-conditions for peace?

- Environments in which peace existed were variable. Some of the peaceful societies were isolated; some involved with neighboring powers. Most were protected by at least some supportive physical barriers.
- The most important political leaders seem to have been not the founders of societies but the consolidators who established the resulting political structures. The consolidators seem to have a character resemblance: pragmatism, tolerance, persistence.
- In an age generally dominated by monarchy, the peaceful societies seem to have had a surprising variety of governmental forms (republics, tyrannies, empires, oligarchies, and a provincial governorship).
- While law codes were developed in a few cases, the more important factor in the peaceful societies seems to have been the establishment of a system that gave a reasonable expectation of justice, at least within classes.
- Peace encourages economic prosperity. Most of the ancient peaceful societies were exceptionally prosperous. This prosperity, however, often waned before peace itself came to an end.
- The peaceful societies were generally active in trade, but this was true of many of their neighbors who were not peaceful.
- Religious and social tolerance were characteristic of most peaceful societies. Egypt, for example, was tolerant of foreign deities and their cults as well as to the foreigners who worshipped them. It later absorbed them.
- Peaceful societies seem to have been creative. They produced a considerable quantity of architecture, sculpture, painting, crafts, music, literature, philosophy, science, and law. They were often centers attracting creative talents from other areas. There was generally tolerance, a willingness to accept a variety of views, an inclination toward pragmatic rather than visionary outlooks, a willingness to compromise. There was often selfishness and sometimes treachery, but also a general commitment to justice and a widespread appreciation of the blessings of peace.

- In foreign policy, the governments of peaceful societies tended to be prudent; relations were cautious; encounters limited; and there were no major military transformations during any of the periods of peace.
- Both in policy and in technique, then, there was a tendency for stability, cautious expansion, limited commitment, and general predictability.
- Peace came to an end because of internal rebellion or external invasion or some combination of the two. In more than half the cases, external invasion was involved. The termination of peace could not be attributable solely to weak leadership. The various crises were met by determined, energetic and capable measures. The basic cause of termination was gradual alteration of balances, either among internal elites, between governors and subjects, or between the societies and the powers surrounding them. One frequent internal change was a tendency toward centralization of power.
- Societies remained peaceful for a long time because leadership assessed situations correctly and established structures appropriate to those situations.

Conditions of Modern Societies (From Melko, 1973: 178-188)

- No one form of government, no one economic system, no one structure of society seems to be essential to peace.
- Good luck is an important element in the longevity of most peaceful societies, and bad luck is often a major factor in their coming to an end.
- Peaceful societies often owe their existence to the combination of a charismatic founder and a shrewd, efficient consolidator. Charismatic founders emerge frequently, but their creations do not last.
- Once a society becomes a going concern, its operation becomes routine and ingenious leadership is not necessary. Geniuses should be given scope in other fields—the arts, sciences, exploration—but not political leadership. Once a society becomes a going concern, mediocrity is what is wanted and needed.

- Mediocre leadership, which so often presides over peace periods, is usually found in periods in which peace comes to an end. Rarely is exceptionally competent leadership found in such periods. This is because genius is rare, but so are centuries of peace. Once the peace period is going, genius is not required to end it. Thus, mediocrity serves the cause of peace.
- Man's natural pugnacity can be neutralized by cultural patterns.
- Inefficient taxation systems preserve peace.
- Peaceful societies have ambiguous, fuzzy, inefficient bureaucracies.
- Tepid ideologies support peace.
- Moderate powers maintain peace more effectively than great powers.
- Peace has been maintained in every conceivable political situation.
- Great reformers rarely preserve peace.
- Peace is often achieved between two neighboring great powers.
- Peaceful states do not make alliances with their neighbor's neighbor.
- Arms control is of little importance in maintaining internal peace.
- Internal peace is not related to population pressure.
- However, peace and prosperity do go together.
- Peaceful societies are usually vital, rarely dull, though leadership is mediocre.
- Peace really does seem to be good for people.
- And peace is the normal condition for most societies on this planet!

Melko (1985: 48) also points out the often crucial role of the "reconciler" (akin to a secular messianic figure) who appears on the scene and brings together conflicting parties: people like Dag Hammarsjkold, Martin Luther King, Jr., Ralph Bunche (but what of Kurt Waldheim?). Reconcilers are inclined to be firm, patient, persistent, and sober rather than jolly, festive, or even charismatic. (Sounds surprisingly like President George W. Bush or former U.S. Secretary of States Henry Kissinger and James A. Baker.)

Once peace is established, leadership tends to become mediocre, even banal, but that is the point: peace is boring, the most wonderful boredom of all. Peaceful societies tend to be tolerant of religious, ethnic and racial minorities; they have periods of high intellectual and aesthetic vitality; and they have stable borders which contribute to peace.

I might add that peaceful societies, rather than being seen as filled with inertia and alienation, are societies that actively seek out peace. Rather than fear, they have courage; rather than paranoiac privacy, they have openness; rather than suppression and denial, they have self-acceptance and self-esteem; and rather than being politically weak, they are politically strong, stable and resilient. (Maybe these societies are not so dull after all!)

Countries such as Sweden, the Netherlands, Canada, India, Switzerland and Costa Rica are all examples of peace-loving societies.

Melko, indeed, has much that is provocative to read and exciting to test. I have tried to address some of these concerns myself. (See Porter: 1982a, 1982b, 1985, 1987, 1991a, 1991b, 1993.)

The U.S.A. and Israel are sadly not on Melko's list of peaceful societies despite their Judeo-Christian and Jewish injunctions to seek peace and pursue it.

But is peace only external, or is it also internal? Can we be externally at war and internally at peace as a nation, or vice versa? Can we be politically and internationally at peace and yet societally and individually at war with each other? Germany is a case of the latter, and so is America—at peace in the world and yet filled with a carnage of death in the urban centers and on TV and in videos. However, peace should mean both externally and internally being at ease. Happily, this has not been an uncommon occurrence in the past. Why, then, is it so elusive in our times?

Perhaps this leads now to the contribution of the Martin Luther King Jr. Center in Atlanta, Georgia, and its contribution to peaceful social change.

Pathways to Nonviolent Social Change: Altruism in Action

Surprisingly overlooked over the years of genocide research has been the work of Martin Luther King, Jr., and the researchers at the Martin

Luther King, Jr. Center for Nonviolent Society Change in Atlanta, Georgia. The following six steps are a summary of Dr. King's nonviolent teachings, which emphasized love in action. Dr. King saw these steps as not only interpersonal and local but also international.

The Six Steps of Peaceful Change

1. **Information-gathering.** In order to understand and articulate the issue, problem or injustice facing the community or society, one must research, investigate, and gather all vital information that will increase an understanding of the problem. Know all sides of the issue but take no sides at first, no matter how much you are biased in one direction or another. This information can be gathered not only from library research but from newspaper articles, inside investigator journalistic accounts, television, various educational and defense organizations and agencies, and personal interviews and focus groups. All this will guide you in the development of appropriate strategy.
2. **Education.** It is essential to inform others about the issue. This minimizes misunderstandings and gains support and sympathy. This can be accomplished through the same sources used for information-gathering. Essential to this step is coalition-building and meetings with all parties to keep lines of communication open. This is often difficult since the press sensationalizes events and the public stays locked into historical stereotypes, guilt, bad faith, and continual punishment for the sins of the past.
3. **Personal commitment.** Regularly check and affirm your faith in the philosophy and methods of nonviolence. Eliminate hidden motives and prepare yourself to accept suffering if necessary in your work for justice.
4. **Negotiation.** Using grace, humor, and intelligence, confront the other party with a list of injustices and a plan for addressing and resolving these injustices. Nonviolent communication does not seek to humiliate but to call forth the good in an opponent. Negotiation can be viewed as a growth and learning experience that can lead to a genuine meeting of the midst.

5. **Direct action.** This approach is used to morally force your opponent to work with you in resolving the injustices; direct action imposes a "creative tension" into the conflict. There are more than 250 different direct-action tactics including boycotts, marches, rallies, rent strikes, work slowdowns, letter-writing, investigative reporting, and petition campaigns, as well as various forms of civil disobedience. These are enhance when they also illustrate or document the injustices.
6. **Reconciliation.** Nonviolence does not seek to defeat your opponent but to seek his/her friendship and understanding. It is directed against evil systems, forces, groups, policies, and acts, not against individuals. Reconciliation includes the opponent being able to "save face." Through reasoned compromise, both sides resolve the injustice with a plan of action. Each reconciliation is one step closer to a peaceful community or society and a peaceful world. Not only are individuals empowered, so too is the entire society; and not only the victim but the victimizer can be turned about. With that comes new struggles for justice and a new beginning.

These, then, are the six steps toward peaceful systems—from individual to community to society to universal understanding. As the well-known bumper sticker says, "Think globally, act locally." Nonviolence is difficult to achieve; perhaps at times impossible, even futile. Against Hitler, nonviolence may have been impossible for direct action; however, these tactics could have been used (and some were) to alert sensitive governments to the dangers of evil or the plight of refugees and victims. Could nonviolent tactics have saved millions of Jews during the Holocaust or Armenians or Cambodians or now Bosnians? That is a question for us to discuss at this conference. However, it is a higher, more moral tactic that must be utilized more often globally, even in the face of genocide . . . and even if it fails.

I hope that this essay has given you something to think about and to test: this melding of the theories of Matthew Melko on peaceful societies and Martin Luther King, Jr.'s theories on nonviolent social change. Let us apply one to create the other. In short, let us create "love in action."

(1994)

Sources

Dr. Matthew Melko, Professor of Sociology, can be reached at the Department of Sociology, Wright State University, Dayton, OH 45435, USA, and the researchers at the Martin Luther King, Jr. Center for Nonviolent Social Change, Inc., can be reached at 449 Auburn Ave. N.E., Atlanta, GA 30312, USA. The B'nai B'rith Anti-Defamation League, 823 United Nations Plaza, New York, NY 10019 or local ADL branches also have a program called "A World of Difference" that is being applied in Germany after a successful run in the USA and Canada. It is another form of nonviolent tactic that should be considered in conjunction with the Martin Luther King, Jr. Center approach.

Westview Press, 5500 Central Avenue, Boulder, CO 80301, USA, has a special list of books on peace studies called the "Westview Special Studies in Peace, Conflict, and Conflict Resolution," Paul Wehr, editor. My own book, *Conflict and Conflict Resolution: A Historical Bibliography* (New York and London: Garland Publishing Company, 1982) contains many useful leads. Important books in the Westview Series include: Israel W. Charny (ed.), *Strategies Against Violence: Design for Nonviolent Change;* Elise Boulding, J. Robert Passmore and Robert Scott

Gassier, *Bibliography on World Peace and Conflict;* and Paul Wehr, *Conflict Regulation.* These books contain numerous groups and research institutes engaged in the study of peace. Paul Wehr's address is Associate Professor of Sociology, Director of the Environmental Conciliation Project, University of Colorado, Boulder, CO 80301, USA.

References

Melko, Matthew. *The Nature of Civilizations.* Boston, MA: Porter Sargent, 1969.

———. "Discovering Peace" and other essays on peace in *Peace Research,* December 1971, January 1972, March 1972, and April 1973.

———. *52 Peaceful Societies.* Ontario, Canada: Canadian Peace Research Institute, 1973.

———. "Peace: A Subject Worth Studying," *The Bulletin of the Atomic Scientists,* April 1975.

———, with Richard D. Weigel, Sally Katary and Michael McKenny. *Peace in the Ancient World.* Jefferson, NC: McFarland & Company, Inc., 1981. The publisher is at Box 611 in ZIP code 28640. Some of the ancient cases of peaceful societies were: The Middle Kingdom Peace (1991-1720 B.C.); The Phoenician Peace (1150-722 B.C.); The Athenian Peace (683-513 B.C.); The Corinthian Peace (655-427 B.C.); The Ptolemaic Peace (332-216 B.C.); The Roman Republican Peace (203-90 B.C.); The Pax Romana (31 B.C.-161 A.D.); and the Hispanic-Roman Peace (19 B.C.-409 A.D.).

———, with Richard D.K. Hord. *Peace in the Western World.* Jefferson, NC: McFarland & Company, 1984.

———. "The Remission of Violence in the West," *International Journal on World Peace* 11(2), April-June 1985, pp. 48-55. With comment by sociologist Robin Williams, pp. 56-60 and rejoinder by Melko, pp. 60-61. The chart used is on p. 51 and is used by permission. The address of the journal is Box 1311, New York, NY 10116, USA.

Porter, Jack Nusan. *Conflict and Conflict Resolution: A Historical Bibliography.* New York and London: Garland Publishing Company, 1982a.

———. *Genocide and Human Rights: A Global Anthology.* Lanham, MD and London: University Press of America, 1982b.

———. "Self-Hatred and Self-Esteem," *The Jewish Spectator,* Fall 1985, pp. 51-55.

——— with Ruth Taplin of London. *Conflict and Conflict Resolution: A Sociological Introduction.* Lanham, MD and London: University Press of America, 1987.

———. "The Roots of Self-Destruction," unpublished paper. The Spencer Institute, 17 Cross Street #2, West Newton, MA 02465, USA, 1991a.

———. "Emblematic Deaths: A Crisis of Our Times," unpublished paper. The Spencer Institute, 1991b.

———. "Genocide is a New Word for an Old Crime" and "The Yellow Star and the Pink Triangle: Sexual Politics in the Third Reich," two essays in Daniela Gioseffi (ed.), *On Prejudice: A Global Perspective.* New York: Anchor-Doubleday Books, 1993, pp. 67-72 and 143-153.

Figure 1
Phases and Outlooks of the Western Interstate Period

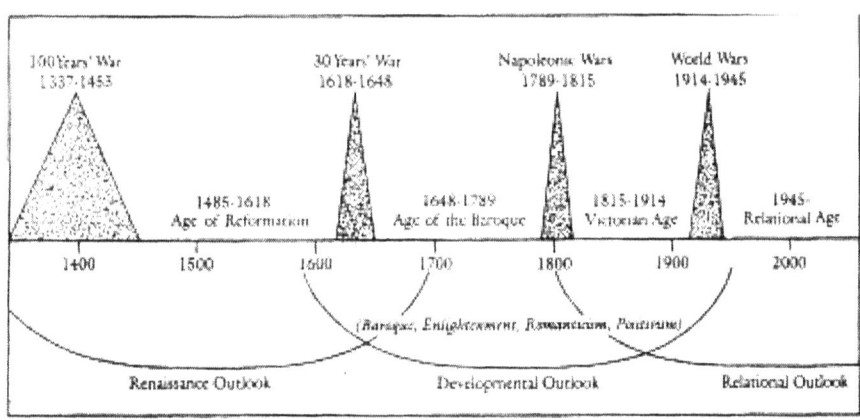

Source: Matthew Melko, "The Remission of Violence in the West," *International Journal on World Peace*, 11:2, April-June 1985, p. 51. Reprinted by permission.

Table 1
PEACE PERIODS IN THE WESTERN WORLD

PEACE	DATES	LOCATION
Venetian	1033-1310	Venice
Hungarian	1312-1428	Hungary
Polish	1410-1606	Poland
Brandenburger	1486-1627	Brandenburg
British	1485-1940	British Isles
Spanish Imperial	1492-1808	Spain, Spanish America
Scandinavian	1262-	Scandinavia, Iceland
Swiss	1865-	Switzerland
Brazilian	1654-	Brazil
Costa Rican	1842-1948	Costa Rica
Canadian	1885-	Canada
Pacific	1788-	Australia, New Zealand, Polynesia, Hawaii

The criteria for peace used in finding these cases have proved to be highly controversial. They are as follows:
(1) Peace is defined as an absence of physical conflict.
(2) The area in which peace occurs may be any definable region.

Source: Mathew Melko, "The Remission of Violence in the West," *International Journal on World Peace*, Vol. II, No. 2, April-June 1985, page 53. The criteria for defining peace is as follows: (1) Peace is defined as an absence of physical conflict; (2) The area in which peace occurs may be any definable region; (3) The period in which peace occurs must last a century or more; (4) Minor interruptions to peace are discounted; (5) If the government of the area of peace is fighting somewhere else, that does not negate the peace of the area. (Melko, op. cit., pp. 53-54.)

Table 2
Duration of Peace Periods

Peace	Dates	Length	Peace	Dates	Length
	Over 400 Years		Roman	BC 31-161 AD	192
Icelandic	1256	716*	1 Laotian	1373-1564	191
Phoenician	BC 1269-725	544	Achemenian	BC 521-331	190
British	1485-1940	455	Australian	1788-	184*
Hispanic-Roman	BC 19-409 AD	428	Brandenburg	1447-1627	180
	Over 300 Years		Hawaiian	1796-	176*
Han	BC 202-184	386	T'ai	1802-	170*
New Kingdom	c. BC 1540-1220	c. 320	Athenian	BC 683-513	170
Mesopotamian	c. BC 1550-1240	c. 310	Manchu	1682-1852	170
Tokugawa	1638-1942	304	Italian	1538-1701	163
Cham	650-952	302	West Indian	1815-	157*
Old Kingdom	c. BC 2650-2350	c. 300	Anglo-Indian	1818-	154*
Fujiwara	c. 600-900	co 300		Over 100 Years	
	Over 200 Years		Kamakura	1185-1331	146
Venetian	1033-1310	277	Dutch	1794-1940	146
Mameluke	1250-1517	267	Arakanese	1546-1684	138

Table 2
Duration of Peace Periods (cont.)

Peace	Dates	Length	Peace	Dates	Length
Scandinavian	1721	251*	Ottoman	1452-1590	138
T'ang	628-868	240	Habsburg	1711-1848	137
Byzantine	838-1071	233	Nepalese	1846	126*
Sung	1004-1235	231	Hungarian	1312-1437	125
Corinthian	BC 655-427	228	Swiss	1848	124*
Sassanian	363- 590	227	Ptolemaic	BC 341-217	124
Ming	1403-1629	226	Mughal	1585-1707	122
Middle Kingdom	c. BC 1990-1785	205	Gupta	336-450	114
	Over 150 Years		Javanese	1830-1942	112
Bohemian	1197-1394	197	Mon	1426-1535	109
Polish	1410-1606	196	Khmer	813-921	108
Burmese	1084-1277	193	North American	1866-	106*
			Costa Rican	1842-1948	106

* Still in process as of 1972
Source: Mathew Melko, *52 Peaceful Societies*, Oakville, Ontario, Canada: Canadian Peace Research Institute, 1973, pp. 34-350

The Ten Commandments of the Holocaust
JACK NUSAN PORTER

1. Thou shalt remember everything and understand nothing
2. Thou shalt record everything—memoirs, diaries, documents, and poetry.
3. Thou shalt teach it diligently to thy children for as Rabbi Emil Fackenheim has said: the survival of Israel is now a sacred duty.
4. Thou shalt teach it to the Gentiles and their children because thou art often at their mercy.
5. Thou shalt not heap abuse upon the children of the ungodly. Though the wicked are to be punished, their children must be forgiven.
6. Thou shalt not judge the victims.
7. Thou shalt not place one set of idols (the heroic) above another (the cowardly). They are to be judged equally before the Lord. As Reb Eli Wiesel of Sighet has said: there is a time to remain silent, so therefore know when to be silent.
8. Thou shalt not dwell heavily upon the sadness of the past. Rejoice for thou hast survived while thine enemies have perished.
9. Thou shalt not lose faith. Amidst all thy doubt and confusion, I, the Lord your G-d, am here among thee.
10. Thou shalt not turn away from thy brothers and sisters; instead reach out and build a paradise on earth so that life and love can prevail.

Copyright © 2003 Jack Nusan Porter

Selected Bibliography on Genocide and the Holocaust

Bauer, Yehuda. *The Holocaust in Historical Perspective.* Seattle, WA: University of Washington Press, 1978.

Bauman, Zygmunt. *Modernity and the Holocaust.* Ithaca, NY: Cornell University Press, 1992.

Chalk, Frank, and Kurt Jonassohn. *The History and Sociology of Genocide.* New Haven, CT and London: Yale University Press, 1990.

Dadrian, Vahakn N. "A Typology of Genocide," *International Review of Sociology,* vol. 5, no. 2, Autumn 1975, pp. 201-212.

Des Pres, Terrence. *The Survivor.* New York and Oxford: Oxford University Press, 1976.

Dobkowski, Michael N., and Isidor Wallimann. *Genocide in Our Time.* Ann Arbor, MI: Pierian Press, 1992.

Fein, Helen. *Accounting for Genocide: National Responses and Jewish Victimization during the Holocaust.* New York: The Free Press, 1979, reprinted by the University of Chicago Press, 1984.

———. *Genocide: A Sociological Perspective.* Sherman Oaks, CA: Sage Publications, 1996.

Gioseffi, Daniela (ed.). *On Prejudice: A Global Perspective.* New York and London: Doubleday Anchor Books, 1993.

Horowitz, I. L. *Genocide, State Power, and Mass Murder.* New Brunswick, NJ: Transaction Books, 1976.

Katz, Steven. *The Holocaust in Historical Context.* New York and Oxford: Oxford University Press, 1994.

Markle, Gerald. *Meditations of a Holocaust Traveler.* Albany, NY: SUNY Press, 1995.

Novick, Peter. *The Holocaust in American Consciousness.* New York: Houghton Mifflin Company, 1999.

Porter, Jack Nusan. *Jewish Partisans: A Documentary of Jewish Resistance in the Soviet Union During World War II.* Two vols. Lanham, MD and London: University Press of America, 1982; reprinted by The Spencer Press, 1999.

———. *Sexual Politics in Nazi Germany: The Persecution of Homosexuals in World War II.* Newton, MA: The Spencer Press, 1999; also appeared as *Sexual Politics in the Third Reich* (pamphlet), Montreal, Quebec, Canada: Concordia University, Montreal Institute for Genocide Studies, 1991.

———, with Steve Hoffman. *The Sociology of the Holocaust and Genocide: A Teaching and Learning Guide.* Revised edition. Washington, DC: American Sociological Association, 1999.

Rosenbaum, Ron. *Explaining Hitler.* New York: Harper Perennial, 1999, paperback. Rubenstein, Richard. *The Cunning of History.* New York: Harper Perennial, 1978.

Tec, Nechama, *Resilience and Courage*, New Haven, CT: Yale University Press, 2002.

Index

A

Abel, Theodore, 47
Aboriginal tribes as victims, 20
Abortion, 6, 38
Abusive-Father Theory, 135
Addictive drugs, 145
Aliyah, 35
Allied Troops, 35
Allport, Gordon, 100
Altruism in action, 239–240
Ament, Susan G., xvi
American Indians, 4, 20, 38, 54
American Sociological Association, xv, 38
Améry, Jean, 148
Amphetamines, 145
Anders als die Andern, 128
Anti-Defamation League, 233
Anti-semitism, 11, 99
Anti-semitism thesis, 218
Anti-Zionism, 99
Anxiety, 186
Arendt, Hannah, 11, 50, 88, 97, 172, 175
Armenians, x, 1, 8, 12, 22, 54
Aryan *volk,* 9
Asch, Solomon, 170
Auschwitz, 40
Australia, 20
Austria, 21
"Auto-genocide," 22

B

"Bad Seed" Theory, 168
Balakian, Peter, xv
Bandura, Albert, 100
Barkun, Michael, 198
Bassiouni, Cherif, 3
Baudrillard, Jean, 74, 84
Bauer, Yehuda, x, xv, 82, 116
Bauman, Zygmunt, 40, 48, 62, 84, 89, 97
Becker, Ernst, 33
Becker, Howard S., xii, 33
Behemoth, 75
Bell, Daniel, 74, 84
Bellamy, Elizabeth J., 89
Belzec, 35
Benedict, Ruth, 100
Benjamin, Walter, 102, 148
Bent, 121
Berlin, Isaiah, 133
Berlin Institute of Sexology, 124
Bettelheim, Bruno, xiii, 50, 148, 207, 227
Bharadwaj, Lakshmi, 32
Bhopal, 72
Biblical genocide, 20
Biological ideology, 14
Black-Jewish relations, viii
Black Muslims, 6
Black Panther Party, 6
Blacks, 5

Blacks and integration, 3
Black slavery, 38
Blade Runner, 84
Blakeslee, Spencer, 72
Bleuel, Hans Peter, 121-122
Blind, 22
"Blood and Soil," 102
"Blut und Erde," 102
B'nai B'rith Anti-Defamation League, 242
Bohr, Niels, 80
Borderland Theory, 133
Borowski, Tadeusz, 148
Bosnia, 10, 20
Boston University, 37, 39
Boulding, Elise, 242
Boulding, Elise and Kenneth, 234
Brandeis University, ix
Brooding, 186
Browning, Christopher, 171
Bruzminski, Stephanya, 34
Brzezinski, Zbigniew, 156
Buber, Martin, 124
Buchenwald, 208
Bullock, Alan, 132, 141
Bullough, Vern, 118
Bureaucracy, 10, 17, 18, 48, 73
Bureaucratic controls, 40
Burns, Jude, xv
Burton, John, 234
Burundi, 22
Butler, Judith, 84
"Butterfly effect," 80
Bystanders, 17, 55

C

Cambodia, 12, 22, 54
Cargas, Harry James, xvi
Catholics (Northern Ireland), 6
Celan, Paul, 148
Center for European Studies (Harvard), 37

Center for Nonviolent Social Change, Martin Luther King, Jr., 233
Chalk, Frank, 39, 57, 116
Chaos Theory, 80, 81, 86
Chaos theory, viii
Charny, Israel, xv, 234, 242
Chelmno, 35
Chemotherapy Theory, 133
Chernobyl, 72
Children in the Holocaust and World War II: Their Secret Diaries, 230
Children's accounts, 230
Chorbajian, Levon, xv
Christianity, 106
Christian-Jewish relations, viii
Chronic Depressive Reactions, 186
Civilization and economy, 73
Clarke, Comer, xiii
Clinton, William, 32, 36
Cognition, Disturbances of, 186
Cohen, Arthur A., 72
Collective Behavior Theory, 183
Colonialization, 12-13
Colonialization, internal, 19
Comparability Thesis, 216
Comparative analysis, 53
Compensation, 56
Concentration camp markings, 130
Confronting History and Holocaust: Collected Essays: 1972-1982, xi, xvi
Consolidators, 236
Convention on the Prevention and Punishment of the Crime of Genocide, 2-5
Coping behavior, 188-191
Coprophilia Theory, 136
Creativity, 236
Croatia, 20, 36
Culture and technology, 73
Czerniakow, Adam, 154

D

Dachau, 208
Dadrian, Vahakn, viii, xv, 47, 54, 116
Dahmer, Jeffrey, 172
Danieli, Yael, xvi
Das Recht auf Lieb, 128
Dawidowicz, Lucy, 117
Deaf, 22
Defeat in war, 15
Definitional Abuse Thesis, 219
Demidenko, Helen, 223, 224
Demjanjuk Trial, 49
Democide, 36, 37, 39
Democratic structure, 15
Depravity, sexual, 40
Derrida, Jacques, xii, 74, 82
Des Pres, Terrence, xiii, 148
Dimmis, 8
Direct action, 241
Disabled, genocide of, 22
Diseased modernization, 73
Distorted history, 223
Disturbances of cognition and memory, 186
Donovan, William ("Wild Bill"), 60
DP Camps, 35
Dresden, 38
Drug use and Nazis, 145
Du Man, Paul, 63, 71, 82
Durkheim, Emile, xiii, 150
Dykish gays, 143

E

Economic prosperity, 236
Education, 240
"Effeminate" gays, 143
Eichmann, Adolf, 172
Eichmann: The Man and his Crimes, 144
Eichmann Trial, 32, 49, 230
Einstein, Albert, 79, 80, 124
Eisenhower, Gen. Dwight D., 35
Eitinger, Leo, xvi, 205
Eliade, Mircea, 63
Ellul, Jacques, 33
Engelmann, Hugo, 32
Environments, 236
Epstein, Helen, 198
Epstein, Leslie, 71
Erickson, Kai, 72
"Ethnic cleansing," 20
Ethnic conflict, 13, 19
Ethnocide, 39
Euthanasia, 22
Evil, 79, 80, 81
  social-psychological theories of, 170
Evil, sociology of, 35, 167
"Exclusionist" approach, 39

F

Facing History and Ourselves, vii
Fascism, 59
"Fate" Theory, 137
Fein, Helen, viii, xv, 8, 40, 47, 54, 62, 72, 234
Feminist theory, 74
Femmes *vs*. Leather Boys, 143
Fields, Rona, 6
Finkelstein, Norman G., 82, 89
Finkielkraut, Alain, 89
Finkler, Rudi, 120
Fisher, Robert, 234
Flaming, Karl, 32
Fogelman, Eva, 194
Fonseca, Isabel, 226
"Foot in the door" theory, 177
Fortunoff Archives at Yale University, 230
Foucault, Michel, xii, 74, 84
Frank, Hans, 125–126
Frankl, Viktor E., 198, 207
Freeman, Michael, 92

Freud, Sigmund, 100
Fromm, Erich, 61, 100, 207
Functionalist Thesis, 215

G
Galway, Ireland, xvii
Gandhi, 234
Gay, Lesbian and Bi-Equal Rights and Liberation, March on Washington for, 33
"Gay subculture," xii
Gay theory, 74
Geheimnisse einer Seele, 129
Gein, Ed, 172
Gemeinschaft, 40
Genealogy Theory, 133
General Systems Theory, 182
Genital Wound Theory, 132
Genocidal mind, 97, 103
"The Genocidal Mind," ix
"The Genocidal Society," ix
Genocide
  author's definition, 11
  components of, 11, 17
  crude, 18
  definition, 7
  factors in, 18, 56
  mixed and emerging types, 13-14
  origin of term, 1
  prediction of, 14
  problem of intent and application, 4, 5-7
  resistance to, viii
  self-inflicted, 22
  in sociology dictionaries, 1
  sophisticated, 18
  and the state, 10
  typology of, 19
  use and abuse of term, 5-7
  when it takes place, 12, 19
Genocide, types of
  auto-genocide, 13

  mixed, 19
  new, 19
  politically based, 13-14
  sexual, 13
Genocide and Human Rights, xi, xv, 73
Genocide-Centered Scholars, 218
"Genocide convention," 2
Genocide Denial, 219
Genocides in history, 20
Genocide Studies, future of, 221
Gerhardt, Uta, 59
The German and National Socialism, 63
German Holocaust of 1939-1945, 54
Germany, 21
Gerth, Hans, 50, 100
Gesellschaft, 40
Gesetze der Liebe, 128
Goebbels, Joseph, 141
Goering, Hermann, 122, 141
Goffman, Erving, xii, 33, 84
Goldhagen, Daniel Jonah, ix, 100
  Controversy, vii, 82, 171, 218
  exclusionist view, 37
  Hitler's Willing Executioners, xiii, 97, 109, 175
  simplistic approach, 16
Goldhagen, Erich, ix, 97-110, 131
  academic background, 97-98
  bibliography of works, 111
  life and writings, 98-100
  Nine Commandments of Nazism, 104-109
Goldhagen-Browning Controversy, 171-172
Goldhagen Controversy, vii, 82, 171, 175-179, 218, 220
Government, forms of, 236
Graeber, Isacque, 61
"Grand narratives," 87
Grau, Gunter, 118, 120

Great Abstractions Theory, 137
Greenblatt, Steven, 194
Greenfield, Sidney, 32
Grimshaw, Allen, 37
Gypsies, x, 8, 21, 116

H
Habermas, Jurgen, 74
Haeberle, Erwin, 118
Half, Barbara, 234
Hall, Peter, 175
Hamid, Sultan Abdul, 22
Haraway, Donna, 84
Hartshorne, Edward Yarnall, 60–61, 63
Harvard University, vii, 32, 97
  Center for European Studies, 37
  Helen Zelaznic Chair in Holocaust and Cognate Studies, 175
Hasidism, 147
Hebrew University, x
Heger, Heinz, 119
Heidegger, Martin, 63
Heines, Edmund, 122
Heisenberg, Werner, 80
Helen Zelaznic Chair in Holocaust and Cognate Studies (Harvard), 175
Helmreich, William, viii
Herzog, Chaim, 36
Hiding, 55
Hilberg, Raul, 40, 47, 82, 88, 100, 117, 223
Himmler, Heinrich, 122, 141
Hiroshima, xi, 37, 38, 40, 47, 72
Hirschfeld, Magnus, 34, 124, 128, 144
Historians, vii
The History and Sociology of Genocide, 39
A History and Sociology of Peace, 233

Hitler, Adolf, 123, 141
Hitler, the mind of, 131–138
Hitler's Willing Executioners, xiii, 97, 109, 175
Hoffman, Stanley, 175
Hoffman, Steve, xv
Holliday, Laurel, 230
Holocaust, 11, 33, 37, 47
Holocaust as overlooked topic, 40
Holocaust as unique event, xi, 36, 38
Holocaust-Centered Scholars, 218
Holocaust Controversies, viii, 215
Holocaust Denial, 219
Holocaust in history, 72
Holocaust literature, 39
Holocaust Memorial Museum and Archives (Jerusalem), ix
Holocaust Studies, viii, 221
Holocaust survivors' symptomology, 185–188
Holocaust to sociologists, 31
Homosexuality, 116
  and Nazis, 142
Homosexuals, xii, 9, 21, 39
Homosexuellefrage, 143
Horowitz, Irving Louis, viii, xv, 47, 62
Housepian, Marjorie, 100
Hsu, Francis, 59
Hussain, Pat, 33
Hutu, 22, 54
Hypnotherapy Theory, 134

I
Id-ego-superego conflict, 169
Ideologists, 18
Ideology, 17, 73
  of the victimizer, 8–9
Ideology, biological, 14
Impaired memories, 223
"Inclusivist" approach, 39

Indians, aboriginal, 13
Indians, North American, 12–13
Information gathering, 240
"Insiders-outsiders," 32
Insomniac drugs, 145
Intentionalist Thesis, 215
International Association of Genocide Scholars, xvii
Irish Centre for Human Rights, xvii
Irish National University, xvii
Irving, David, 71, 131
Isherwood, Christopher, 118
Isolation, tendency to, 186
Israelis, 49

J
Jacobs, Steve, xv
Jehovah's Witnesses, 21, 116
Jellonnek, Burkhard, 120
Jerusalem, Israel, ix
Jewish Partisans, 50
Jewish Partisan unit, 31
Jewish radicalism, viii
Jews, 1, 8, 20, 21
Jonassohn, Kurt, viii, 39, 57, 116
Judeophobia, 99
Justice, system of, 236

K
Katz, Steven, ix, x, xv, 37, 88
Kelman, Herbert, 100, 109, 170, 234
Kershaw, Ian, 47
Khmer Rouge, 13
King, Martin Luther, Jr., 233, 234
Kitsuse, John, xii
Kleist-Kasino, 123
Koestler, Arthur, 148, 152
Konishschuk, Nikolai, 226
Kosinski, Jerzy, xiii, 148, 226–227
Kovel, 31
Kreisberg, Louis, 234
Kruk-Maks Group, 226
Kruk Otryad, 31
Kultur und Technik, 73
Kuper, Leo, 234
Kutner, Luis, 234

L
Langer, Larry, xvi, 223
Lanzmann, Claude, 50
Lauritsen, John, 119
Lautmann, Rudiger, 117
Legacies, 56
Legitimization, 18
Lemkin, Raphael, 1
Lesbians, xii, 143
Le Suicide, xiii
Levi, Primo, xiii, 148
Lifton, Robert J., 63, 198, 207
Linenthal, Edward, 216
Lipper, Kenneth, 175
Lipstadt, Deborah, 71, 82, 83
Lorenz, Edward, 81
Lubavitcher Rebbe, 147
Lutze, Viktor, 123
Lyotard, Jean-Francois, 74, 84

M
Maalot, 38
Mandela, Nelson, 234
Maniewicze, 31
Mann, Thomas, 124
Mannheim, Karl, 50
Mann oder Weib, 128
March on Washington for Gay, Lesbian and Bi-Equal Rights and Liberation, 33
Markings of camp inmates, 130
Marx, Karl, 33
Marxian theory, 75
Masters & Slaves, 143
Maxwell, Robert, xiii, 148, 156, 227
Mayer, Hans, 148

McLuhan, Marshall, 79
Media, 91
Meiklejohn, Alexander, 63
Melko, Matthew, xvii, 233, 234–235, 242
Melson, Robert, xv
Memorialization, 56
Memory, Disturbances of, 186
Mengele, Josef, 63
Mentally ill, 22
Merton, Robert K., 32
Metaphysical Theory, 168
Milgram, Stanley, 100, 109, 170
Military, dependence on, 14
Mills, C. Wright, 16, 33, 50, 59, 100, 147, 150
Milwaukee, University of Wisconsin-, 32
Milwaukee, Wisconsin, 5, 32
Minorities, strong and healthy, 15
Minority groups, 14
Modernization, 40, 73
Modern societies, 237–239
Mommsen, Hans, 131
"Moral tradition," 39
Mormons, 21
Mosse, George, 118
Muenther, Axel, xiii
Muller, Claus, 118
Muslims, 20
My Lai, xi, 38
Mystification Thesis, 217

N

"Nacht und Nebel," 102
Nagasaki, 72
National Socialism, 59
Native Americans, 39
"Nazi decalogue," 98
The Nazi Doctors, 63
Nazi Germany, 13
Nazi ideology, 101

Nazi leaders and sexual orgies, 144
Nazi medical staff, 22
Nazi Party of America, 5
Nazis
  and drug use, 145
  and homosexuality, 142
  and sex, 145
  sexual aberrations among, 141
Nazi *Weltanschauung,* 100
Necrophilia Theory, 135
Negotiation, 240
Neumann, Franz, 75
New Zealander Indians, 20
"Night and fog," 102
"Nine Commandments" of Nazism, 103–109
Noel, Donald, 32
Nonviolent social change, 239–241
North American Indians, 12–13
Northern Ireland, 233
Northwestern University, xii
Novick, Peter, 82
Nuremberg Trials, 2

O

O'Brien, Darren, 223
Olympia, 102
Omnicide, nuclear, 36, 39
Ordinary Men, 177
OSS (Office of Strategic Services), 60

P

Pais, Abraham, 80
Palen, J. J., 32
Pandora's Box, 129
Paradigms, 39
Paragraph 175/175a, 116
Parsons, Helen W., 59
Parsons, Talcott, 59, 60, 150
Passivity of victims, 54–55
Passmore, J. Robert, 242

"Pattern variables," 150
Peaceful change, 240–241
Peaceful societies, pre-conditions of, 235–237
Peace in the Western World, 234
Percy, Bill, 118
Perpetrators, 55–56
Personal commitment, 240
Personal identity, alterations of, 186–187
Planck, Max, 80
Plant, Richard, 118
Plural meanings, 87
Political parties, dominant, 15
Politicide, 36, 37, 39
Polonsky, Antony, 155
Pornography Theory, 134
Porter, Irving, 225–226
Porter, Irving and Faye, 35
Porter, Jack Nusan, xv, xvi, 62, 73
  parents of, 31
Porter's Theory of Genocide, 17
"Porter's Two-Step Theory," 16, 177
"Post-modern" approach, vii
Postmodernism
  discussion of, 82–93
  meanings of, 85–87
  what is, 84–85
Postmodernism
  and power, 86
  and "*representation*," 85
  and *sexuality*, 86
  and "*simulation*," 85
  and S&M, 86
"Postmodern political science," 90
Postmodern Theory, 74
Postmodern thinkers, xii
Post-traumatic stress, 56
Power relations, 87
Proctor, Robert N., 63
Projection theory, 169

Propaganda, 91
The Protocols of the Elders of Zion, 71
Psycho-analytical Theory, 183–184
Psychoanalytic or Psychological Theory, 169
"Psychohistory," 131
Psychological implications of Survivor's Syndrome, 181
Psychosomatic conditions, 187
Psychotic states, 187

Q
Quantum Theory, 80

R
Race is everything, 104
Racial Hygiene, 63
Racial ideology, 14
Racism Thesis, 218
Radical Judaism, viii
Rapaport, Chanan, 234
Rational Choice Theory, 90
Rationalization and modernity, 40–41
Ravven, Robert, xvi, 212
Reaction of victims, 54–55
Reconciliation, 241
Rector, Frank, 119
Reich, Wilhelm, 62
Remembrance, 56
Rescuers, 17, 55
Resistance, 17
Resistance Controversy, 220
Resistance of victims, 55
Retaliation, possibility of, 15
Rinder, Irwin, 32
Robinson, Jacob, 2
Roehm, Ernst, 119, 124
Roma gypsies, 20
Rorty, Richard, 84
Rosenbaum, Alan S., x, 54

Rosenbaum, Ron, 131
Roth, Guenther, 48
Rovno, 31
Rubenstein, Richard, 37, 40, 47, 89, 92, 118
Rwanda, x, 10, 22

S

Sack, John, 225
Savran, Bella, 194
Scholem, Gershom, 147
Schoppmann, Claudia, 120
Scientific Humanitarian Committee, 124, 128
Scott, Ridley, 84
Scott, Robert, 242
Segey, Tom, 49
Serbs, 20
Sereny, Gitta, 35
Serial-Killer Theory, 135
Sex
  and gender, xii, 84, 87
  and Nazis, 145
  and power, 91
Sexual aberrations
  among Nazis, 141
Sexual depravity, 40
Sexual harassment, xii
Sexual orgies and Nazi leaders, 144
Sexual Politics in the Third Reich: The Persecution of the Homosexuals During the Holocaust, xv–xvi
Sexual rights, 116
Sexuelle Zwischenstufen, 128
Sharp, Gene, 234
Sherman, Martin, 119
Sherwin, Byron L., xvi, 155, 212
Shoah, 40
Silber, John, 82
Silhouette, 123
Silverberg, Robert, 32

Simmel, George, 50
Smelser, Neil, 72
Smith, Roger, xv
Sobibor, 35
Sobiesek, Joseph, 226
Social adaptations, 188–191
"Social deviance," xii
Socialism, 147
Social organization, 18
Social-Psychological theories of evil, 170
Social theory, 39
Sociological construct of Holocaust, 47
Sociological theory and social praxis, viii
Sociological treatment of Holocaust, 48
Sociologists
  meaning of Holocaust to, 31
  and unique events, 37
Sociology
  and comparative genocide, 36
  as discipline, xi, 53
  of evil, 167
  of the Holocaust, xi
Sociology of Genocide and the Holocaust, 38
Sociology of Genocide as a course, 38
Sociology of Jewry, viii
The Sociology of Jewry, 39
The Sociology of Modern Anti-Semitism, 61
The Sociology of the Holocaust and Genocide, xv, 73
Socio-Political implications of Survivor's Syndrome, 181
Socio-Political Theory, 183
Soviet historiography, 99
Soviet Partisans, 226
Spiegelman, Anya, 148

Spiegelman, Art, 148
Spielberg Foundation, vii, 230
SS Einsatzgruppen, 31
SS under Hitler, 21
Stability, 237
Stangel/Stangl, Franz, 35, 172
Staub, Edwin, 170
Steakley, James, 118
Stigma, 54
Strugnell, John, 71
Stumke, Hans-George, 120
Styron, William, 71–72
Suicide, Le, xiii
Suicide drugs, 145
Suicides, Holocaust, 147–160
Sunshine, Peggy, xv
Survivor, what is a, 184–185
Survivor-children, coping behavior
  psychological adaptations, 192–195
  social and political adaptations, 198–200
Survivor-children groups, 204–206
Survivor's Syndrome, 181, 200–202
  Socio-Political implications, 181
Symbolic Meaning Theory, 90
Symptomology of Holocaust survivors, 185–188
Syphilitic Theory, 136

T

Tec, Nechama, viii
Technologists, 18
Technology, 9–10, 17, 73
Temperate attitudes, 15
Territorial ambitions, 15
Theological Theory, 168
Therapy, 203
Thorstad, David, 119
Tibetan genocide, 20
Tolerance, 15, 236
Totten, Sam, xv
Trade activity, 236

Transvestitism, 144
Treblinka, 35, 40
Trevor-Roper, Hugh, 132
Tribal conflict, 13, 19
Tribunals, 56
Triumph of the Will, 102
Turkish genocide of 1915, 54
Turks, 12
Tutsi, 22, 54
Two-Step Theory, 10, 11, 16, 138, 177
Tyrnauer, Gabrielle, 116

U

U. N. Convention, 3
U. S. Holocaust Memorial Museum, vii, 32
Ukrainian police, 31
Ukrainians, 20
Uncertainty Theory, 80, 90
Unique events and sociology, 47
"Uniqueness-comparability" approach, 39
Uniqueness Thesis, 216
United Nations General Assembly, 2
Ury, William, 234
Uztashi, 36

V

Varon, Benno Weiser, 49
Vashem, Yad, ix, x
Venema, Adriaan, 119
Verba, Sidney, 175
Victims,
  characteristics of, 17
  passivity of, 54–55
  reaction of, 54
  resistance of, 55
Vietnam War, 3, 40, 47, 72
Visconti, Luchino, 119
Volks Gemeinschaft, 103
Von Papen, Franz, 122

W

Walesa, Lech, 36
War, 12, 19
"War" Theory, 138
Watt, Donald, 223–224
Weber, Max, 40, 89
Wehr, Paul, 234
Weissenberg, Gershon (Jerry), xv
Weissmark, Mona, 32
Weltanschauung, 98, 100
West, Cornel, 84
Western Civilization, xi, 73, 79
  role of the Holocaust in, 71
Western World, peace in, 234
Wiedergutmachung, xiii, 116, 206
Wiesel, Elie, x, 31, 33–34, 88, 234
Wilkomirski, Benjamin, 223
Wills, George, xii
Wirth, Louis, 50
Witches, 38
Withdrawal, 186
Wolfe, Alan, 39
Wolf Girl of the Polish Forests, 226

Women, 21, 38
World League for Sexual Reform, 128
World War I, 1
World War II, vii, 1
Wrong, Dennis, 7

X

X Factor, 138

Y

Yale University, Fortunoff Archives, 230
Young Turks, 22

Z

Zelaznic, Helen, 175
Zimbardo, Philip, 100, 109, 170
Zionism, 147
Zivilization und Wirtschaft, 73
Zweig, Stefan, 148
Zyglboim, Arthur, 154

About the Author

Jack Nusan Porter has been a sociologist for nearly 40 years as well as a writer, editor, businessman, and social activist. He received his B.A. from the University of Wisconsin-Milwaukee in 1967 and his Ph.D. in sociology from Northwestern University in 1971. Born in the Ukraine in 1944 to Soviet Partisan parents, Dr. Porter escaped the Nazis with his parents and moved first to Austria and then to America, eventually settling in Milwaukee, Wisconsin in the late 40s.

He is a former Vice-President of the International Association of Genocide Scholars, has received the Distinguished Scholarly Career Award from the American Sociological Association Section on the History of Sociology, and is a former Research Fellow in Ukrainian Studies at Harvard University.

He lives in Newtonville, Massachusetts where he is Director of The Spencer School. He has published over 30 books and over 600 articles and reviews including *Genocide and Human Rights: A Global Anthology*, *Confronting History and Holocaust*, *The Jew as Outsider*, *Sexual Politics in the Third Reich*, and *The Sociology of the Holocaust/Genocide*.

This volume is the first in a proposed six volumes of Dr. Porter's work. Others will deal with sociology, culture, American Jewry, Black-Jewish relations, and radical thought.

Dr. Porter can be reached at jacknusan@earthlink.net or (617) 965-8388.

About the Author

Also by Jack Nusan Porter

Non-fiction

Student Protest and the Technocratic Society (1971)
Kids in Cults, *with Irv Doress* (1977)
Notes of a Happy Sociologist (1980)
The Jew as Outsider (1981)
Confronting History and Holocaust (1983)
Conflict and Conflict Resolution, *with Ruth Taplin* (1987)
Sexual Politics in the Third Reich (1997)
A Life of Mitzvah: Rabbi Joseph Mayer Jacobson: Boston's Premier Orthodox Jewish Leader (1997)
The Death of Sociology? Social Theory and Social Praxis (2005)
The Sociology of Jewry: A Post-Modern Interpretation (forthcoming)
The Radical Writings of Jack Nusan Porter (forthcoming)

Anthologies

Jewish Radicalism, *with Peter Dreier* (1973)
The Sociology of American Jews (1978)
Genocide and Human Rights (1982)

Sourcebooks

The University and its Community: A White Paper for De Paul University in Chicago (1969)
Handbook of Cults, Sects, and Self-Realization Groups (1982)
Jewish Partisans: A Documentary of Jewish Resistance in the Soviet Union During World War II, two volumes, with *Yehudah Merin* (1982)
Sexual Politics in Nazi Germany (1991)
The Sociology of Business (1991)
The Sociology of Jewry (1992)
The Sociology of Genocide/The Holocaust, *with Steve Hoffman* (1992)
Women in Chains: A Sourcebook on the Agunah (1996)
The City of Lowell: Social Problems and Social Issues (2004)

Bibliographies
Jews and the Cults (1981)
Conflict and Conflict Resolution: A Historical Bibliography (1982)
The Speeches and Writings of Jack Nusan Porter (2005)

Screen Treatments
Happy Days Revisited: The Milwaukee-Hollywood Connection (2001), documentary
Key West Rabbi (2002), comedy
Partisans (2002), drama
C. Wright Mills: An American Radical (2005), documentary

Textbooks and Encyclopedias (contributor)
Annual Editions: Readings in Sociology (1972)
The Study of Society (1974)
Encyclopedia of Sociology (1974)
Encyclopedia of American Jewish Women (1995)
Handbook of Pastoral Care (1996)
Encyclopedia of Italian-American Life (1997)
Encyclopedia of Genocide (1999)
Encyclopedia of Genocide and Crimes Against Humanity (2004)

Journals (Founder and Editor)
Journal of the History of Sociology, with Glenn Jacobs (1977-1983)
The Sociology of Business Newsletter (1977-1979)

Reports
Gay, Lesbian, and Bisexual Writers Issues Survey (1992)
Quincy 2000: A Report on Urban Trends for the City of Quincy, Massachusetts (1998)
Newton 2000: A Report on 21st Century Trends for the City of Newton, Massachusetts (2000)

www.ingramcontent.com/pod-product-compliance
Lightning Source LLC
Chambersburg PA
CBHW021821300426
44114CB00009BA/263